Rock Mountain Creed

Jesus' Sermon on the Mount

by

Phillip A. Ross

Pilgrim Platform
Marietta, Ohio

Copyright ©2011 Phillip A. Ross
Edition: 4/25/2011
All rights reserved.

ISBN: 978-0-9820385-8-1
Edition: 9-12-2020

Published by

Pilgrim Platform
149 E. Spring St., Marietta
Ohio, 45750
www.pilgrim-platform.org

Biblical quotations are from the *English Standard Version*, Standard Bible Society, unless otherwise cited.

Cover art: James J. Tissot (1836-1902), "Jesus Preaches the Sermon on the Mount," watercolor.

Printed in the United States of America

For Tom & Sara
brother & sister in Christ

And Paul
friend and confidant in Christ

Toward the clarification
of all things
Mark 13:23

BOOKS BY PHILLIP A. ROSS

The Work At Zion—A Reckoning, Two-volume set, 772 pages, 1996.

Practically Christian—Applying James Today, 135 pages, 2006.

The Wisdom of Jesus Christ in the Book of Proverbs, 414 pages, 2006.

Marking God's Word—Understanding Jesus, 324 pages, 2006.

Acts of Faith—Kingdom Advancement, 326 pages, 2007.

Informal Christianity—Refining Christ's Church, 136 pages, 2007.

Engagement—Establishing Relationship in Christ, 104 pages, 1996, 2008.

It's About Time! — The Time Is Now, 40 pages. 2008.

The Big Ten—A Study of the Ten Commandments, 105 pages, 2001, 2008.

Arsy Varsy—Reclaiming The Gospel in First Corinthians, 406 pages, 2008.

Varsy Arsy—Proclaiming The Gospel in Second Corinthians, 356 pages, 2009.

Colossians—Christos Singularis, 278 pages, 2010.

Rock Mountain Creed—The Sermon on the Mount, 310 pages, 2011.

The True Mystery of the Mystical Presence, 355 pages, 2011.

Peter's Vision of Christ's Purpose in First Peter, 340 pages, 2011.

Peter's Vision of The End in Second Peter, 184 pages, 2012.

The Religious History of Nineteenth Century Marietta, Thomas Jefferson Summers, 124 pages, 1903, 2012 (editor).

Conflict of Ages—The Great Debate of the Moral Relations of God and Man, Edward Beecher, 489 pages, 1853, 2012 (editor).

Concord Of Ages—The Individual And Organic Harmony Of God And Man, Edward Beecher, D. D., 524 pages, 1860, 2013 (editor).

Ephesians—Recovering the Vision of a Sustainable Church in Christ, 417 pages, 2013.

Galatians: Backstory/Christory, 315 pages, 2015.

Poet Tree—Root, Branch & Sap, 72 pages, 2013.

Inside Out Woman—Collected Poetry, Doris M. Ross, 195 pages, 2014 (editor).

God's Great Plan for the World—The Biblical Story of Creation and Redemption, 305 pages, 2019.

John's Miracles—Seeing Beyond Our Expectations, 210 pages, 2019.

Essays on Church—Ordinary Christianity for the World, 385 pages, 2020.

TABLE OF CONTENTS

INTRODUCTION

What difference does Jesus make? Did His teaching and ministry change anything? Or did Jesus' teaching simply uphold the Old Testament law without changing a jot or a tittle, as He is sometimes understood to have said in Matthew 5:18? Do the Ten Commandments still stand today? Or did Jesus change them? The question is so huge and important that there must be a clear biblical answer. If you know of a easy, clear answer about this, please point me to it.

Most Christians believe that the Ten Commandments are still in force, as do I. And yet, if they are still in force, why do Christians not worship on Saturday, the Sabbath?

> "Six days you shall labor, and do all your work, but the seventh day is a Sabbath to the LORD your God. On it you shall not do any work, you, or your son, or your daughter, your male servant, or your female servant, or your livestock, or the sojourner who is within your gates. For in six days the LORD made heaven and earth, the sea, and all that is in them, and rested on the seventh day. Therefore the LORD blessed the Sabbath day and made it holy" (Exodus 20:9-11).

The seventh day is Saturday, not Sunday. But does a change of day mean that the Fourth Commandment is no longer in effect? Not at all!

But it does mean that something has changed, that Christ brought a very important change to God's law, at least to part of it.

My intention here is not to answer the Sabbath question in full, but to simply use it as an example that points out that the birth, life, ministry, teaching, death, and resurrection of Jesus Christ has brought an important change to the world—to the whole world. Suffice it to say here as a way to tickle your curiosity that Christians worship on the Eighth Day.[1]

If you are not familiar with the Eighth Day or with God's eternal Sabbath, your own lack of familiarity should suggest to you that something in your life, in your Christian education, and your church is amiss. If God said that the Ten Commandments are eternal, and He did, and if Jesus Christ changed something so fundamental and essential as the day of worship, which He did, then Christians everywhere should understand and be able to explain it. But in my experience, this is not the case. I doubt that one in a thousand Christians could provide a rational explanation about the change of Sabbath worship.

But I don't want to get stuck on the Sabbath. There is much more to this issue than Sabbath considerations. What about the First Commandment and religious toleration? What about the Second Commandment and icons? Does that include the various trinkets that can be found in Christian bookstores? What about the Third Commandment and movies, television, CDs and DVDs? Should Christians expose themselves and their children to the trash that passes for entertainment today? Where do children learn to honor their parents today? At school? Think again! What about adultery, theft, bearing false witness, not to mention covetousness? Not a recent high school graduate in ten thousand will have any idea about what I'm talking about.

Providing real answers for these questions may mean the difference between human survival and destruction. Have I overstated the issue? I don't think so. And yet, my intention here is not to answer all of these questions. A lot of people write books in order to provide answers because readers like to have answers. Questions are harder. Questions make people think. Questions make people uncomfortable.

---

1   Christians worship on the Eighth Day for a variety of reasons, central to which is the fact that Christ fulfilled the Sabbath and that fulfillment inaugurated God's eternal Sabbath, which stands outside of time itself. See: Exodus 22:30; Leviticus 9:1; 12:3; 14:10,23; 15:14,29; 22:27; 23:36,39; Numbers 6:10; 7:54; 29:35; 1 Kings 8:66; 12:32,33; 2 Chronicles 7:9; 29:17; Nehemiah 8:18; Ezekiel 43:27; Luke 1:59; Acts 7:8; Philippians 3:5.

After thirty years in Christian ministry I'm convinced that the Bible itself does not simply provide answers. The Bible asks questions that confound us and our most qualified scholars, who spend lifetimes trying to untie the intellectual knots provided by other scholars so that they can tie their own knots in different and noteworthy ways. But, God did not simply give the Bible to scholars. He has given it to His church, to His people, to those who are inhabited by His Holy Spirit. And in fact it is the Holy Spirit through regeneration who answers the questions that the Bible asks.

The power and presence of the Holy Spirit through personal regeneration is absolutely essential to the correct, orthodox understanding of Scripture. The whole point of the Bible is to invite or in some cases drive people to the personal relationship with Jesus Christ that is the foundation of Christian faith. God Himself must—and will—answer the questions He poses in His Word. My answers cannot satisfy you, nor will yours satisfy me. We must each hear from God Himself. Have I overstated the case? I don't think so, but I do think that hearing from God is nothing like what people imagine it to be. It is not magical or mystical, but is actually quite ordinary. At least God intends it to be quite ordinary.

It is, however, a lot of work. God needs it to be that way because there is a lot to understand. The world is not as simple as our ancestors thought. I'm not suggesting that previous generations of Christians were wrong. They were not! But their answers are not our answers, and inasmuch as we try to rely on their answers to the deep biblical questions, we will continue to find those answers to be inadequate to the complexities of our contemporary world. It has always been this way. Every person and every generation needs, not to reinvent Christianity, but to understand it for themselves.

Today we find that the ineffectiveness of the church in our world is tied to our own regurgitation of old answers. The answers themselves don't change, but our languages and circumstances change all the time— and faster every year! It is not that we need new Christian answers, but that we need renewed hearts and minds to engage God's answers through regeneration.

All this having been said, we must also understand that God does not forbid nor discount scholarship. In fact, it can be a great help. But scholarship is not a substitute for faith. However, it is a relatively common understanding among Christians that God's enemies will often attempt to substitute scholarship for faith, especially among church leaders. Indeed, seminary students are all too often easily coaxed to do exactly this. I know because I was one. Seminaries are too often more faithful to academics than they are to the gospel of Jesus Christ. I say this with great fear, shame, and trepidation because no seminary staff person would ever suggest such a thing of their own seminary, though they might suggest it about others. The point of this observation is not to devolve into name calling and mud slinging, but to call all Christians to a renewed self-evaluation in the light of Christ by the power and presence of the Holy Spirit in regeneration and according to Scripture. The healing and unity that Christ offers is not something that Christians *find*, it is something that we *assume*.

We can—and must—help one another find biblical answers for our world's problems. That's how God's Holy Spirit works. He doesn't simply give you and me answers privately. He gives them publicly. God interacts with Himself through our engagement of His Word (the Bible) by the power of the Holy Spirit and in the light of Jesus Christ. Christ's church is a corporate thing, and necessarily so. But the goal is not to have a grand systematic or biblical theology that defeats all comers for all time. The goal is discussion and growth in the midst of relationship, first with Christ and then with one another.

God's intent in Scripture is to change our minds through disillusionment, and to continue that change all our lives. God intends for us to outgrow our childish and immature beliefs and illusions. And that growth, that sanctification, does not end in this life, which means that we are always growing, always learning and always changing. But the changes that we are to undergo are not a kind of flip-flopping reversals about what we believe. Rather, Christian growth is always a matter of growing deeper in faithfulness.

Indeed, Peter assures us that the revelation of God in Christ is progressive, that it will continue to unfold in both depth and breadth over time—eternally. The revelation of God in Christ will continue to develop over time and in history because Christians will continue to grow and mature, and that growth and maturity will continue to unfold the depth and richness of God's blessings spiritually, personally, corporately, scientifically, and technologically.[2]

---

2   See *Peter's Vision of Christ's Purpose in First Peter*, by Phillip A. Ross, Pilgrim Platform, Marietta, Ohio, 2012.

Here, we will examine Jesus' understanding of how the human manifestation of His Sonship, and His impending sacrifice (at the point He gave the Sermon on the Mount) and how its propitiation for sin affected God's moral law. Jesus understood and accepted His role in the Trinitarian Godhead. How could He not since it is His reality? This also means that He understood the complex character of human identity as having both individual and corporate poles, as well. Remember, He was both fully divine and fully human, both at the same time without mixing or confusing His divinity with His humanity. This is the orthodox, historic, inherited, Christian, and universally accepted teaching. Indeed, belief in the doctrine of the Trinity is essential for Christian identity.

My presumption in these pages, garnered from Scripture and confirmed by my own ongoing regeneration, is that the image in which humanity has been created is in some way trinitarian. When God created Man (Adam), God said,

"Let *us* make man in *our* image, after *our* likeness" (Genesis 1:26).

God used a plural referent to Himself. The next verse also indicates the plural character of Man.

"So God created man in his own image, in the image of God he
created him; male and female he created them" (Genesis 1:27).

The fact of the two biological sexes of Man confirm that we are necessarily social beings who have a corporate element to our individual identities.

Why take this as an axiom of human character? Because God's Trinitarian character is the most unique thing about God, and it is the one thing that identifies God as completely and ultimately unique. God's Trinitarian character is in a sense the one thing that makes God God. Therefore, it is this image that should come to mind when we think of God, in whose image we have been created. And it is the necessity of the corporate character of human identity that gives rise to human morality.

Human morality is an essential element of Jesus' sermon on the mount. What Jesus will say about human morality is that it issues from the reality of our simultaneous individual and corporate character. And that this simultaneity itself issues from the fact of our creation in God's likeness. Humanity was created to be a kind of reflection of God's character, both as individuals and socially or corporately. And this is why Jesus focused on right worship, which issues out of the positional relationship with Jesus Christ held by the born-again (twice-born or regenerate), and the moral relationships between and among Christ's people.

These are the topics that Jesus addressed in this sermon. Yet, there is an additional issue or problem presented by the sermon on the mount. In order to understand what Jesus was talking about requires, in contemporary parlance, an understanding of the context and the subtext of Jesus' words. In order to understand what Jesus was talking about (or what anyone talks about for that matter), we must share to a convincing degree Jesus' perspective. We must have some understanding of where He was coming from in order to understand what He means by His words. In order to understand Jesus we must stand under Him. We must account ourselves to be His people, both individually and corporately.

You and I must belong to Jesus Christ personally, which means everything that the orthodox, historic idea of being personally and individually saved, born-again and/or regenerated by the power and presence of the Holy Spirit means. And at the same time we must belong to the corporate body of Christ, the church. We must find and establish our identity as individuals in Jesus Christ and as a people in His church. To fail in this regard is to stand outside of Jesus Christ, not under Him. To fail in this regard is to not have access to Jesus' context, subtext and/or perspective, which will preclude people from seeing God's kingdom or even God Himself, as Jesus told Nicodemus (John 3:3, 5).

Therefore, I pray that you, my reader, will already have this perspective. And if you don't or if you aren't sure, I pray that what follows will help you stand under the Lord of the Universe who is manifest in the human flesh of Jesus Christ, and who lives and reigns forever. And I pray for your patience with me as I delve into issues that are far more complex than our ancestors ever imagined. Just as medical science has revealed the dizzying complexity of the human body, so God in Christ is still revealing the astonishingly simple faith that unlocks the infinite complexity of God in Christ. To this God Jesus prayed (and Jesus' prayers are efficacious),

> "As you sent me into the world, so I have sent them into the world. And for their sake I consecrate myself, that they also may be sanctified in truth. I do not ask for these only, but also for those who will believe in me through their word, that they may all be one, just as you, Father, are in me, and I in you, that they

also may be in us, so that the world may believe that you have sent me. The glory that you have given me I have given to them, that they may be one even as we are one, I in them and you in me, that they may become perfectly one, so that the world may know that you sent me and loved them even as you loved me" (John 17:18-23).

Phillip A. Ross
March 2011
Marietta, Ohio

1. The Vision Thing

*Seeing the crowds, he went up on the mountain, and when he
sat down, his disciples came to him. And he opened his mouth
and taught them, saying: "Blessed are the poor in spirit, for
theirs is the kingdom of heaven. Blessed are those who mourn,
for they shall be comforted."* —Matthew 5:1-4

In all likelihood, the Sermon on the Mount didn't actually happen as
it was recorded in Scripture. Of course, Jesus taught these things to
His disciples, but probably not in one sitting (or setting). Luke
recorded these teachings as the Sermon on the Plain (Luke 6:17-ff).
Don't get me wrong, these are true teachings of Jesus. We can be sure of
this because Scripture truly represents and teaches the character of God.
However, in order to access the true meaning of Jesus' teachings we
must read them faithfully.

By this I mean that we need to assume that they are true, that they
truly teach God's character and wisdom, and that we can completely
depend upon them. If we begin with doubt we will end with doubt
because we will read our own doubts into these words of Jesus. We are
not going to do that here. We are going to begin this study of the
Sermon on the Mount by consciously assuming that the text we
encounter is true and can be trusted to teach God's truth. This assumption, which is the central act of faith in Christianity, will be our guide
and the foundation upon which our understanding will rest. Why do
this? Because apart from this assumption or presupposition Christian
faithfulness cannot stand.[3]

---

3   Assuming the truth of the Bible as is done here involves what I call presupposi-
    tional trinitarianism or presupposing the reality of the Trinity. For more on this
    see *Arsy Varsy—Reclaiming the Gospel in First Corinthians* (2008), *Varsy Arsy—*

There is no Christianity apart from biblical Christianity. Christian faith rests upon the biblical context, and that context issues from a unified whole, from the uniquely Christian Trinity. The beginning of Christian faithfulness comes from God, from the Trinity, who created the world, and gave His Word to the various Old Testament prophets. In the fullness of time He sent Christ, who in turn sent His Holy Spirit to regenerate His people. All of these various things and events work to provide the context in which the assumption of faithfulness can take root.

Of course, this context, which originated in the Trinitarian Godhead, is not established apart from human involvement. And the primary instance of human involvement that has provided this necessary context within human history was the advent of Jesus Christ—His fleshly birth. Jesus Christ was born to Mary in Bethlehem in a manger, died as a propitiation for sin on the cross, and was raised from the dead to be seated at the right hand of God almighty with all earthly power and authority. Jesus Christ is the fulcrum or pulley that by God's grace moves the whole world through the participation of believers in Christ, through faith in Christ.

The world cannot be moved by human effort alone. The world is moved by the fulcrum or pulley of the Trinitarian God in Christ. All such movement is the work of God in Christ. God in Christ moved Jesus to faithfulness, as God in Christ moves all of Christ's disciples to faithfulness. The faithfulness of Christ and of His disciples, both the divine faithfulness of God and the human faithfulness of Jesus at work in His people, then moves the world. Ultimately, it is all God's work in Christ. Proximately, it is Christ's work through Christians.

Understanding and/or making good use of the Sermon on the Mount requires that we begin with the proper context of faithfulness, which is where Jesus began, where God began, in the Trinitarian Godhead. Similarly, having been created in God's image, we also begin with the Trinity. We begin in Christ. And that is the secret of the Sermon on the Mount: it was given by Christ for those in Christ. Deep speaks to deep (Psalm 42:7).

NOT NEW

Contrary to popular opinion the various teachings of the Sermon on the Mount are not new. Jesus did not originate them in this Sermon.

They can all be found in the Old Testament. So, rather than being different because they were new, Jesus set them in relief in the Sermon by comparing them with common misunderstandings of the times in which He lived. Sometimes that comparison was stated—"You have heard that it was said..." (Matthew 5:27, etc.). And sometimes it was the result of shocking His hearers out of their usual expectations by showing them that the values of God's kingdom were the reverse of the values of the world—"Blessed are the poor in spirit... (Matthew 5:5).

The Pagan and Greek understanding of blessedness was a function of individual freedom. The Pagan and Greek gods were blessed because they were not bound by the laws of this world, neither the laws of physics nor the laws of justice. They could do what they pleased, and that freedom was understood as a great blessing. The Greeks and Pagans wanted to become like their gods. That kind of freedom was the hope and aspiration of many people in antiquity. It still is today.

Contrary to Christian teaching, but in harmony with the subversion of multiculturalism, people today tend to cling to this Pagan under-standing regarding the blessings of freedom. People think that being free means that they can do whatever they want. The poor think that the rich have this kind of freedom because they can afford to do what-ever they want. And the rich think that the poor have this kind of freedom because they are not encumbered by the obligations of wealth maintenance.

Contemporary people generally think that freedom means not being bound or obligated by anything, and particularly not being bound by God's law. Freedom in our day is, by popular definition, anti-nomian.[4] People mistakenly believe that by faith and God's grace Chris-tians are freed from all laws, including the moral standards of culture, many of which conform to biblical morality.

But this is not what Jesus taught. People tend to read this under-standing into the Sermon on the Mount, but it is a faithless reading. It assumes a Pagan or Greek worldview and then reads that worldview into Scripture. Much of the difficulty understanding the Sermon on the Mount comes because people don't assume the worldview of biblical faithfulness, as Jesus did. People begin with a different set of unbiblical presuppositions and find that Jesus' teachings don't make sense on the basis of those presuppositions unless they spiritualize the Sermon to the

---

4   Antinomian: any view which rejects laws or legalism and argues against moral, religious, or social norms, or is at least considered to do so. The term has both re-ligious and secular meanings

point that it doesn't say what Jesus said, or doesn't apply to this world. Too many people believe the Sermon to set an ideal that is intended for heaven and not for this world.

Rightly Dividing

There is an easier way to make better sense of the Sermon: by assuming that it is faithful to Scripture, to the Old Testament, by assuming that it is not antinomian. As we shall see, Jesus taught in the Sermon on the Mount that God's blessings are the fruit of obedience to God's Word, as originally taught in the Old Testament.

Jesus did not put an end to Old Testament law in such a way that it has no further application. Rather, He was Himself the end or purpose of the law. In Christ the purpose of the law was fulfilled, and that fulfill-ment of the law brought about a new administration of God's covenant, an administration for people who now stand on the other side of Christ's advent and His historical fulfillment of the law.

Old Testament law can be divided into three parts: moral, ceremo-nial, and civil. This division is neither perfect nor exclusive, which means that almost every part of the Old Law contains moral, ceremo-nial, and civil aspects. The division is not clean, though there is much truth to it. Jesus changed or ended parts of the ceremonial and civil aspects of the law, and many of those changes are the subject, directly or indirectly, of His Sermon on the Mount. But more than changing various aspects of the law, Jesus changed hearts and minds, which gave people a completely different perspective regarding God's law.

Jesus taught differently than the Scribes and Pharisees (Mark 1:22), but not differently than the Old Testament. The newness of the New Covenant in Christ is not a function of its difference from the Old Covenant, but is a function of its fulfillment of the Old Covenant in Christ, and of the new people with whom the New Covenant is made, people who are renewed or regenerated in Christ.

Unseen

What was new was Christ's fulfillment of the Old Covenant as He died on the cross, and the dispensation of God's Holy Spirit to the Gentiles (Matthew 12:18, Acts 10:44-45, Romans 15:16, Galatians 3:14). God's covenant in Christ does not exclude the Jews or the conditions of the Old Covenant. Christ has not abrogated God's law, He fulfilled it Himself, and provided the means for its fulfillment by His people through the manifestation of the Holy Spirit through regeneration.

Christ fulfilled God's covenant and died as a propitiation of sin for His people, which recreated a way for people to grow in grace by drawing near to God.

But the Scribes and Pharisees who interacted with Jesus in the New Testament stories didn't see this reality. They didn't believe it, didn't accept or understand that Jesus was the fulfillment of the Old Testament.

We can't blame them for not seeing it. It couldn't be seen until it was complete, until the death and resurrection of Christ had fully manifested in history. That's why it was necessary for Jesus to die on the cross. Had He not finished the revelation of the Trinity in human flesh, it would never have been seen. Consequently, at the time that this Sermon on the Mount was given, the time of Jesus' earthy ministry, they didn't see it. They couldn't see it because it had been veiled (2 Corinthians 3:13-18).[5] Paul didn't see it either, not until after it was complete and he met the resurrected Christ on the road to Damascus. Paul didn't see it until Christ knocked him off his high horse and explained it to him.

This Sermon came pretty early in Jesus' ministry. In chapter four of Matthew's gospel, Jesus had just started preaching, after having been tempted by Satan. He was just beginning to preach and gather His disciples. Matthew said that Jesus preached this Sermon on the Mount, said these things, because He *saw* the crowd, because He took notice of the multitudes of people who had followed Him. This sermon was Jesus' response to seeing the people, seeing their needs, seeing their hopelessness, and their faithlessness.

Jesus began preaching in earnest as He took over the message and leadership of John The Baptist.

> "From that time Jesus began to preach, saying, 'Repent, for the kingdom of heaven is at hand'" (Matthew 4:17). John was the last of the Old Testament prophets. And John's job was to prepare the way for the Messiah, for Jesus, which he did. With this message of repentance Jesus began to call for disciples, promising to make them "fishers of men" (Matthew 4:19).

He began teaching and healing and drawing crowds of people. And as multitudes of people were drawn to Jesus, He saw them. He saw their needs, their potential, their interests, and their weaknesses.

---

5   For more on the veiling of the gospel see the corresponding sections of *Varsy Arsy—Proclaiming the Gospel in Second Corinthians*, Phillip A. Ross, Pilgrim Platform, Marietta, Ohio, 2009.

ON THE MOUNTAIN

So, He "went up on the mountain" (v. 1). His purpose in going up on the mountain was at least two-fold. He needed a platform from which to teach. He needed His voice to carry so that the multitude could hear Him. And yet He knew that they needed "ears to hear" (Matthew 11:15), as well. There is more to hearing Jesus than acoustics. The platform also needed to be a symbolic place that would help His message reverberate, a place from which His teaching would resound or echo in history.

Part of that echo was to remind people of God's law, the laws that Moses had brought down from the mountain. Jesus' Sermon on the Mount was an echo of the law of Moses, an echo of the Ten Commandments. It wasn't a simple reproduction of that law, but was reminiscent of it. God's law, the Ten Commandments, would echo through Jesus' teaching by design and intention. It has proven to be more of a clarification than a simple recapitulation.

By going up on the mountain Jesus also put Himself in the symbolic place of Moses, the law giver. But Jesus' teaching would not be a pontification like that of Moses, who simply carried to the people the law that God had written with His very finger upon tablets of stone (Exodus 31:18). That law, which Jesus would not change, not even a jot or a tittle (Matthew 5:18), had already been given.

Jesus did not rescind it. Rather, Jesus' purpose was to clarify the law and teach its principles, its application from the perspective of its fulfillment, from a fully revealed Trinitarian perspective. His purpose was to help His people, His disciples, better understand and practice God's law. Jesus would reiterate or echo God's law from the mountain, showing it in the light of Christ. The advent of Christ cast the Law in a different light through His fulfillment of it.

To emphasize the fact that in Christ God Himself had come down to the people to provide further clarification of His law, Luke remembered this sermon as being on the Plain (*pedinos*, or level place—Luke 6:17). Luke's version has Jesus off the mountain and down with the people, where He could speak with them directly, man to man. Luke's symbolism is important because it emphasized the humanity of Jesus during a time that He was functioning out of His divinity as lawgiver. Nonetheless, we are going to follow Matthew's presentation rather than Luke's. We will refer to Luke when he provides additional perspective.

So, was Jesus actually on the mountain or in the plain? Because we understand the gospel writers to have provided a collection of Jesus' teachings rather than a blow by blow account of exactly how it happened, we can easily imagine that these teachings took place both on the mountain and in the plain. Indeed, these are the central teachings of the Lord, which He taught everywhere He went to anyone who would listen.

Before speaking, Jesus "sat down" (v. 1). This seemingly minor detail demonstrates that Jesus taught in the tradition of the Rabbis. Unlike modern times, in the days of the Lord, Rabbis addressed their congregations from a sitting position. The teacher would sit at the head of the table, or in a prominent position facing the people.

Jesus was always out ahead of His disciples, showing them the way, or preparing things for them. And so here, I imagine Jesus being ahead of them, up the hill, looking for the right spot from which to address the crowd. And when He found it, He sat, and waited for the disciples and the crowd to catch up. As they did, as they came to Him, He opened his mouth and began teaching them (vs. 1-2).

BLESSED

The first word out of His mouth was *blessed*, (*makarios*). The Greek word means *supremely favored* and by extension fortunate, well off or happy. Blessed is a description of context and circumstance. Jesus spoke about those who are favored by God, and by implication, those who are faithful to God, those upon whom God smiles. The reference is Deuteronomy 28:1-14, the declaration of God's blessings upon His people, upon those who "faithfully obey the voice of the Lord" (Deuteronomy 28:1). Jesus provided the principles of blessedness, lessons about how to be on the receiving end of God's blessings.

So, the first question to ask is, Who does God bless? And the answer is that God blesses those who "faithfully obey the voice of the Lord" (Deuteronomy 28:1), if I may repeat myself—and I must because God does. But, you may wonder, isn't this idea of being blessed for one's obedience an Old Testament teaching? It is. But what we see here in the Sermon on the Mount is that Jesus has made it a New Testament teaching as well, which makes it a both testaments teaching, which makes it doubly important. Repetition of God's Word is good for the soul.

Is this a kind of salvation by works teaching? No. Salvation is only by grace through faith (Ephesians 2:8). But the faith here is the faith of those who obey the voice of the Lord. While salvation is by faith alone, by the singularity of faith, blessing—sanctification or growing near to

God—comes through obedience. In Deuteronomy 28 God spoke to His people, not to individuals alone but to His people as a group. The blessings are for *them* in the plural, as a whole. Of course those blessings will manifest for individuals as well, but they are not for individuals exclusively. These blessings are for the people of God, for the body of Christ, the church, in all of its Trinitarian complexities.

The full measure of God's blessing is reserved for His people as a people. The full measure of God's blessing manifests more fully when His people are in unity, in Christ, when obedience is measured corporately rather than merely individually. And yet corporate obedience requires individual obedience, but is more than mere personal obedience. Such obedience, the corporate blessings of God's people, also comes by grace through faith. And while God's blessings are for God's people, for the church, they impact more than the church. God's blessings will have a positive impact upon the world (Luke 2:14, 2 Corinthians 5:19-21), upon all people, even the ungodly.

Poor In Spirit

> "Blessed are the poor in spirit, for theirs is the kingdom of heaven" (v. 3).

At the first hearing our ears are rankled because this is not what we expect to hear. Those who first heard it were undoubtedly shocked, perhaps even confused. Those who had followed Jesus tended to be poor, uneducated, and unhealthy. They were people who were dominated by problems of various sorts, and they followed Jesus hoping to solve some of their problems, to get healing for themselves or their loved ones. They were less interested in learning what Jesus had to teach, than they were in getting particular problems fixed. Many had health problems or came on behalf of someone who had health problems. So, Jesus healed some of them.

But Jesus' primary concern was not fixing their problems. He healed in order to get their attention and to establish His credentials. Rather than simply giving hungry people a fish, Jesus wanted to teach them how to fish, if I may build upon the well-known aphorism. Speaking to Peter and Andrew, He said,

> "Follow me, and I will make you, not fishermen—they were already fishermen, but 'fishers of men'" (Matthew 4:19).

In Christ, they would expand their existing skill set and apply it to the mission of Christ. The blessings of God would come with the growth and maturity of His people. This is what Jesus taught on the Mount.

While the Sermon on the Mount is not composed of explicit principles for Christian evangelism, it is composed of principles for Christian evangelists because Christians must actually practice Christianity before they can engage in evangelism. The teachings and principles of the Sermon on the Mount are not for unconverted sinners, as if Jesus was teaching works-righteousness to the unsaved. Not only are these principles beyond the reach of those who are not Christian, they have proven to stretch the grasp of most Christians, as well. They can only be practiced from a Christian perspective. They don't make sense apart from Christ's Trinitarian perspective. All Christian understanding is necessarily trinitarian, which is unique to Christianity. Apart from Christ this understanding is impossible, but in Christ it is inevitable. In addition, faithfully engaging these principles takes practice and discipline. They are simple, but not easy.

Of course, everyone will benefit from faithfully engaging these principles, from learning and applying these principles in their own lives. But the truth is that only those who are actually animated by God have the interest and ability to do so, and too few of those to date—at least in the contemporary world—actually manifest the fullness of that ability. Gilbert K. Chesterton said that

> "Christianity has not been tried and found wanting; it has been
> found difficult and not tried."

The promise of Jesus Christ is that the faithful exercise of these principles will be common to all in the kingdom of God. So, in anticipation of that kingdom we are to learn and practice them as individuals, as families, as churches. Christ fixes sin through His propitiation on the cross. And through the practice and perfection of these principles by those who are saved, God will fix the rest of our problems by providing His many blessings. God's blessings are the fix that the world needs now.

Jesus did not use the Sermon on the Mount to inspire the masses who had followed Him up the mountain to become Christians. That's not what He was doing here, nor did that happen. These Beatitudes are not all that inspiring. The discipline and work of sanctification are not things that people naturally want to engage. Most people are unaffected, confused, or disgusted by them, not inspired. Jesus was not trying to reach people who wanted to be inspired.

Inspired people are not poor in spirit, the inspired are rich in spirit. They are filled with their inspirations, their hopes and dreams. Those who are inspired are full, not empty, rich in spirit, not poor. Jesus was not speaking to the rich in spirit. Christianity is not about inspirational messages for people who feel bad. Christian hope is not like worldly hope.

Rather, Christianity is for the poor in spirit, for those who don't have much spirit, who are uninspired. That's why they are poor in it. Paul, quoting Jesus, mentioned this to the Corinthians.

> "My grace is sufficient for you, for my power is made perfect in weakness" (2 Corinthians 12:9).

Jesus was not simply talking about people who need God, but about people who know that they need God, people who know their own sinfulness and their own inability to do what needs to be done. In contrast, people who think themselves to be basically good, people who are proud of their Christianity or their spirituality or their faithfulness or their inherent goodness, are not poor in spirit.

The poor in spirit are humble. They are meek, modest, not arrogant or prideful. They are patient and kind. They do not envy or boast. They are not arrogant or rude. They do not insist on their own way. They are not irritable or resentful. They do not rejoice at wrongdoing, but rejoice with the truth. They bear all things, believe all things, hope all things, endure all things (1 Corinthians 14:3-7).

These are the kinds of people who compose the kingdom of heaven, who will build the kingdom of heaven on earth (as it is in heaven), who will inherit the kingdom of God. Jesus' Sermon on the Mount is not about simply providing directions for people who want to go to heaven, but is descriptive of those who are engaged in Christ's mission to bring the kingdom of God to earth, "for theirs is the kingdom of heaven" (v. 3)—*is* not *will be*.

THOSE WHO MOURN

> "Blessed are those who mourn, for they shall be comforted" (v. 4).

This verse is very much like the previous verse. Again, we see Jesus standing godless common sense on its head. How can mourning be a blessing? What sort of blessing is grief and sorrow? Questions like these reveal a godless common sense perspective, not a faithful Christian perspective. The person who asks questions like these has hold of the issue by the wrong end. Jesus did not say that it is a blessing to mourn, to feel sadness.

People mourn in the face of loss—the loss of a loved one, the loss of a job, the loss of a home or something of value. There is no blessing in an act of mourning. It is a painful and sad experience. And everyone knows it because it is a universal experience. Everyone mourns in this life because everyone experiences losses in this life. Mourning is a universal experience. Some mourn more and some less, but everyone mourns.

Those who mourn in Christ will be comforted in Christ. So, it is not the fact of mourning that is a blessing. Rather, the blessing is the comfort that comes to those in Christ. The use of the word *shall* here conveys the idea that the comfort is assured. Nothing can keep the comfort away. The *comfort* (*parakaleō*) that Jesus has in mind is a matter of calling near, which is the literal meaning of the Greek word. Blessed are those who mourn, for they shall be called near. Near to what or who? To Jesus, of course. Being near to Jesus is a blessing.

In these two verses Christ has called attention to humility and sadness, and suggested that there is an up side to these things in Christ, that we should not fear humiliation or sadness. Rather, if we can engage them in Christ, if we can hold on to faithfulness in the midst of such things, there will be a benefit, a blessing. Faithfulness is the key to the comfort. The comfort comes through faithfulness. It is a product of faithfulness.

Paul spoke of a similar idea when he wrote to the Romans.

> "Therefore, since we have been justified by faith, we have peace with God through our Lord Jesus Christ. Through him we have also obtained access by faith into this grace in which we stand, and in which we rejoice in hope of the glory of God. More than that, we rejoice in our sufferings, knowing that suffering produces endurance, and endurance produces character, and character produces hope, and hope does not put us to shame, because God's love has been poured into our hearts through the Holy Spirit who has been given to us" (Romans 5:1-5).

In Christ the bitterness of such experiences is transformed into fuel for character development and hope, both of which are blessings. The pain of mourning is mitigated by faithfulness in Christ. Yes, but more than that, faithfulness dissolves the pain of mourning into hope, and hope is the fuel of sanctification for the engine of salvation by grace through faith in Christ alone. The pain of loss in this sinful world cannot be avoided. But it can be changed into the joy of growth and maturity in Christ—and that is the blessing that awaits those in Christ who mourn.

2. The Return of Righteousness

Blessed are the meek, for they shall inherit the earth. Blessed are those who hunger and thirst for righteousness, for they shall be satisfied. Blessed are the merciful, for they shall receive mercy. Blessed are the pure in heart, for they shall see God.
—Matthew 5:5-8

There are two definitions of meek: 1) showing patience and humility, gentleness; 2) easily imposed on, submissive. Contemporary Christians will likely feel fine about the first definition because it is full of Christian qualities—patience, humility, and gentleness. But the second definition may give people a harder time. Being submissive and easily imposed upon will get you taken advantage of. People will use you and walk all over you. Meekness is not a popular character quality. Yet, submissive is also a well-defined biblical character quality that is intended for all Christians (Romans 10:3, Hebrews 13:17). It's funny how people like the idea of patience, humility and gentleness, yet reject the idea of submission.

Paul called for universal submission.

> "Therefore do not be foolish, but understand what the will of the Lord is. And do not get drunk with wine, for that is debauchery, but be filled with the Spirit, addressing one another in psalms and hymns and spiritual songs, singing and making melody to the Lord with your heart, giving thanks always and for everything to God the Father in the name of our Lord Jesus Christ, submitting to one another out of reverence for Christ" (Ephesians 5:17-21).

Paul called for men to submit to their elders, wives to submit to their husbands in the Lord, children to submit to their parents, and for everyone to submit to Christ through one another. Indeed, universal submission is a directive of the first order. Christianity apart from such submission is not Christianity.

Obviously, this doesn't mean that everyone is a boss and gets to command other people. In fact, the call for submission isn't related to any commands but Christ's. Submission is a prerequisite for service. The Greek word (*hupotasso*) is composed of two words meaning *under orders* or an arrangement, a system. To submit to something is to find your place in a chain of command in which you are not at the top.

It is more about taking orders than giving them. In fact, in a chain of command the only person giving orders is the person at the top. Sure, those orders are to be conveyed to those down the chain. But the conveyance of orders that have been received is not at all like giving original orders. Of course, the captains and lieutenants will have to interpret and adjust the orders to fit the circumstances of their mission.

Interestingly, as the orders move down the chain of command they get more specific, more narrow, more particular. The general commands all of the battalions and gives orders to the battalion commanders. The battalion commanders parse those orders and divide out the responsibilities to their company commanders. And the company commanders further parse the orders they have received for their squadron leaders. No single squadron is expected to do what has been given to the battalion to do. And yet, each squadron contributes to the general cause. This is the kind of submission that is called for in the gospel. Christ is the general, the only general. And the rest of us take orders and contribute to the cause of Christ.

Some people have more responsibility than others, and that's just the way it is. Leadership is a responsibility and a burden. Real leadership is hard work in many ways, and most people don't want it. People, who are like sheep, tend to shy away from leadership. Most people prefer to follow and avoid the hassles, dangers and stresses of leadership. People require a boost from something in order to get the courage and energy required to lead. That boost ultimately comes either from God or from Satan. Leadership is never neutral. It always moves people in one direction or another, toward God or toward Satan.

THE MEEK

The word *meek* in this verse describes how we are to follow orders. We are to do so not reluctantly but willingly, eagerly. The meek have a gentle disposition. The meek are sheep-like. Jesus likened us to sheep (Matthew 9:36) because people are so much like sheep in many ways.

Sheep are timid, fearful, easily panicked. They are stupid and gullible, very vulnerable to fear, frustration, pests, and hunger. They stampede easily and are vulnerable to herd psychology. Sheep have little or no means of defense. They can only run, and not very well at that. Sheep are easily killed by their enemies. They are jealous and compete for affection and attention. They constantly need fresh water and fresh pastures. But they have very little discernment in choosing food or water. Like goats, they eat just about everything. Sheep are stubborn and will insist on their own way, even when it harms them. Sheep are easily "cast"—flipped over on their backs or sides and are often unable to get up. In so many ways sheep are helpless. They look for easy places to rest, and don't like to be sheared or cleaned up.

Unfortunately, too much wool can cause sheep to be easily "cast." They are creatures of habit and easily get into destructive behavioral ruts. Of all livestock, sheep need the most care. They need to be constantly on the move to keep from overgrazing a field and destroying their own food source. And yet, sheep are very gregarious, social animals. They love to be with the herd. It's not hard to see why Jesus referred to us as sheep. Sheep are domestic animals and would not survive in the wild.

The meek in this verse suggests those who are Christ's sheep, those over whom He is Shepherd. Yet, in spite of our human weaknesses, there are many people who will not submit to the Lord (or His representatives), who refuse to be meek and who strut and boast as if they are tough and independent—who don't think they need a shepherd. But in reality there are no tough sheep, just as there are no waterless clouds (Jude 1:12). A waterless cloud, like a tough sheep, is an oxymoron, a contradiction of terms. But that doesn't stop some stubborn sheep from acting tough. Paul said that

> "the mind that is set on the flesh is hostile to God, for it does not submit to God's law; indeed, it cannot. Those who are in the flesh cannot please God "(Romans 8:7-8).

> "For, being ignorant of the righteousness of God, and seeking to establish their own, they did not submit to God's righteousness" (Romans 10:3).

What happens to a sheep that doesn't submit to the shepherd? Death. It's only a matter of time because sheep cannot care for themselves. That's who *we* are—all of us, not just Christians. All people are like sheep. The only difference is that Christians know that they are sheep. Christians know the Shepherd. We know His voice. Unbelievers don't.

Meekness is revealed by patience and poise in the midst of injury. The meek are most identifiable by their lack of irritability, anger, and revenge. The meek don't get even. They don't get irritated, and that is what leads to peace. The meek are peacemakers, and will inherit the earth.

It is interesting that the meek will inherit the earth and not simply the kingdom. The poor in spirit will have the kingdom of heaven, while the meek will inherit the earth. Why this difference between the earth and the kingdom of heaven? Because the difference between earth and the kingdom of heaven is great, but one day there won't be such a difference. One day earth will be as it is in heaven because Christ has inaugurated the coming of the kingdom of God to earth.

Being meek means doing nothing in response to insult or injury. I might even suggest that being meek is a matter of staying focused on your orders, and not getting distracted by the difficulties and vicissitudes of life. Meekness is knowing your place in the chain of command, and of performance in that place. Being meek is a matter of obedience and quick response to orders. A good Sargent is not only good at barking orders to the troops, he is also good at receiving orders from his lieutenant. A good Sargent is good at receiving orders and carrying them out. He knows what needs to be done, and he does it without getting distracted. A good Sargent is a meek Sargent.

HUNGER AND THIRST

> "Blessed are those who hunger and thirst for righteousness, for they shall be satisfied" (v. 6).

Jesus was surely speaking to hungry and thirsty people. Crowds, like sheep, eat and drink all the time. But it was not ordinary hunger or thirst that Jesus spoke of. The object of the hunger here is critical. Jesus was adding His blessing upon those who desire righteousness, those who endeavor to uphold biblical moral principles.

People have no moral principles of their own. Sin has made us unable to discern truth or true moral principles. Sin has skewed our judgment. Apart from Christ, apart from the Shepherd, people will drain whatever resources are available to them and tear each other apart for whatever resources are left between them. Apart from Christ people are self-righteous, proud, irritable, and afraid (fearful). Apart from Christ people know at some level that they are destined for death and Hell (Romans 1:20). People will stubbornly cling to their old habits of selfishness and godlessness. Nothing but their own death and rebirth in Christ can change them. That is the major point of the Bible and the singular mission of Jesus—nothing but Christ can change people.

Education only makes us smarter sheep. It has no effect on our selfishness, stubbornness, or our blindness to the things of God. Educated people are only better able to justify their old habits. An educated Christian is a blessing, an educated heathen is not. Education does not change our essential character. It only brings out what is naturally in us.

Similarly, wealth only makes us richer sheep. Wealth has no effect on our stubbornness or our blindness to the things of God. Wealthy people are only better able to fund their old habits, not change them. A wealthy Christian is a blessing, a wealthy heathen is not.

Health is no different. It only keeps us from getting sick. Being healthy means being able to be what you are and do what you want. A healthy sheep is better able to be a sheep than is a sick sheep. Healthy sheep are better able to do sheeply things, but it doesn't make them other than sheep. Health doesn't change our character or habits, it just allows us to better engage them.

Education, wealth and health are all offered as panaceas for a better world, as the means for improving ourselves and our world. And all of these things are good, but none of them are able to change our godless habits, our selfish desires, or our godlessness. Education, wealth, and health only make us better able to be who we naturally are. They cannot change our sin nature.

Apart from Christ, apart from Scripture, people would have no idea about real goodness or godliness because sinful people are neither good nor godly. Godliness is not our natural condition. We cannot become better people or more godly by looking within ourselves, or at one another. The human heart is a cesspool of sin and corruption.

> "The heart is deceitful above all things, and desperately wicked:
> who can know it? "(Jeremiah 17:9).

Too many people think that human beings are naturally good, and that we are corrupted by the world. But that is backwards to what the Bible says. Scripture teaches that people are naturally sinful, naturally evil, and depraved. Scripture teaches that our sinfulness and depravity corrupt the world. It's not that the world corrupts us, but that we corrupt the world. Of course, God created everything good. But people ignore and disregard the fact of the Fall, the reality of sin.

Adam fell and sin has been our natural condition ever since. The fix for the corruption of the world is not political action. That's not the first step, anyway. The first step is confession of our sin, acknowledgment that we are the problem, that we are so lost that we are not worth saving. This is what it means to be poor in spirit. Only when we see the actual depth of our own personal depravity can we begin to contemplate the degree of our own wickedness. Only when we grasp our iniquity, added together with (or maybe multiplied by) all of the wickedness of other people and the wickedness of human history, can we own the hopelessness of looking within ourselves. Whether we look into our own individual hearts or look to the great literature of human history, we see the same thing—unrepentant wickedness.

While people don't like seeing this about themselves, seeing it, owning it, is a necessary part of salvation. Those who turn away from Christ, those who ignore the gravitas of human iniquity, of their own depravity, their own culpability, their own ignorance, deny the truth of God. And God is the only thing that can save them—us. The truth of our situation, best seen on the cross, is the man Jesus Christ. His death is our salvation. There is no other way. That's the way God designed it. That's the way God designed us. So, to reject the reality of human sin, to deny one's own sin, is to reject God's truth, God's man, Jesus Christ.

SATISFACTION

> "Blessed are those who hunger and thirst for righteousness, for
> they shall be satisfied "(v. 6).

Human unity is a powerful thing. People working together can accomplish just about anything. The modern world is a testimony to the power of people working together. The modern world is built upon the foundation of Christian values, of Christianity. That's what Christianity is: the expression of Christian values. Science and technology blossomed in Christendom, not India or China, not in Persia or Babylon. In fact, human unity is such a powerful thing that God destroyed it at Babylon when that unity was not built upon genuine godliness.

Babylon was the seat of Nimrod's power, and Nimrod was not in the lineage of faithfulness. The Babylonians were trying to reach up to heaven from the earth, without God's blessing. They would have brought sin into heaven. But God cannot tolerate sin and evil. So, their attempt to reach heaven while engaged in sin and evil could have ended in no other way. They had no righteousness, and were trying to storm heaven without it. God could not allow it.

In contrast, God reached down through Jesus Christ with the gift of righteousness in order to mend the breach between heaven and earth. And it is only by the gift of Christ's righteousness—not ours—that we sinners are able to receive grace, confess our sins, receive forgiveness, and be united with Christ on earth, as it will one day be in heaven (Matthew 6:10). It is the desire for that righteousness, as the deer pants for the waters (Psalm 42:1), that brings, not heaven nor earth, but fullness and satisfaction.

The Greek word translated as *satisfied* (*chortazo*) literally means *gorged*. The desire for Christ's righteousness will make us full, very full. So, will we be filled with Christ's righteousness? Yes and no. Yes, that desire will increasingly dominate our hearts and minds as we grow in grace. Christians do become more righteous, more holy, over time. We get better at it as we mature in it, as we follow the Lord. So, it fills us, but we don't fill it. There is more to Christ's righteousness than we can ever know or experience in this life. So, it is not that we reach some summit of righteousness where we can bask in the light of Christ and snarl at those who are less righteous. It just doesn't work like that.

Rather, the more we grow in the righteousness of Christ, the more we come to realize what depraved sinners we actually are. The more holy we become, the more we realize how far we are from any sort of real holiness. Just as the road leading upward takes us down, as it took the Babylonians down, so the road leading downward in Christ, in service and humility, takes us up. This is no great mystery, but is only common sense. Jesus taught that the way to greatness never ventures off the path of humble service. This is true because it is right. To seek this kind of service is the hunger and thirst for righteousness that Jesus mentioned.

MERCIFUL

"Blessed are the merciful, for they shall receive mercy" (v. 7).

You may have heard it this way: you get what you give. This can be seen in everyday life. Smile at someone and they will smile back at you. Snarl at them and they will likely snarl back. Of course, you don't *always* get what you give. But that's the general idea behind the Golden Rule, which Jesus taught in Matthew 7:12,

> "So whatever you wish that others would do to you, do also to them, for this is the Law and the Prophets."

In verse 7 however, the *whatever* is specified as mercy. If you wish mercy from others, give mercy to them. Don't wait for them to give it to you.

The mercy (*eleēmōn*) in view here is not mere forgiveness, but is compassionate forgiveness. It is forgiveness with a passion. It is not the forgiveness that is begrudgingly given after an infraction has occurred. It is the prevenient forgiveness that is given *carte blanche*. Jesus was teaching the importance of the Old Testament understanding of mercy (*chêsêd*). This Old Testament understanding of mercy regarded mercy as a covering for sin. God cannot countenance sin, which is why the law alone does not bring us near to God. The law only condemns us by revealing the degree of our sin in the face of a righteous God. When we understand God's law we see ourselves from God's point of view (to an extent). The law shows us how far we fall short of real righteousness.

Christ, then, provides a covering for our sin, which allows us to draw near to the Lord in spite of our present imperfections. As long as we remain under Christ's cover, Christ's authority, we are okay. But once we draw near to God in Christ, if somehow we slip out from under that covering through disobedience or neglect, we are then more exposed to the burning light of God's perfection and His wrath against sinners. To some extent we are drawn nearer to God while we are under Christ's authority, so to then abandon that covering makes us worse off than if we had never known Christ.

Of course, God's mercy is a good thing because it allows us to grow in sanctification while under the protection of Christ. Apart from God's mercy we would simply have to be perfect as Christ is perfect, which is impossible because of our sin. But to abandon Christ in the midst of our sanctification exposes us to greater light and heat, and removes His protection. So, to abandon Christ is not a good thing. Those who abandon Christ are worse off than those who never knew Him.

We grow in God's mercy by being merciful ourselves, by practicing mercy. Jesus also said it this way,

> "For if you forgive others their trespasses, your heavenly Father will also forgive you, but if you do not forgive others their tres-

passes, neither will your Father forgive your trespasses" (Matthew 6:14-15).

Pure In Heart

"Blessed are the pure in heart, for they shall see God" (v. 8).

Here the wisdom of Christ flies in the face of the wisdom of the world. In the world happiness is accorded to those who get what they want. *Blessed are those who know how to get what they want*, spouts worldly wisdom. The world values the ingenuity and craftiness that hones the art of deceit without engaging in boldfaced lying. Such artisans of dazzle know how to bend and shape the truth to indirectly accomplish their own ends, while convincing others that they are working for them, or for the downtrodden and helpless. Indeed, there is no lower moral decrepitude than bilking the poor in the name of justice and righteousness. Such are the very opposite of the pure in heart. This is the heart of the gambling industry which peddles false hope to the poor and downtrodden.

Jesus referred to them as the pure in *heart*, not the pure in *head*. Jesus has the heart in mind—the will, the intentions, not pure thoughts or ideas. Jesus did not call them the pure in *hand*, either. Jesus was not talking about pure actions. Our actions issue out of our hearts. Jesus was talking about the root, not the fruit. Nor did He call them the pure in *mouth*. There is more to purity than talk. It involves talk, but there is more to it than that.

Matthew Henry calls this the most comprehensive of the beatitudes. The Psalmist noted that this purity of heart was essential for all who would worship God.

> "Who shall ascend the hill of the Lord? And who shall stand in his holy place? He who has clean hands and a pure heart, who does not lift up his soul to what is false and does not swear deceitfully. He will receive blessing from the Lord and righteousness from the God of his salvation" (Psalms 24:3-5).

No one can approach God without this purity of heart.

Of course, only Christ could fulfill this requirement, and He did. He did it for us. But Christ's fulfillment does not absolve us of our responsibility. It just shifted it from our responsibility to God to our responsibility to Christ. Through Christ's death and resurrection He is bringing humanity into maturity and perfection (wholeness, completeness), whereas prior to Christ the demands of God's perfection were simply revealed in the law without facilitation. The law said, *Here it is, do it! Be ye perfect!*

But no one could. The demands of God's perfection are more than people can bear. God's perfection is too far out of reach. In Christ, however, people can avoid the consequences of their own sin and failures before they have outgrown them. In Christ, spiritual growth is possible, whereas apart from Christ it is not. Apart from Christ complete maturity and perfection are simply expected, demanded of beings who are imperfect and unable to reach perfection.

Because judgment ensues for any and all sin, people are condemned by the Old Testament. And because no one—save Christ alone—is perfect and everyone is a sinner, there is no result but damnation. Paul saw this clearly and wrote to the Romans about it.

However, in Christ growth in grace, growth in righteousness, is possible because Christ covers our sin. Christ shields us from God's wrath by covering us with His perfection and authority until we reach perfection ourselves, in glory. To be under Christ's authority is to be shielded from God's wrath. Christ provides more than an opportunity for growth, He provides the means for growth. Again, apart from Christ people face God's demand for immediate perfection on their own, and must face the consequences for their failure to achieve it.

God gave Moses the Ten Commandments, but no one could do them. The gift of God's law was a demand for perfect righteousness. The law is good and helpful, but apart from an opportunity to grow into it, it is a curse that leads only to damnation.

When a bank forecloses on your house, it demands immediate payment of the loan. If you don't have the money, you lose the house. You don't have any choice. The case is closed. But Christ is like a mortgage company who steps in and pays off your loan for you. The foreclosure is then off the table because the mortgage company now owns the house.

Like it or not, agree to it or not, you have then incurred a moral (if not actual) debt to the mortgage company, who now has the right to dictate the terms by which you may continue to live in the house. The mortgage company made the choice to redeem your house. You didn't because you couldn't. You had no choice in the matter. You had no ability to pay the debt. If you did, you would have.

Christ, your new landlord, then determines whether you may continue living in the house. And He is gracious and merciful beyond our wildest expectations. But there are still rules for occupancy. Christ did not change the law, not a jot or tittle (Matthew 5:18). Basic household occupancy rules still apply. Christ is laying out these rules in this Sermon on the Mount. They are the same as the old rules, and yet they are also new because they have been given to a renewed people, a people who have the help of the Lord. What is new about the New Covenant is that past infractions have been forgiven, and the consequences for new infractions are being held at bay, until the Lord returns. So, you now have a choice. You can now live by Christ's rules, with Christ's help, or suffer the consequences on your own. That's the choice you have, and it's your choice. You are completely free to make it.

Today, we still live in this interim period, the time after Christ came and announced the new mortgage plan, but before He takes full possession of the house. Christians are only stewards, living in the Master's house and caring for his property until He returns. Our situation today is that Christ has already come and has already made the redemption deal with God thousands of years ago. When He closed that deal on the cross, the interim period began. It is still in process until Christ returns to take possession and wrap up the details. And while we don't know exactly when that will be, we are closer to that time than any previous generation. So, we best get ourselves ready.

3. HEALING THE CHEESEMAKERS

*Blessed are the peacemakers, for they shall be called sons of
God. Blessed are those who are persecuted for righteousness'
sake, for theirs is the kingdom of heaven. Blessed are you when
others revile you and persecute you and utter all kinds of evil
against you falsely on my account. Rejoice and be glad, for
your reward is great in heaven, for so they persecuted the
prophets who were before you.* —Matthew 5:9-12

In the Monty Python movie, *Life of Brian* (1979), Jesus was
preaching the Sermon on the Mount. Brian was way back in the
crowd. Mel Brooks, the director, focused on this rear end of the
crowd, on several people talking together. They were arguing and bickering about a variety of things. There were several significant points
made by this scene.

First, if crowds then were like crowds now, it would have been
difficult to hear Jesus' unaided voice in that environment if it happened
as Matthew suggests. Second, the kind of people Jesus spoke of were the
complete opposite of the kind of people in the crowd, at least those in
the back of the crowd. And third, misunderstanding was common.
Those near Brian couldn't hear and were speculating about what Jesus
may have said when a fellow in front of them turned around and said, "I
think it was: blessed are the cheese-makers."

A woman turned to her obviously educated, upper class husband
and asked, "What's so special about the cheese-makers?" Her husband
replied with disdain, "It's not meant to be taken literally, but obviously
applies to any manufacturer of dairy products." Brooks has put his finger
on an important aspect of Jesus' Sermon on the Mount by showing how

easily misunderstood it is, and how far people take their misunderstandings. It's a riot, funny, but sadly funny because it is so true.

The point was in part the importance of context, and in this case it
suggested that there was no context for the crowd to understand what
Jesus was talking about. That context could be lost or obscured in Jesus'
day, as it can be in our own. The context must be informed by biblical
faith and apart from that faith Jesus makes no sense. People should
understand Jesus better today than people did in the first century
because we know more about the Bible and about their culture than
they did. But we don't, not generally. People are distracted by all sorts of
things. And whether that was the point made by this Monty Python
scene or not, it is an important observation for us.

In the absence of correct context, people simply supply their own.
We all do it, and we cannot help but do it because language and
communication require a meaningful context. And where context is
missing or obscured, the brain naturally searches its available memory
for something relevant, or not. Right understanding requires right
context. The combination of human intelligence and imagination gives
us the ability to justify or rationalize anything. A lot of humor involves
playing with context, taking things out of context, insinuating,
assuming, or inserting things into a wrong context.

The Peacemakers

So, who was Jesus referring to? Who were the peacemakers?
Jerusalem was occupied by Roman military might at the time. So, the
Romans would not have been the peacemakers. And the Zealots were
calling for rebellion, which would exclude the Zealots. Was Jesus referring to the Pharisees, who had made peace with Rome by compro-
mising the biblical message in order to maintain their positions of privi-
lege? No, it was none of these. Rather, Jesus was imposing the future of
the kingdom upon his listeners. He was saying, these are the kinds of
people who will inherit the kingdom of God. So, these are the kinds of
people you should want to be.

Curiously, Muslims sometimes employ this verse (and others) for
themselves, believing that the followers of Islam are imposing peace
upon the world through Jihad and thereby hope to receive God's
blessing. But this Islamic imposition of peace appears to the rest of the
world to be the very opposite of peace. Thus, the Muslims provide an
example of how we poor misguided human beings can turn an idea on
its head in order to make it fit some presupposed context. The Muslim

version of peace is Pax Islama, where Islamic law enforces peace through political domination.

Indeed, presuppositions can be dangerous. It is remarkably easy to presuppose what is not actually the case, and then interpret various facts on the basis of that presupposition. To guard against this danger, our presuppositions like our faith must be dependent upon the correct object of faith in order to be true. It is not the presupposing or the believing (faith) that makes a thing true—not at all. Many people believe false things and harbor inaccurate, faulty presuppositions, and get all sorts of things mixed up.

Rather, it is the correctness or ultimate objectivity, the object to which the presupposition or faith depends upon that provides the self-authentication that is accorded to absolute truth. Having faith is important, but having faith in the right thing is essential. Faith in the wrong things is worse than no faith at all. The absence of faith provides no assurance, and false faith provides faulty assurance.

We cannot help but presuppose many things, rightly or wrongly. We are hard wired for it. The process of thinking requires us to make various presuppositions, which may or may not be true. But only correctly presupposing the Trinitarian truth of Jesus Christ is ultimately self-authenticating. In other words, God's truth always proves to be true in the long run.

We see this in the scientific process when we formulate an hypothesis, when we make an assumption or presupposition regarding something, and then set out to establish it experimentally. Scientists intentionally try to disprove the thesis by doing various experiments to determine if it is always true. As long as the results of the experiments do not contradict the theory, it is assumed to be true. True theories over time authenticate themselves when no circumstances or experiments contradict them. This is what it means for a theory (presupposition) to be scientifically true.

"Blessed are the peacemakers, for they shall be called sons of God
"(v. 9).

Peacemakers (*eirēnopoios*) make peace by reconciling parties that are at variance. Peacemakers reconcile differences of opinion. They work to harmonize those who are out of accord with one another. However, by calling these peacemakers sons of God, Jesus indicated that the correct context for peacemaking is the Word of God.

He did not mean that peacemakers should simply find the mean or average between conflicting opinions or suggest that the truth lay somewhere in the middle, between the differing opinions, as if the truth can be averaged like a column of numbers. This kind of peacemaking is called equivocation. Equivocation finds a mean position that is not completely false but that cleverly avoids an unpleasant aspect of the truth. Equivocation doesn't reconcile differing opinions, it conflates them by taking a little of this and a little of that in order to hide various unpalatable elements of the truth.

Real peacemaking, on the other hand, reconciles differing opinions by harmonizing them with objective truth, God's truth, God's Word. This is why Jesus called them sons of God, because they were to represent God's truth. Peace, then, comes from the harmonization of our opinions—our presuppositions and our faith—not with one another, but with objective truth, ultimate truth, God's truth, God's Word. And Scripture teaches that ultimate truth is the Trinitarian Person, Jesus Christ. Thus, real peacemaking always brings us into accord with Jesus Christ, on His terms, not ours. Peacemaking begins with reconciliation with God, and there is no way to do this apart from Christ. This reconciliation comes with God's blessing. This is what this Beatitude means.

PERSECUTED

> "Blessed are those who are persecuted for righteousness' sake, for theirs is the kingdom of heaven" (v. 10).

Verse 10 follows verse 9 for a reason. Verse 9 sets the context for which verse 10 is to be understood. Matthew here introduced the idea that Christians will be persecuted, but not persecuted for crimes or for any legitimate or lawful reasons, but for righteousness' sake. They will be persecuted for adhering to moral principles, but not just any moral principles, the moral principles of the Bible.

It might seem odd that people are persecuted for being good and right, for honoring the truth. Daniel Webster defined *righteousness* in his 1828 dictionary as:

> "Purity of heart and rectitude of life; conformity of heart and life to the divine law. Righteousness, as used in Scripture and theology, in which it is chiefly used, is nearly equivalent to holiness, comprehending holy principles and affections of heart, and conformity of life to the divine law. It includes all we call justice,

honesty and virtue, with holy affections; in short, it is true religion."

And who might these religious persecutors be? Jesus didn't say, but there are a bunch of them.

This Beatitude has proven to be true throughout history. Christians have always been persecuted and despised by the majority of people in any society. We might want to doubt that this statement has been true in America because most people believe that most people in America have always been Christian. And that may be true. But being a Christian is different than being a *faithful* Christian. Usually, the more faithful a Christian is the more persecution is experienced. In fact, most Christians are not faithful Christians, and this has pretty much always been the case, at least over the past few generations. Faithfulness has always been a serious problem in the church. It was that way when Jesus preached, and when Paul preached. The many creeds and confessions of the churches are the fruit of faithfulness speaking to unfaithfulness. This is what an honest reading of the Bible teaches.

It is the faithlessness of Christians that gives Christianity a bad name among so many people. Many people observe faithless Christians and determine that Christianity must, therefore, not be what it purports to be. This is a huge problem, and is the number one factor that retards genuine Christian evangelism.

People prefer being faithless Christians to being faithful Christians because faithlessness does not expose them to difficulties or persecution by the world. So, shallow people who would rather avoid persecution than honor Christ, hold to a shallow Christianity, an easy Christianity, a positive Christianity. Christianity-lite avoids difficulties of all sorts, and especially persecution. Shallow people are easily converted to an easy Christianity, a false Christianity, or it might be better to describe it as an inadequate or incomplete Christianity.

Many misunderstandings of Christianity are not completely false, but neither are they completely true. Unfortunately, too much of what passes for Christianity today is actually some version of Christianity-lite, half true. It's a kind of half-way covenant[6] where beliefs and behaviors can be segregated, compartmentalized from one another.

People rationalize, *We're all sinners. No one is perfect, and no one expects us to be perfect.* And like most lies, this one is mostly true. We

---

6   *Essays On Church—Ordinary Christianity for the World*, Phillip A. Ross, Pilgrim Platform, Marietta, Ohio, 2020, "The Halfway Covenant," p. 115.

are all sinners and no one is perfect, save Christ. But someone does expect Christians to be perfect—God (Matthew 5:48). God wants to be in relationship with His people, but He cannot tolerate sin. And because people are full of sin, He cannot tolerate the people He loves. It's a problem.

So, He sent Jesus to provide propitiation, to atone for the sin of humanity so that the broken relationship between God and humanity can be restored. Jesus has done all that. Now God can relate to people through Jesus Christ, but only through Jesus Christ because He alone is God's mediator. He alone is perfect. And all authority has been given to Christ.

So, in Christ, then, God expects His people to be perfect because if they are not, He cannot relate to them. The point is this: God expects people to be perfect in Christ. It is not that God has now lowered His expectations because of what Christ did, but that Christ has fulfilled God's expectations. In Christ, God expects Christians to be faithful, to be the best Christians they can be. God expects us to do our best, to live the best lives possible, not to cut corners, not to be shallow, but to strive for excellence in all things (1 Corinthians 12:31). But God also knows two other things: 1) that our best will not be good enough because it will not be perfect, and 2) that Jesus will make up for what we lack.

Yet, there are two issues with this scenario that must be addressed. First, Jesus will only make up for the difference inasmuch as we actually do our best to completely trust Him and make the effort to live up to His expectations. This is the faith issue. He knows when we are fully trusting Him, when we are actually doing our best, and when we aren't, because He can read our hearts. And while Jesus is indeed the ultimate fudge-master because He fixes our flaws, He will not tolerate half-baked belief or half-assed efforts. He requires our wholehearted confidence, loyalty, and engagement.

Of course, Christians don't begin with a fully mature faith, but we had better end with it because Jesus is also the ultimate heart-master who requires that we give all we have, that we don't hold back, that we don't dissimulate. He gives us the power to believe, and then the opportunity to trust Him, to trust God's Word. He's after our hearts, our minds, our lives. He will surely make up for what we lack, but only inasmuch as we give all that we have. Jesus doesn't require great faith, just honest faith. A little is plenty as long as we are not holding anything back.

This might sound like works-righteousness, but it isn't. And it isn't because the second issue that needs to be addressed is that we can do nothing apart from God's election and the power and presence of the Holy Spirit through regeneration. All of the work related to our righteousness has been done, is being done and will be done by Christ Himself, through His Trinitarian Holy Spirit. God decreed the redemption of His people from sin, and eventually the whole world will be freed from it. He sent Jesus Christ to atone for our sin, and then sent the Holy Spirit to sanctify us. There is nothing left for us to do but to give our assent to God's plan and process. Giving that assent, however, is not a little thing. Rather, it's a big deal.

ANANIAS AND SAPPHIRA

Ananias and Sapphira held back (Acts 5:1-18). They gave generously, but held back, not their property but their trust, their faith. They were outwardly members of the church, but did not discern the body of Christ (1 Corinthians 11:29). Their church membership was *sarx* not *soma*.[7] The Lord was not after all of their property or all of their money, but all of their hearts, all of their faith. The property and the money were incidental to the point of the story. The point was their dissembling, their intention to deceive the Lord and His representatives, their holding back. No doubt they had been trusting in their own worthiness, and not in the worthiness of Christ.

In fact, the story of Ananias and Sapphira illustrates this Beatitude rather well. Acts 5:11 tells us that great fear came upon those who heard the story that God had struck Ananias and Sapphira dead on the spot for holding back. It is a terrifying story and we should not water it down or domesticate it to our own sensibilities. *They withheld, God killed them on the spot, and people became afraid.*

Scripture acknowledges that there were "many signs and wonders" that were "regularly done" (Acts 5:12), and the story of Ananias and Sapphira is simply accounted to be one of them, and accepted without further consideration. The lesson of this story was assumed to be obvious and further explanation was not necessary.

But let's think about it. The critical observation was that

> "none of the rest dared join them, but the people held them in
> high esteem" (Acts 5:13).

---

7   See *Arsy Varsy—Reclaiming the Gospel in First Corinthians*, Phillip A. Ross, Pilgrim Platform, Marietta, Ohio, 2008, p. 211-13, etc.

There are two groups differentiated here. There were *the rest* who dared not join, and there were those who were already members, who had already joined them. The idea of joining a group suggests that a group existed. The point of the story is that Ananias and Sapphira had their membership in the group withdrawn by the Lord.

The group was the early church, in which the apostles and other unnamed people were members. The church was the group that the rest dared not join (v. 13), but at least they held the church in high esteem. Christians understood, and non-Christians at least held the church in high esteem or respect, probably out of fear.

Notice in Acts 5:14 that, though the rest dared not join,

> "more than ever believers were added to the Lord, multitudes of both men and women."

This is quite curious. While none of the rest dared to join, nonetheless multitudes of believers, both men and women, were added to the membership roster. What was going on here? Did Matthew forget what he said in verse 13? No, he was showing the difference between these two groups (believes and unbelievers), making a point about real church membership.

One explanation could be that the story of Ananias and Sapphira was such an odd and disturbing story that it was ignored or suppressed because people couldn't make any sense of it, and what they did under-stand they didn't like. It is a disturbing story. These were the people who dared not join. These people were afraid. They didn't understand, but couldn't deny the death of Ananias and Sapphira. So, they stayed away, but held the church in high esteem.

Nonetheless, the gospel continued to march forward providing signs and wonders on a regular basis, which attracted new people, people who did not know the story of Ananias and Sapphira. The Bible was not in existence yet. And these new people were the ones who were attracted by the signs and wonders and added to the roles. That's one explanation.

Another explanation might be that those who had been added to the roles were actually driven by superstitions and not by the truth of the gospel. We see a lot of this today, but are usually hesitant to think that such a thing was going on in the Early Church. We have idealized the early Christians by thinking that they provide the model of faithfulness that we are to follow. But this is only partially true. We are not to follow other Christians, no matter when they lived. Rather, we are to follow Christ alone. And indeed, this is a common problem that has plagued the churches in every age.

SHADOWS AND SUPERSTITIONS

Some of these people were so superstitious that

> "they even carried out the sick into the streets" (Acts 5:15)

in the hope that they would be cured by Peter's shadow! I know that there has been a lot of spiritualizing about this verse by a great many great Christians, genuine Christians. And I am not trying to suggest that God couldn't heal people with Peter's shadow (Acts 5:15).

Rather, I'm suggesting that the "all" who were healed in verse 16 might not refer to those they carried out in the hope of being healed by Peter's shadow. What if that was not Luke's point? Could his point have been that the people who had been brought into the church by the multitudes were so filled with superstition that they actually believed that Peter's shadow could heal? Doesn't that sound superstitious? Isn't superstition a lingering problem for Christians, even today?

Note that Luke did not say that Peter's shadow ever actually healed anyone, nor are there any other instances of anyone being healed by a shadow in Scripture. Such a healing would be a unique biblical event, not impossible but without precedent, reference, or explanation. Look again. Luke said that the

> "people also gathered from the towns around Jerusalem, bringing
> the sick and those afflicted with unclean spirits, and they were all
> healed" (Acts 5:16).

It doesn't say that these were the same people as those in verse 15 or that they were healed by Peter's shadow. So, it could be making the point that in spite of the foolish superstitions of those who thought that healing could come by Peter's shadow, the Apostles healed them anyway.

The only other occurrence of the word *shadow* in Luke's gospel was in Zechariah's prophecy about the child Jesus:

> "And you, child, will be called the prophet of the Most High; for
> you will go before the Lord to prepare his ways, to give knowl-
> edge of salvation to his people in the forgiveness of their sins, be-
> cause of the tender mercy of our God, whereby the sunrise shall
> visit us from on high to give light to those who sit in darkness

and in the shadow of death, to guide our feet into the way of
peace" (Luke 1:76-79).

There are many other references to the word *shadow* in the Bible,
some positive and some negative. Nonetheless, prior to Christ's advent
the multitudes were sitting in darkness and in the shadow of death. The
reference to shadow was generally not a good thing. It was to these
multitudes that Christ brought hope and healing, not by shadow or
darkness, but by light. People are healed, not by the shadow of Peter,
but by the light of Christ. We are to look, not to Peter or his shadow,
but to Christ alone. The light of Christ came in the service of healing
and peace.

It could be that this verse about Peter's shadow provides a kind of
fulfillment for Zechariah's prophecy. The darkness and power of superstition is a major biblical theme in that Jesus was sent, not only for our
salvation, but to dispel darkness and shadow, sin and superstition.
History continues to reveal that many people are hell-bent on clinging
to superstitions and shadows, on bringing the darkness of their old
habits and beliefs into the church with them. This is a recurring theme
in Paul's writings. Indeed, Paul himself was a blessed peacemaker who
had been persecuted for righteousness sake (2 Corinthians 4:8-10) by
those who clung to darkness and superstition.

REVILE AND PERSECUTE

"Blessed are you when others revile you and persecute you and
utter all kinds of evil against you falsely on my account" (v. 11).

Jesus added reviling and slander to the list of persecutions that
would come against His people. Reviling is spreading false information
about someone, so it's not much different than uttering all kinds of evil
against someone falsely. The difference is that the information is not
merely false but also evil. While many people might wonder why
Christ's righteousness would be such a target of vituperation by so many
people, it is actually quite common, though not taken to such extremes
in our day.

Imagine a run down house in a poor neighborhood. The windows
are many and filthy. One day a window washer comes by and washes a
window inside and out, but only one. The people in the house and their
friends in the neighborhood who had gotten used to the windows and
didn't even notice they were filthy. But now that one is clean the others

are seen as filthy. While before they had grown used to seeing them as filthy and dismissed their filthiness from their minds, now in the presence of a clean window the others are judged to be filthy. The clean window by being clean, brings judgment against the dirty windows without a word being spoken. Whereas before, as long as they are all dirty, no one notices.

A new union employee comes online at the factory and wants to make a good impression, so he works hard—too hard. His associates let him know that he's working too hard, and that his hard work makes them look bad by comparison. So, in order not to stir up trouble the new employee is asked to slow down. And if he doesn't, there will be trouble. The light of honesty and integrity reveals the lack of honesty and integrity.

> "And this is the judgment: the light has come into the world, and
> people loved the darkness rather than the light because their
> works were evil "(John 3:19).

People love the darkness, the shadows and superstitions, and many people don't like letting go of them in the light of Christ—so they don't. They cling to the darkness. And if they come into the church, they bring their love of darkness and superstition with them.

> "'Rejoice and be glad,' said Jesus, 'for your reward is great in
> heaven, for so they persecuted the prophets who were before
> you'" (v. 12).

Everyone knows how Israel persecuted her prophets. The prophets had a hard time because Israel did not want to hear what they had to say. The prophets came on behalf of the poor and downtrodden to the wealthy who oppressed them. They came with the Word of God, a judgment for freedom and mercy, and against greed and oppression.

By telling people that their reward would be great in heaven, we see that Jesus diverted whatever expectations people might have for some kind of earthly reward for their faithfulness. It is not that there are no earthly rewards for faithfulness, but that such rewards cannot be guaranteed. Generally, faithful societies are more blessed than unfaithful societies, but God's blessings are not always immediate.

The world is a complex place, and things don't always unfold as we expect them to or as we think that they should. Nonetheless, in the final analysis, at judgment, God will mandate justice. Rewards and punishments will be dispensed. And those in or under Christ will be protected from God's wrath against injustice by the righteousness of Christ, and those who aren't won't be.

The upside of God's judgment is that those in Christ don't merely avoid God's curses, but they also acquire His blessings and rewards. Indeed, heaven itself is a great reward. But it should also be noted that while God's grace is free, His rewards are meritorious. John

> "heard a voice from Heaven saying… Write, Blessed are the dead who die in the Lord from now on. Yes, says the Spirit, they shall rest from their labors, and their works follow them" (Revelation 14:13).

While we all pass naked from this earth into death, without gold or property, we do take our character and our history with us—good or bad, whether we are destined for Heaven or Hell. Character and history are eternally attached to the soul. God's grace accompanies His people into heaven. Wherever we go we always take ourselves and our history —and God's grace. Or not.

So, cultivate your character in Christ. Marinate yourself in Christ alone, in the Trinitarian God who is Father, Son and Holy Spirit.

4. SALTWORKS

You are the salt of the earth, but if salt has lost its taste, how shall its saltiness be restored? It is no longer good for anything except to be thrown out and trampled under people's feet. You are the light of the world. A city set on a hill cannot be hidden. Nor do people light a lamp and put it under a basket, but on a stand, and it gives light to all in the house. In the same way, let your light shine before others, so that they may see your good works and give glory to your Father who is in heaven.
—Matthew 5:13-16

There have been many explanations about why Jesus compared His people to salt, and they help us understand the importance of the analogy. Salt is essential to human health. Salt adds flavor to food. Salt was an ancient preservative to keep food, usually meat, from spoiling. Salt was used in the place of money, etc. And these explanations are all helpful and good.

It must also be noted here that the phrase "covenant of salt" was an important idea in the Old Testament. And because the general subject of the Sermon on the Mount is the clarification of God's law or covenant, which was to shape the character of God's people, and because Jesus would have been familiar with the Old Testament and with that phrase, I suspect that He had Numbers 18:19 in mind:

> "All the holy contributions that the people of Israel present to the Lord I give to you, and to your sons and daughters with you, as a perpetual due. It is a covenant of salt forever before the Lord for you and for your offspring with you."

In this section of Numbers the Lord had given the Levites to Aaron and the priests (his sons) to help them with religious duties. Aaron and the priests were to tend to the worship of the Lord, and the Levites were to tend to the needs of the priests, to collect the tithes and offerings of the people, and to redistribute the largess collected from tithes and offerings to support the Temple, the priests, and themselves, and to provide for the poor and needy among the people of Israel.

The other important reference to the covenant of salt that Jesus surely had in mind is 2 Chronicles 13:1-11. Jeroboam was in rebellion against God. The Chronicler asked,

> "Ought you not to know that the Lord God of Israel gave the kingship over Israel forever to David and his sons by a covenant of salt" (2 Chronicles 13:5)?

God's covenant, this covenant of salt, was an eternal covenant, an enduring covenant. The well-being of God's people was tied to the covenant—forever. Jeroboam had the approval of the majority in Israel and thought that was enough.

> "And now you think to withstand the kingdom of the Lord in the hand of the sons of David, because you are a great multitude and have with you the golden calves that Jeroboam made you for gods" (2 Chronicles 13:8).

The point of the Chronicler was that neither the will of the majority nor the pedigree of the false gods they chose to believe in could defend them against the claims of God's covenant. The phrase "covenant of salt" referred to the eternal covenant that God has with His people. If it is an eternal covenant and the Bible is true, it is still binding. Christians understand that God's instructions themselves are the

> "covenant of salt forever before the LORD for you and for your offspring with you" (Numbers 18:19).

Jesus' reference to salt pointed back to God's eternal covenant in order to indicate that the New Covenant with Christ or through Christ was not a different covenant, but a renewal of the eternal covenant. And yet, it was not just another instance of covenant renewal, the kind that is sprinkled throughout the pages of the Old Testament. Rather, this covenant in Christ was not a renewal because the terms of the covenant had not changed, it was a covenant fulfillment because Jesus Christ

Himself had fulfilled the terms of the covenant. It was more than a covenant renewal because it was also a covenant fulfillment.

Thus, Jesus was summing up or clarifying God's covenant with His people in this Sermon on the Mount. He was cutting through the accumulated barnacles that had accrued and obscured the heart of God's law, God's covenant, among those ancient people of Israel. And Jesus was applying it to His renewed and regenerated people. As God's Word was a covenant of salt, so Jesus' Word in this Sermon provided a clarification of God's covenant of salt that was made both new and complete in Christ, or through Christ. Prior to Christ's advent, God's eternal covenant had lost its saltiness, its covenantal power among the Jews, and was being renewed by Christ and given to the whole world.

In the Old Testament, one of the primary functions of the Levites was to provide for the various Temple sacrifices. And of course, those sacrifices were at the very heart of God's Old Testament covenant. The people of Israel brought various animals and grains to be offered in sacrifice as an atonement for their sins. The priests did the bloody work of sacrifice, with the help of the Levites. The priests did the ceremonial stuff, and the Levites did the preparation and cleanup. And as part of the cleanup, they preserved and distributed the sacrificed meat and grain to feed the priests, themselves, and others in need.

So, where did the salt come into this process? The Levites surely finished by butchering the animals into pieces that could be handled and stored until they could be distributed. The most common ancient method of preservation involved rubbing salt into the meat. The salt was a preservative, but it needed to be absorbed into the meat in order to provide protection. The salt killed the microbes that caused the meat to spoil.

God described His instructions as a covenant of salt. And Jesus took what applied to the doctrine of the covenant, the saltiness of biblical doctrine, and applied it to His people, so that the people could absorb the essential characteristics of Jesus' salty teaching of the covenant. Jesus said that His people were themselves the covenant of salt (v. 13).

Christ's people, dead meat that they were prior to this New Covenant, were to be rubbed down with the salt of the covenant, so that they could absorb the essential character of the covenant, which contributed, not merely their preservation, but provided structure for new life in Christ. This New Covenant was not merely a preservative, but it provided for the structure and character of their new lives in Christ.

Christ's people are not only the salt of the earth, they are salt *for* the earth. Christ's people are God's covenant, and His covenant is for the earth. So, through Christ's humanity, God's covenant is of the earth. Peter alluded to this human dimension of the covenant when he wrote,

> "Like newborn infants, long for the pure spiritual milk, that by it you may grow up into salvation—if indeed you have tasted that the Lord is good. As you come to him, a living stone rejected by men but in the sight of God chosen and precious, you yourselves like living stones are being built up as a spiritual house, to be a holy priesthood, to offer spiritual sacrifices acceptable to God through Jesus Christ" (1 Peter 2:2-5).

Paul alluded to it in 2 Corinthians 3:2-3:

> "You yourselves are our letter of recommendation, written on our hearts, to be known and read by all. And you show that you are a letter from Christ delivered by us, written not with ink but with the Spirit of the living God, not on tablets of stone but on tablets of human hearts."

LOST SAVOR

But, asked Jesus,

> "if salt has lost its taste, how shall its saltiness be restored? "(v. 13).

When salt looses its *savor* (Authorized Version—*mōrainō*), it becomes insipid, bland. Such salt lacks interest, significance, and impact. The loss of taste means the loss of the ability to relish something intellectually, or enjoy it. It means the loss of a particular quality or character. On the other hand, to have taste means, according to Webster (1828), having judgment, discernment, good perception, or the power of perceiving and relishing excellence in human performance. Taste is the faculty of discerning beauty, order, congruity, proportion, symmetry, or whatever constitutes excellence, particularly in the fine arts. Taste is not wholly the gift of nature, nor wholly the product of art. Rather, Webster said, it is a function of culture. Christians themselves are the covenant of Jesus Christ and the salt of Christian culture. So, when Christ's people lose their saltiness, their covenantal savor, their Christian character, they are

> "no longer good for anything except to be thrown out and trampled under people's feet" (v. 13).

Lord, have mercy.

Indeed, the salt to which Jesus referred is the culture of the covenant, the culture of the church. And when the culture of the covenant has lost its savor among God's people, not only is it worthy of being trampled underfoot, but Jesus pronounced the judgment that it *shall be* so trampled. The loss of the saltiness, the savor of the covenant in the lives of God's people, constitutes the loss of the covenant itself. The loss of the saltiness of salt is the loss of the central characteristic of salt. Similarly, the loss of the tastefulness of the covenant constitutes the loss of the central characteristic of the covenant, the character of the covenant in the people of God. It is a judgment against the church.

RESTORATION

How then is this salt of the covenant to be restored once it has been lost? Not easily. And while the elements of the covenant can be restored little by little, the culture of the covenant will one day be restored in its wholeness. The covenant itself is or represents a Trinitarian whole that is greater than the sum of its parts. It provides God's holistic, Trinitarian solution for the problem of humanity, both the sin of humanity as a whole or type, and the various sins of humanity's individuals. At some point, as well as the restoration of individuals into the covenant, there will be the restoration of the wholeness of the covenant in the world. And that will be a great day (Revelation 21:10)!

Sure, this church and that church can restore Christ's covenant in their respective churches, and they should. But one church cannot restore it for another. Rather, each church must restore it individually, just as each Christian must be individually restored to God through Christ. And yet, the covenant has been established through Christ as the federal head, as a new prototype of humanity as a whole. According to Scripture, all authority has been given to Christ (Matthew 28:18). The full extent of the covenant has been given for all humanity.

But don't mistake this for universalism. It is not! God has already restored His covenant with humanity through Christ. That has already been done through His life, death, resurrection, and ascension. Christ is already sitting on the throne waiting for the end.

> "The one who conquers, I will grant him to sit with me on my throne, as I also conquered and sat down with my Father on his throne" (Revelation 3:21).

> "But of that day and hour no one knows, no, not the angels in
> Heaven, nor the Son, but the Father" (Mark 13:32).

Christ, like all of us, is waiting for the end, but the end that Christ is
waiting for is not the destruction of the world.

> "For God did not send his Son into the world to condemn the
> world, but in order that the world might be saved through him"
> (John 3:17).

Christ is awakening and awaiting the fulfillment of the purpose of the
world, the *telos*, the completion of the wholeness of God's decree.
Thankfully,

> "The Lord is not slow to fulfill his promise as some count slow-
> ness, but is patient toward you, not wishing that any should per-
> ish, but that all should reach repentance" (2 Peter 3:9).

As the gospel of Jesus Christ overwhelms the world it will crowd
out unbelief over time. Some unbelievers will die in their unbelief and
others will be converted. But over the long haul belief will win out
because God will win. Christ cannot be defeated. Regardless of what it
looks like to you and me. Dawn follows the night, and Christ is
bringing the light not the night, illumination not shadow.

LIGHT OF THE WORLD

> "You are the light of the world. A city set on a hill cannot be hid-
> den" (v. 14).

It's not just that Christ is bringing the light of God to the world,
not just that Christ is the light of the world. But Jesus said that *His
people* are the light of the world. He said that His people are a city set
on a hill that cannot be hidden—not just Christ, not just Him, but His
people. A single person does not a city make. Those who are in Christ
are together the light of Christ. The city is a culture. Christ shines
through His people, in unity in Christ. The salt of Christ flavors His
people. The covenant of Christ shapes their character. It salts them,
enhances their flavor and preserves their identity.

But in order for the salt to preserve the dead meat of the body, it
must be rubbed into it and absorbed by the body, the meat. A sprinkling
of the covenant will not suffice. Rather, the covenant must be vigor-
ously rubbed into every nook and cranny, every crevice and cleft of the
dead meat, or the body will rot.

Today, we see moral rot everywhere God's covenant is forgotten or denied. The covenant applies to all of life and living. There are no areas where it does not apply. And if it is not applied to any area of life, that will be the area that begins to rot. If the rot is left unchecked, no matter how small the breach, it will eventually spoil the whole piece of meat. In this Sermon on the Mount Christ was rubbing the salt of the covenant into the body of Christ, showing us both how to do it and what it means. And there is no end to the practice of covenant preservation because every new individual body in every generation needs to be rubbed down with the salt of the covenant to keep the body of Christ from rotting.

However, where salt preserves dead meat from rot, Christ's covenant preserves the body of Christ that has been crucified and resurrected. Note that Christ's covenant is for the flesh (*sarx*). It is not simply for spiritual people (*soma*). Rather, it is for making people spiritual. It is for dead meat, but more than that. Christianity is about continuous covenantal renewal through the process of covenantal preservation by rubbing down the body of Christ in the covenant of salt. Christ's covenant is for the preservation and renewal of dead meat.

We can't do that, of course. Only God can provide new life, and He does so by His grace alone. His preferred methods of dispatching that grace are through Word and Sacrament. He uses His Word to communicate His grace to His people and the Sacraments to empower and maintain it/them. And the content of what He communicates is His New Covenant with Christ, which is salvation by grace through faith in Christ alone. Of course, the aloneness of Christ is always manifest through the Trinity. The Trinitarian Godhead is the central characteristic of Christ and the central distinction of Christianity.

THE WHOLE COVENANT

We know that the covenant or gospel of Christ only functions salvifically for the regenerate, but it also has a function among the unregenerate. In order to see this, we need to understand that the covenant is the gospel. They are one and the same. The good news of God's grace is the news of His New Covenant with His people. Apart from the New Covenant through Christ there is no good news.

The gospel, or covenant, must be applied to everyone, to all flesh.

"And the angel said to them, 'Fear not, for behold, I bring you
good news of great joy that will be for *all the people*'" (Luke 2:10,
emphasis added).

Everyone needs to hear the gospel of Christ's good news, His New
Covenant with God, because the hearing of the gospel awakens the
Spirit that has been given by grace (Romans 10:17).

We know that the Spirit has not been universally given, at least not
yet. Many people still reject the gospel because there is no Spirit in them
to awaken. They are, in the popular idiom "dead men walking." For
whatever reasons, God is no respecter of persons and gives His grace as
He chooses (Exodus 33:19, Romans 9:18). Nonetheless, His preferred
means of dispatching that grace continues to be Word and Sacrament.

Therefore, the focus of the church and of Christians regarding the
advancement of the gospel needs to be on Word and Sacrament. We
must use the means that God blesses. The use of other means constitutes
disobedience to God's Word. For the most part the faithful, historic
church has always understood Word and Sacrament in terms of worship.
Engaging in Christian worship, private and public, is the most effective
way to advance the gospel in the world. When worship is engaged
biblically—correctly—it is the most attractive and effective way to
advance Christ's cause in the churches and in the world. The most effective means of growth—both character growth or sanctification and
church growth or evangelism—are Word and Sacrament.

This does not mean that Word and Sacrament will appeal to
everyone. Many people will reject such an emphasis because they find it
irrelevant, out of date, archaic, behind the times, etc. However, such a
determination constitutes a personal judgment against Scripture and
history. It amounts to the elevation of one's own personal opinion over
Scripture, which is, of course, the natural position of the unbeliever. But
such a view (the dominance of personal opinion) is not to be tolerated in
the church because it is a violation of the authority of Scripture and
demonstrates a refusal to submit one's self to the authority of Scripture.

The dominance of personal opinion is a tare in a field of wheat, a
pretender that is not what it first appears to be. To confuse weeds for
wheat leads to a harvest for the fire. Jesus said,

"If anyone does not abide in me he is thrown away like a branch
and withers; and the branches are gathered, thrown into the fire,
and burned" (John 15:6).

There will be many withered, broken branches that will be burned up.

Such a fire is not the end of the world, but it is the end of the tares and unfruitful branches (Matthew 13:40). Such a fire is not the purpose of Christ, either. Such a fire produces more heat than light. The smoke from such a fire covers the land like a dense fog. No, such a fire is not the light of Christ, for the light of Christ burns pure and clean, and illuminates the darkness (Revelation 22:5). Christ's focus is not on the weeds and tares, but on the wheat. Christ's purpose is to get the wheat into the barn. The burning of the tares is incidental (Matthew 3:12, 13:30)—but real.

Lampstand

> "Nor do people light a lamp and put it under a basket, but on a stand, and it gives light to all in the house. In the same way, let your light shine before others, so that they may see your good works and give glory to your Father who is in heaven" (vs. 15-16).

These verses are quite interesting and, as we will see, quite different than what people usually think. Let's review the Lord's Sermon to this point so we can understand the context of verses 15-16. Jesus has blessed various kinds of people—the poor in spirit, those who mourn, the meek, seekers of righteousness, the merciful, the pure in heart, the peacemakers and those who are persecuted for righteousness' sake. These kinds of people are on the blessing end of God's covenant.

Jesus indicated that He is the renewal of God's eternal covenant in the various "I am" passages in John (John 6:41, 6:48, 6:51, 8:24, 8:28). And by personalizing the covenant, Christianity in the sense of the living of a Christian life is not the mere expression of this covenant, but Jesus said that Christians are themselves the covenant (v. 13). This idea of being the covenant or of being in Christ (united with or in unity with Christ) can be best understood from a Trinitarian perspective.

There is an identity between the Father, the Son, and the Holy Spirit that unites them without amalgamating them into a single person or thing. Their unique identities or Persons are preserved in the midst of unity. Their identity or personhood is more covenantal than ontological. It's more about covenant than being. This Trinitarian characteristic of God is also reflected in man, in humanity because we have been created in God's image. The union or unity of Christians in Christ then extends this covenantal identity to cover or include those who actually are in Christ, in union or unity with Christ.

SERMON ON THE MOUNT

These people who are called Christians

"are the light of the world. A city set on a hill (that) cannot be hidden" (v. 14).

Note that the word *you* must be plural because it refers to a city, a multitude. However, all plural yous (groups) are made up of singular *yous* (individuals). The corporate you is a collection of individual yous. That is an important trinitarian point that should not be missed because it intertwines our identities with one another as well as with Christ. We are already all together one, in unity in Christ. Who we are, our identity, both individual and corporate, should not and cannot be hidden from the world. Christianity is not a secret society or an underground cult. We must live publicly, openly, and honestly—regardless of the difficulties or the cost.

These verses command Christians to live openly and publicly as Christians by letting their little lights shine openly and publicly before others. Christ wants other people, public people not just your friends, to see what you are doing and how you live. The Lord wants to put your beliefs and your character on public display.

But wait a minute! That sounds a lot like pride, doesn't it? It does! That's what prideful people do, right? So, how is this kind of public shinning of our little lights different from pride? Simple, it's the same process, but without the attitude. You see, pride is an attitude, not an activity. While a prideful person and a faithful person might do the same things, the same kinds of good works, the two things are actually quite different. The prideful person does it as an expression of pride, but the godly person does it in service to Christ.

And at this point in Jesus' Sermon, we have another difficulty to consider: the doing of good works and works-righteousness. Isn't that what the Pharisees did? We don't want to be like the Pharisees, do we? Yes, in part we do! The Pharisees actually did good works like helping other people, contributing to good causes, etc. But Jesus didn't like the Pharisees. So, that means that we should not be like them, that we should not help people or contribute to good causes and the like. Right?

Well, partly yes and partly no. Yes, we should not be like the Pharisees in the sense of being full of pride. But no, we actually are commanded here and elsewhere to do good works.

But don't prideful people do these kinds of things and then parade themselves in front of others looking for accolades?

They do. Nonetheless, here Jesus tells us, not only to do good works, but to do them publicly so that others can observe us doing them. So, how isn't this like pride? Again, it's the same thing but without the attitude.

Christ's people are humble, meek, pure in heart, striving for righteousness, seeking perfection, and are hated and persecuted because of it. But Christ's people are not looking for accolades. Our reward is from Christ alone. Christians are to do good works *where* they can be seen, but not *in order* to be seen. We are to engage good works openly and publicly, but humbly. We are not to do them in order to advance our personal standing or position in the community. Rather, our goal, beyond the particular social needs that we are addressing, is the glorification of God. All praise, honor, glory, credit, and accolades go to God alone. Christians are to make sure to the best of their ability that all praise, honor, glory, credit, and/or accolades relative to good works are given to the Lord. The glory is God's, not ours.

EVANGELISM WORKS

This shining of our lights, this city on a hill is also an act of evangelism. It is a model for evangelism, for witnessing to God's goodness and glory to those who don't yet understand why we do what we do. Christian outreach should be a function of the good works department. Does your church have a good works committee? Shouldn't good works be funded and supervised by the church just like evangelism and youth ministry are funded and supervised? Shouldn't they at least be encouraged? Isn't that what Jesus was saying here?

> "Let your light shine before others, so that they may see your
> good works and give glory to your Father who is in heaven" (v.
> 16).

Doesn't this sound like a really important part of what Christians are to be doing? Doesn't this sound very much like both actual ministry and evangelism?

Of course it does! So, in these few verses we see that the expression and engagement of God's New Covenant in Christ through worship and doing good works, not only accomplishes God's purpose for His people, but these things are also to be the primary methods of Christian evangelism.

"Again Jesus spoke to them, saying, 'I am the light of the world. Whoever follows me will not walk in darkness, but will have the light of life'" (John 8:12).

The light of Christ illuminates the way.

5. Downloading The Upgrade

*Do not think that I have come to abolish the Law or the
Prophets; I have not come to abolish them but to fulfill them.
For truly, I say to you, until heaven and earth pass away, not an
iota, not a dot, will pass from the Law until all is accomplished.
Therefore whoever relaxes one of the least of these
commandments and teaches others to do the same will be called
least in the kingdom of heaven, but whoever does them and
teaches them will be called great in the kingdom of heaven. For
I tell you, unless your righteousness exceeds that of the scribes
and Pharisees, you will never enter the kingdom of heaven.*
—Matthew 5:17-20

The Sermon on the Mount has confused a lot of people because on
the one hand it seems as if it is putting down the Old Testament
and offering a new teaching, as if Jesus was saying, "Out with
the old and in with the new." And, while this provides an easy way to
understand what Jesus was saying, it is wrong. Yes, Jesus' life and teachings did produce some changes in the way that the Old Testament is to
be understood. But it cannot be said that He opposed the Old Testament. Rather, He fulfilled the law and the prophets (or prophecies), and
that fulfillment has shed additional light by which to see and understand
Old Testament doctrine and practices. The Old Testament now stands
in the light of Christ.

Jesus said,

> "Do not think that I have come to abolish the Law or the
> Prophets" (v. 17).

So, if you have been thinking that Christianity means the end or abandonment of Judaism, you have been mistaken. Christianity does not mean the *end* of Judaism, but its fulfillment. Christianity cannot be understood apart from the Old Testament.

The building of a house does not require the destruction or abandonment of its foundation. Nonetheless, when the house is built it significantly effects the foundation. Before the house is built people can relate directly to the foundation, but after it is built people relate directly to the house, and only indirectly to the foundation. The house depends upon the structural soundness of the foundation, and at the same time it covers it by resting upon it. The Old Testament is not obsolete. Rather, it provides the foundation upon which Christianity exists. Christianity does not and cannot exist apart from the foundation and structural integrity of the Old Testament.

Jesus had "not come to abolish them but to fulfill them" (the law and the prophets of the Old Testament, v. 17). Because Paul was a master of the Old Testament he was able to see or understand how and why Jesus fulfilled the Old Testament law and prophecies. And this was what Paul's letters and teaching were about. Paul was helping us understand what he understood about Jesus. Of course, it wasn't just Paul. Jesus Himself taught that He fulfilled the Old Testament when He instructed two despondent followers going home after His crucifixion on the road to Emmaus (Luke 24:27). Jesus had fulfilled (*pléroö*) the law and the prophecies. He satisfied them, executed them, carried out their legalities, completed them.

NOT REBELLION

Jesus was not a Jewish rebel who had been working against Judaism to abolish or eclipse the Old Testament. He was Himself a Jew, who had provided the highest possible service to the cause and fulfillment of Judaism (Luke 24:44, John 1:45, 5:46).

However, Judaism prior to its fulfillment was different than Judaism after its fulfillment in the same way that a sales order is different prior to its fulfillment and after. It's the same sales order, but after it has been fulfilled it stands in a different relationship to the customer, to the sales person, and to the company. The fulfilling of the order changes everything. Yet, the customer is still a customer, the sales person is still the sales person, and the company is still the company.

Jesus was not a revolutionary working to overthrow the system. Nor was He a radical trying to undermine it. His teachings were as ordinary as the Old Testament itself, and in the society in which He lived, the Old Testament established all the social norms.

It was common in Jesus' day, as it is in ours, that people tend to think that whenever a new teaching comes along, it overthrows all of the old teachings. People tend to think that every new teaching is a kind of Copernican revolution. But Jesus did not produce a Copernican revolution regarding the Old Testament. God was still God, the law was still the law and the prophets were still the prophets.

Something changed, but it was not a matter of turning the Old Testament upside down or inside out. Nonetheless, when people heard the preaching of the gospel, they expected that the new way would assume a completely different form from the old. This, however, is a very dangerous idea because it undermines genuine historical progress by destroying or devaluing the accumulated wisdom of the past.

It is a curiosity that liberals call themselves "progressives" because the kinds of radical revolutions that they proffer against tradition actually harm genuine progress, both social and scientific progress, by refusing to learn and adopt the lessons of history. Revolutionaries want to come in and turn over the tables of accumulated knowledge, as if the wisdom of history is responsible for the failures of humanity. So-called Progressives actually retard social and scientific development by denying both Christ and history. They should be called "regressives" because they actually reuse old ideas by dressing them up in new explanations. The descriptive language and rationalizations change, but the actual ideas remain essentially the same.

Most of the Temple Jews and Pharisees misunderstood Jesus, by mistaking him to be a revolutionary or a radical—many people still do, including Liberals and Progressives. This view pits Jesus against Judaism. But Jesus is not anti-Semitic, nor is Christianity anti-Semitic.[8] That's like saying that those who fulfill sales orders are against sales orders or against the company they work for, because by fulfilling them, they change the status of the sales order. It is a nonsense argument, but is made by some otherwise very intelligent people.

In contrast, Jesus depended upon the veracity and integrity of the law and the prophets.

---

8   William Nicholls in his book, *Christian Antisemitism—A History of Hate*, Aronson, New Jersey, 1995, has documented the fact that many Christians have seriously misunderstood this concern. But rather than correct it, he has added to the misunderstanding by suggesting that Christianity is itself antisemitic.

Production

> "For truly, I say to you, until heaven and earth pass away, not an
> iota, not a dot, will pass from the Law until all is accomplished
> "(v. 18).

The law and the prophets stand as being true and trustworthy. It
was necessary for Jesus to fulfill the law as it had been written in the Old
Testament in order to fulfill God's demands for sinful humanity. Actually, Jesus was fulfilling a sales order. You are not your own, for you
were bought with a price (1 Corinthians 6:19-20, 7:23), said Paul to the
Corinthians. Our salvation is the result of Christ's purchase (1
Corinthians 6:19).

In fact, Jesus did come to earth to alter the status of the Old Testament law. He altered it by fulfilling it, just as a sales order is altered by
fulfilling the offer. And, again, after the order has been fulfilled, the
meaning changes. The order cannot be fulfilled more than once. Once
the order is delivered it is canceled. It's done. It's no longer in effect. A
fulfilled sales order no longer makes any demands on the company. Jesus
didn't change the original order, He simply fulfilled it.

And having fulfilled it, He was then in the position to issue a new
sales order, which He was doing here in the Sermon on the Mount. He
was ordering the kind of people that He would keep: the poor in spirit,
those who mourn, the meek, seekers of righteousness, the merciful, the
pure in heart, the peacemakers, and those who are persecuted for righteousness' sake. And just as God's original order had laid out the specifications for the perfection of humanity, which Jesus fulfilled, so Christ's
new order would rely upon those original specs, but would modify
them in the light of Christ. Christ's fulfillment of the original specifications of the old order means that He is the human prototype that was
ordered in the Old Testament.

Continuing with this analogy, following Christ, production began
in earnest as the factory (church) began producing replicas of the prototype. "Be imitators of me, as I am of Christ" (1 Corinthians 11:1), said
Paul. The word *Christian* means little Christ. Christians are created in
the image of Christ, a dim image—not as divine imitations, but as
human imitations.

These new models or imitations coming off the factory line needed
a new manual because their specs are somewhat different. The Christian
model is similar to the Jewish model. They are very closely related, but
different. So, a new manual, a shorter manual was issued to accompany

the new imitations—the New Testament. Much of the old manual—the Old Testament—still applied because the new model was not a complete redesign, so it was also included for reference. Jesus was here in this Sermon on the Mount providing the new specs for the new line that was to be in His image, the specifications for the new production line in Christ.

Jesus was very much aware of how easy it is for flaws and errors to creep into the design and the manufacturing process. He knew personally how difficult yet important it would be for Him to follow the original Old Testament specs, to fulfill the law and the prophets. He knew personally that every detail needed attention. "Therefore," He said,

> "whoever relaxes one of the least of these commandments and teaches others to do the same will be called least in the kingdom of heaven, but whoever does them and teaches them will be called great in the kingdom of heaven" (v. 19).

His reference to "these commandments" pointed to the whole or the spirit of God's law, the Old Testament. The Pharisees had divided the law into greater and lesser commandments, as if some were more important and some were less important. We know this kind of division as compartmentalization.

> "The Pharisees tithed mint and dill and cumin, but neglected the weightier matters of the law: justice and mercy and faithfulness. These you ought to have done, without neglecting the others" (Matthew 23:23).

Of course, Jesus was referring to the Ten Commandments because that was common parlance at the time. But more than the bare Ten Commandments, Jesus had the spirit or the intent of God's law in mind. The Pharisees had missed the spirit or intent of God's law by treating the law in a wooden, contrived, or artificial way. They had the letter, but missed the spirit.

Consequently, Jesus was altering the law of God because of the accumulation of error and faulty human traditions that had accrued to it (Matthew 15:3). Yet, He was not changing the essential teachings of God's law. How do we know that Jesus was making some changes? In a few verses He will say,

> "You have heard that it was said to those of old... But I say to you" (vs. 21-22).

Several times He contrasted the old teachings with His new teachings. However, His new teachings weren't actually new, but were God's original teachings, renewed for a renewed people, and purged of their errant traditions.

MERCY

Note also that at least some of those who will relax one of the least of the commandments will nonetheless be in the kingdom of heaven. They must be in the kingdom in order to be called the least in the kingdom. God's grace is amazing! Perfect obedience is not a requirement for entry into the kingdom of heaven—thank God! Rather, said Jesus, those who actually practice these commandments and teach them will be called great. Practice is not perfection. Some missing of the mark will be tolerated, but not without consequences. The consequences pertain to one's status in the kingdom, whether great or least.

According to Calvin it is an error to think that Jesus was talking here about heaven in the after life.

> "The kingdom of heaven means the renovation of the Church, or the prosperous condition of the Church, such as was then beginning to appear by the preaching of the Gospel."[9]

The kingdom of heaven is a reference to Christ's church, which will endure into the afterlife, of course. But the point here is that what applies to the kingdom of heaven also applies to the church. It applies now, here in this Sermon on the Mount and elsewhere in Scripture. Not every reference to the kingdom is about the church on earth, but many are. The key to understanding this is to understand that the church carries over from this world into the new world (Matthew 6:10). Not only is Christ's church the Israel of God, it becomes the kingdom of God, as well.

Christ did not reject or annul God's Old Testament law or prophecies. Rather, by fulfilling them He announced His victory as the Messiah of God who had both the ability and the authority to speak for God. Had He come as a revolutionary to overthrow Old Testament doctrine, He would have undermined the accumulated historical authority of God in the world. And that would have undermined His own authority and teaching. But by fulfilling the law and the prophecies of the Old Testament, He assumed and acquired the authority and historical momentum of God's cause in the world.

---

9   *Calvin's Complete Commentary*, Matthew 5:21, eSword.net.

Jesus did not come to deny, overthrow, or ignore the Old Testament, nor to eliminate God's demand for righteousness. The Jews had proven themselves, as humanity's representatives before God. But they were completely unable to fulfill God's plan for humanity. God's intent was to heal the breach between Himself and humanity that had resulted from Adam's sin, and to restore righteousness to the character of humanity. God knew that righteousness was necessary for sustainable development in the world, and that apart from righteousness, the world would be stuck in a cycle of death and destruction emanating from the character and activities of humanity. Righteousness is the cure for sin, but we—humanity—have no righteousness of our own. Rather, our lives and wills are dominated by sin. Human perception, human thinking, and understanding are skewed by sin.

God's own people, Israel, could not avert the momentum of Adam's sin—human sin, though God had provided them with everything that they needed to do it themselves. God had given them the law and the Temple, the sacrificial system, and the prophets. Of course, God knew that success would not be possible apart from Christ, but Israel didn't know that yet. And that was the central lesson that humanity needed. The primary lesson of the Old Testament is the failure of Israel, the failure of God's own people who represented humanity, to heal the breach of sin. Israel could not do what God required. God had called Israel apart so that their history would provide the lessons that would eventually facilitate God's ultimate revelation to the world. The central lesson was man's inability, which led to the failure and destruction of the Temple and the nation of Israel. That lesson is about human inability, not simply the failure of Israel.

FULFILLMENT

Nonetheless, that failure and subsequent destruction did not end God's demand for righteousness. God's grace did not replace God's law as the way of salvation, it facilitated it. Of course, salvation is by grace alone. But let's not forget the other *solas* of the Reformation. Salvation is by *Sola Scriptura* (Scripture Alone), *Solus Christus* (Christ Alone), *Sola Fide* (Faith Alone) and *Soli Deo Gloria* (God's Glory Alone). God's grace does not negate the law, but rather demonstrates the inability of the law alone, and the necessity of the law in Christ (Galatians 6:2), and does so by fulfilling it. God's law shows us our need for God's grace. But God's grace does not negate God's law, it enables it.

So, the failure of Israel and the consequent destruction of Jerusalem in A.D. 70 facilitated the transition between the old administration, the old way or method for the establishment of God's righteousness and the new administration, the new way or method in Christ. And it did so without contravening the Old Testament, but by fulfilling it.

God needed to change the administration of His eternal covenant without abrogating it or changing its central characteristics. By fulfilling the law and receiving the sentence of death for the sin of humanity on the cross, Christ was able to fulfill God's eternal covenant without changing its central character. Then through Christ's resurrection, He was able to carry the central character of the Old Covenant into the New Covenant in such a way that the fulfillment of the Old became the establishment of the New.

His death on the cross brought new life to the covenant, and the destruction of the Temple and of Jerusalem, the nation of Israel, opened the way for the salvation of humanity as a whole. Thus, Israel's failure and destruction became the central object lesson for humanity's salvation. Israel's failure opened the door of salvation to the Gentiles, to humanity at large, which was God's plan from the beginning (Genesis 17:4). Because of this, Jesus could tell his disciples,

> "unless your righteousness exceeds that of the scribes and Pharisees, you will never enter the kingdom of heaven" (v. 20).

It was not that Jesus was railing against the corruption of the Pharisees. They were actually very holy people! The point was not their corruption, but their holiness. Judaism had produced the best that humanity could offer, even with God's help. The point was that the best that humanity had to offer was not good enough to stand before God's righteousness.

Rather, Jesus was railing against their self-righteousness, not because they were unrighteous from a human perspective but because even the best human righteousness cannot stand before the righteousness of God. Verse 20 was not a comment about the corruption of the Pharisees, though surely some of them were corrupt. Rather, it was a comment about the complete inability of human righteousness and the absolute need for Christ's righteousness.

Jesus upheld the Law (the Ten Commandments), the Prophets (or prophecies), and the Old Testament demand for perfect righteousness. Not an iota or a dot of that Old Law could be changed prior to its fulfillment. And because its fulfillment was still in the future, Christ had yet to suffer and die on the cross. He had yet to be resurrected from the dead or be taken up through His ascension. Thus, the Law stood as it was. It was not the law that needed to change, but humanity.

> "For I tell you that Christ became a servant to the circumcised to
> show God's truthfulness, in order to confirm the promises given
> to the patriarchs, and in order that the Gentiles might glorify
> God for his mercy" (Romans 15:8-9).

By fulfilling God's law Christ established Himself as the long antici-
pated and now revealed Messiah. And that gave Christ the authority to establish the New Covenant with God's renewed people, a renewed instance of the same covenant—but fulfilled, which makes a big differ-
ence! Following Christ's revelation as the Messiah, people would look back upon His life and teachings to see how the Messiah had fulfilled the law and the prophets. People would then be able to see His relationship with the Old Testament, and how He had been present everywhere through it, and what adjustments He had made to it.

INSTRUCTION

Of course, His people didn't come to these realizations until the Holy Spirit had come upon them and instructed them. So, He appeared to two disciples who had lost heart, given up hope, and were headed home on the road to Emmaus.

> "And he said to them, 'O foolish ones, and slow of heart to be-
> lieve all that the prophets have spoken! Was it not necessary that
> the Christ should suffer these things and enter into his glory?'
> And beginning with Moses and all the Prophets, he interpreted to
> them in all the Scriptures the things concerning himself" (Luke
> 24:25-27).

He showed them His Trinitarian character, and how He had been involved in the Old Testament through the Holy Spirit. This provided them with a huge insight. Now they could see the Old Testament in the light of Christ, and they went back to tell the others.

Seeing the Old Testament in the light of Christ was like reading in a darkened room where various shadows had before occluded the text, making reading difficult, and then turning on the overhead light. Suddenly, everything that had been previously obscured by shadows became clear in the light of Christ. Suddenly they saw, not something different but the same thing, only more clearly. It's the same thing, but the clarity, the new light in Christ, made a significant difference in what they saw and understood about what they had seen.

And so it was for Paul and the Apostles. They began to see the Old Testament in the light of Christ, and it changed everything. But it changed things without changing the direction of historical development or the nature of God's eternal covenant. They saw, not only through new eyes, but through trinitarian eyes. The world suddenly took on a depth and character that they had not seen before. It was the same world, but they had new eyes in Christ.

And one of the first things that Jesus told them was that their righteousness needed to exceed that of the Scribes and Pharisees, the priests and intellectuals who defended the Old Testament. But again, this was not simply a criticism leveled against the Scribes and Pharisees, as much as it was the announcement of something new. The Messiah, had shed new light on old truth. The message or gospel of Jesus Christ is not antisemitic, and has never been antisemitic. Rather, it is meta-semitic. It is not opposed to the Old Testament or to Judaism. Rather, Jesus stands on the shoulders of the law and the prophets.

6. Margin of Validity

You have heard that it was said to those of old, 'You shall not murder; and whoever murders will be liable to judgment.' But I say to you that everyone who is angry with his brother will be liable to judgment; whoever insults his brother will be liable to the council; and whoever says, 'You fool!' will be liable to the hell of fire. —Matthew 5:21-22

Jesus was obviously engaged in some sort of contrast in verses 21-22. Of this there can be no doubt. But there are varying interpretations about the things being contrasted. Were the things of old a reference to the Old Testament law, or to the misunderstanding of that law by His contemporaries. The words in these two verses alone cannot answer that question. So, we need to examine the context.[10]

---

10 Calvin's comment is germane: "It now remains for us to see, what Christ condemns in the Pharisees, and in what respect his interpretation of it differs from their glosses. The amount of it is, that they had changed the doctrine of the law into a political order, and had made obedience to it to consist entirely in the performance of outward duties. Hence it came, that he who had not slain a man with his hand was pronounced to be free from the guilt of murder, and he who had not polluted his body by adultery was supposed to be pure and chaste before God. This was an intolerable profanation of the law: for it is certain that Moses everywhere demands the spiritual worship of God. From the very nature of the law we must conclude, that God, who gave it by the hand of Moses, spoke to the hearts, as well as to the hands and to the eyes. True, our Lord quotes the very words of the law; but he does so in accommodation to the view which was generally taken of them by the people. 'Till now, the scribes have given you a literal interpretation of the law, that it is enough, if a man keep his hands from murder and from acts of violence. But I warn you, that you must ascend much higher. Love is the fulfilling of the law, (Rom. 13:10;) and I say that your neighbor is injured, when you act towards him otherwise than as a friend.' The latter clause

The larger context, as I have previously suggested, is the Old Testament law, which also applies to these verses. But it is more difficult to say with any precision exactly what aspect of the Old Testament law is in view here. That is a more precise question than can be answered by Jesus' words alone. We are inquiring into, not the context of the Scripture, but the context of that particular social situation and the presuppositions of those involved, the exact nature of which we simply cannot know with the precision we sometimes desire with our contemporary computer informed mentality. The text just doesn't provide it.

Therefore, because Scripture is true and trustworthy, we must assume that this lack of precision is intentional on God's part. Indeed, questions of legality can, and often do, get carried away under microscopic examination, allowing the spirit or intent of a particular law or teaching to get lost or occluded in a barrage of nitpicking or tangential concerns. This kind of hyper-legality is quite common among contemporary lawyers.

Of course, there is sufficient precision provided in the Bible with regard to the gospel, to the Scriptures and to God's law in terms of both general use and personal application. But the details needed for every individual application are not simply a matter of reading the letter of the law (Romans 7:6), but require personal interaction with the Holy Spirit through regeneration.

Through regeneration the Spirit informs the conscience, as the Scriptures are read in the light of Christ. God does not simply provide all of the answers in a mechanical way that negates the value, freedom, or responsibility of each individual before God. We have been given the ability and the freedom to think, and this gift cannot be overemphasized. It is endemic to the human condition and at the very heart of human identity, both individual and corporate.

God has not created us to be robots who are without essential freedoms in the face of an automated or unresponsive destiny. Indeed, we have been created for the sole purpose of exercising freedom in the light of Christ to the glory of God. Nothing makes us more human or more free than the genuine exercise of conscience in the light of Christ (Deuteronomy 30:19).

---

which he quotes, he who kills shall be liable to the judgment, confirms what I said a little before, that Christ charges them with turning into a political scheme the law of God, which had been given for the government of the heart."
(*Calvin's Complete Commentaries*, Matthew 5:21, public domain)

MURDER

> "You have heard that it was said to those of old, 'You shall not
> murder; and whoever murders will be liable to judgment'" (v.21).

This is a clear reference to Exodus 20:13: "You shall not murder."
The Hebrew word translated *murder* (רצח) refers to the murder of
human beings. The Authorized Version translation as *kill* is technically
correct, but inadequate for the precision required by contemporary
people. While the command is directed specifically against the unlawful
taking of human life, its intent corresponds to the prohibition of
revenge. Revenge, also called vengeance (נקם) in the Old Testament, is
the prerogative of the Lord and is specifically forbidden everywhere in
Scripture, Old Testament and New (Deuteronomy 32:35, 32:42; Psalm
94:1; Hebrews 10:30).

Murder is almost always the acting out of revenge, if not by the
perpetrator then by someone who has manipulated or paid the perpetrator. Most murders are not random acts of violence, but are specifically
directed acts of anger and revenge. Jesus did not invent this interpretation. It was not a new teaching for the Jews or the Gentiles. It is thoroughly grounded in the Old Testament in many ways and in many
verses.

Moses asked and taught Israel,

> "What does the Lord your God require of you, but to fear the
> Lord your God, to walk in all his ways, to love him, to serve the
> Lord your God with all your heart and with all your soul, and to
> keep the commandments and statutes of the Lord, which I am
> commanding you today for your good? Behold, to the Lord your
> God belong heaven and the heaven of heavens, the earth with all
> that is in it. Yet the Lord set his heart in love on your fathers and
> chose their offspring after them, you above all peoples, as you are
> this day. Circumcise therefore the foreskin of your heart, and be
> no longer stubborn" (Deuteronomy 10:12-16).

If anything, Jesus was reminding the Jews and perhaps instructing
the Gentiles that God's law had always been concerned about more than
mere behavior. It has always been about shaping human character,
human attitudes.

The demand to love God completely, totally, is every bit as much a
demand that pertains to human emotion as it does to human behavior.
So, to say that the Old Testament is about behavior and the New Testa-

ment is about motivation is simply inaccurate. There is just as much concern and instruction regarding motivation in the Old Testament as in the New. The command to circumcise the foreskin of one's heart simply means to cut away all callousness and emotional insensitivity toward God and His love. It is a demand for emotional sensitivity or emotional receptivity toward God. It is the demand to stop stubbornly rejecting God, rejecting His love and His jealous demand for exclusive devotion.

> "You shall not take vengeance or bear a grudge against the sons of your own people, but you shall love your neighbor as yourself: I am the Lord" (Leviticus 19:18).

This concern is about much more than murder or revenge. It is about holding a grudge against someone. It is about being offended, about resentment. God said, you shall not! And yet people still get offended. People still harbor resentments. People still hold grudges—even in the church! This should not be the case. However, Jesus was not simply advising that people stifle their feelings. Rather, He was providing a way to deal with these things in the church, to adjudicate them before they turned into civil suits or crimes. Jesus wanted to keep people out of civil court (Luke 12:58). Jesus said,

> "that everyone who is angry with his brother will be liable to judgment" (v. 22).

There is a translation issue here in that the Authorized Version includes the Greek word *eikē*,

> "whosoever is angry with his brother *without a cause* shall be in danger of the judgment" (emphases added).

This is an important issue and the modern translations are in error when they leave it out. Why is it important? Because all anger in and of itself is not sinful, as Jesus taught when He looked on the Pharisees

> "with anger, being grieved for the hardness of their hearts" (Mark 3:5)

and when He overthrew the tables of the moneychangers (Matthew 21:12-13). There is such a thing as righteous anger in the face of stupidity and injustice.

Jesus' response was not in opposition to the Old Testament, nor to God's law as a whole or in general. If there is any opposition here it is to the persistent stubbornness that continues to deny and/or ignore God in the light of Christ. Jesus is opposed to the failure to engage God seriously, the failure to engage God's Word honestly. Jesus was opposed to the customs and traditions that had accrued over the centuries and obscured the original intent or Spirit of the law. God's truth should always trump tradition, even religious tradition, because it is often the codification of religious ideas that interfere with the exercise of individual conscience.

The difficulty is that the codification or systematic arrangement of the various elements of God's law tends to harden our understanding of God's Word in a way that insists upon universal agreement and application, and fails to allow for the variation that is often required by particular circumstances and the exercise of personal conscience in the light of Christ.

This is not to deny that there must also be a body of common law or a common understanding of the law that all people honor and respect. Not at all! Rather, such a body of common law belongs to the jurisdiction of civil government, and is not the subject of our present inquiry. Clearly, murder should be against such a common law, and subject to the jurisdiction of civil law. Of this there can be no doubt.

However, other more subtle and less central elements of God's Word that effect personal morality in the light of Christ must remain uncodified in civil or common law. Civil law should not proscribe morality or intention because it cannot enforce such concerns. Rather, morality falls under the jurisdiction of the church and family. Thus, as God has done in the Old Testament and as Jesus was doing here in the New Testament, the determination and maintenance of common or community standards of morality are the responsibility of the church and her members. Jesus was modeling this responsibility in His Sermon on the Mount by showing us how to teach morality in the light of Christ.

The Christian church, by following Christ's model, is called to teach and establish the moral standards of local communities without infringing into the jurisdiction of civil government. There must always be a division of jurisdictional authority between the church and state in order to keep both church and state from joining together. Such a merger or an overlapping of civil and religious authority and jurisdiction provides a concentration of social power and authority that tends toward totalitarianism. And their separation mitigates against that tendency.

Much history is about the struggle between civil and church governments for the totalitarian control of societies for various reasons. And the lessons of history are that the dominance of either church or state tends to be socially lethal in a variety of ways. If power itself doesn't corrupt, it most certainly invites corrupt people to the exercise of their corruption. Monopolistic social influence, whether church or state, invites abuse. Fortunately for us, the wisdom of the U.S. Constitution insisted on various divisions of power, authority, government, and influence to prevent such monopolization of power and influence. Unfortunately for us, those divisions have been increasingly blurred, crossed, and violated over the past hundred years or so.

CONSCIENCE

There is another element of this issue of God's law that Jesus was teaching. That element is the growth and development of individual conscience in the light of Christ. This growth and development is a function of personal exercise. The exercise of conscience tends to grow and mature it, while the lack of exercise produces moral atrophy. In addition, where the exercise of morality is absent there can be no freedom. The issue here is not justification, which is by grace alone. The issue here is sanctification or growth, which also issues out of God's grace into the lives of believers. Here I am talking about the intersection of God's sanctifying grace with the life of the believer and its fruit— obedience. Our obedience is always a response to God's grace, and is never perfect nor complete, but it does improve over time.

Chapter Twenty of the *Westminster Confession of Faith* provides for the exercise and development of personal conscience in the light of Christ. There we see that God alone is the master of the conscience, and that the Lord has left sufficient wiggle room in His Word for such exercise. Were the Lord to have nailed all morality down so tight as to preclude individual evaluation and application, neither morality nor freedom would exist in any meaningful way. If everything is laid out according to the letter of the law, whether civil or religious, there would be no need for the development of personal morality, and conscience would tend to atrophy from lack of use.

This position is argued from Christ's silence and from the degree of precision provided in the biblical text. The Bible does not provide a set of rules that can be simply cut and pasted without thought and consideration about options and consequences. There is sufficient clarity and definition in Scripture to encourage individual consideration and evalu-

ation in the light of Christ that will then provide the specifics necessary
to guide individuals without imposing a false unity that shuts down
open and honest discussion. Often, the desire for doctrinal unity in the
church imposes a doctrinal narrowness that is not found in Scripture.
And that narrowness in turn creates a rigidity that tends to shut down
honest inquiry and genuine discussion of certain issues for fear of
crossing commonly accepted norms that are not actually found in Scripture. Such inquiry and discussion is not a threat to biblical Christianity
in the light of Christ. Rather, it is the means of genuine growth in
grace.

This is not a denial that orthodoxy provides important limits
regarding various beliefs and behaviors. Faithlessness and apostasy are
very real threats to Christianity. Orthodoxy does have limits. However,
faithfulness is not a matter of simply avoiding certain areas of discussion,
but is a matter of studying classic issues and positions in order to
discover for one's self the fallacies of erroneous beliefs. Such errors can
only be seriously defeated when they are seriously considered. Straw
men are easily defeated, genuine heretics are more difficult to convert.
Christ can be trusted to steer His people safely through all dangerous
doctrinal waters. God will not fail to complete what He has begun. Nor
can we get to our destination without actually taking the journey.

Rules

Scripture doesn't always provide the degree of clarity we desire or
require for some personal application, nor the clarity to be able to codify
Scripture into particular rules that will apply for all people at all times.
God is not looking for us to develop a religious rule book, He is looking
for the kind of obedience in grace that seeks the wisdom and guidance
of the Holy Spirit.

God's desire is to establish a relationship of love, trust, and honor
with humanity, both individually and corporately because of God's
Trinitarian character. Human diversity is practically infinite. No two
people are the same. This magnificent diversity of character applies not
only to human beings, but it also applies to the various situations and/or
contexts of human life. Human diversity is necessary for the success of
human adaptability to various situations and environments.

Obviously, some common rules of behavior (civil government) are
necessary for social commerce. And other rules or principles (church
government) are given for the beauty and effectiveness of corporate life
and worship. And some areas of obedience are reserved by the Lord for

personal evaluation and application that develop individual conscience in the light of Christ.

Rather than a world in which uniformity of conscience is demanded of all people, God has created a world wherein the diversity of conscience in the light of Christ provides for a glorious multiplicity and diversity of character and circumstance that not only produce the fruits of the Spirit (Galatians 5:22-23), but depends upon the free exercise of those fruits within bounds that are illuminated by the light of Christ. The love of God in Christ provides not only the highest expression of human freedom, but completely depends upon the reality of that freedom.

Christianity is not a journey without an end. It has a very specific end and purpose, which is the establishment of the kingdom of God on earth as it is in heaven. However, that end or purpose is not a termination point, as if it were the destination of a journey. Rather, the end and purpose of Christianity is the development and maintenance of the social structures and freedoms that allow this end or purpose to unfold over time. Indeed, Christianity provides the best possible foundation for sustainable social and economic development. And at a time when that foundation is threatened its principle elements must be strengthened by more widely embracing the ancient social practice of covenant renewal.

JUDGMENT

The alternative to covenant renewal provided by Jesus in verse 21 is judgment. While this verse is specifically about murder, it has a much wider application when understood in the larger context of Scripture. The avoidance of this judgment requires the manifestation of the love of God in Christ. God's love actually retards the development of sins like anger, revenge, grudge holding, etc.

Imagine the beauty of human relationships, of human society and culture, without the irritations of anger, revenge, or grudges. Now imagine how good things could be without

> "quarreling, jealousy, anger, hostility, slander, gossip, conceit, and disorder" (2 Corinthians 12:20).

Imagine the possibilities for economic development in a world where honesty and integrity reign, a world without the deceit, greed, corruption, and vice that eat away at social and economic value. Of course, the complete elimination of such sins is impossible this side of Christ's return. But, even though sin cannot be eliminated, it can be reduced. And that is one of God's goals in the light of Christ.

Not only does anger make one liable to God's judgment, but all of the biblical sins bring similar liabilities. Anger is often at the very heart of sin. Anger causes slander, malice, and revenge. If lies and deceit don't issue out of anger, then surely anger issues out of a bed of lies and deceit. Anger and gossip are similarly related. They are reciprocally cause and effect to each other. Anger often causes people to gossip about others, and that gossip also makes others angry and temps them to gossip in return. What about the relationship between extortion and anger, injustice and anger, adultery and anger? The list goes on and on. Indeed, anger is often at the very heart of sin.

But, people say, *I get angry, and I can't help it. It just happens.* And it does! We can deny a lot of things, but not anger. It simply asserts itself in spite of our efforts to contain it. Sure, some people can bottle it up better than others, but it doesn't just go away. So, what are we supposed to do with our anger?

Paul recommended that we

> "put away falsehood, let each one of you speak the truth with his neighbor, for we are members one of another. Be angry and do not sin; do not let the sun go down on your anger, and give no opportunity to the devil" (Ephesians 4:25-27).

Put away falsehood. Obviously, this means that we need to stop lying and deceiving others and ourselves. But it also requires that we take up truthhood. Falsehood cannot simply be abandoned, but must be replaced. We must study and know the truth, God's truth because there is no other. We must fill our hearts and minds with truth in order to crowd out the falsehood.

NEIGHBORS

We must then speak this truth, God's truth, to our neighbors, those who are nearest to us physically during our day. It is not that we should gather in affinity groups and reinforce our affinities, our common beliefs and views about life. Rather, we are to speak God's truth with our nearest neighbors, with the people that we come into contact with day by day. We must interact with the people who don't think like we do, with people who disagree with us. But as we interact with them, we must not simply shove our worldview down their throats. We must actually interact with them, listen to them, and adjust our views in the light of the truth that they bring to us. If we want to be heard, we must first be able to hear, to listen. And the most important thing to hear is God's Word.

People will listen to us inasmuch as we listen to them, God willing. We can teach people how to listen by modeling it. Of course, we must take care not to adapt ourselves and our views beyond the bounds of orthodoxy in the light of Christ. Nonetheless, we must take the initiative because God has commanded it. Godless and lost people are for the most part godless and lost because they don't understand God's truth or they understand it wrongly. They can't hear because they don't know how to listen.

Paul said that we are members one of another, us and our neighbors. We have our humanity in common. We have been created in God's Trinitarian image. This is not just a social nicety, it is our salvation because it touches upon our membership in the body of Christ. Salvation is not just me and Jesus, but is me and Jesus in the body of Christ—the church.

> "Be angry and do not sin" (Ephesians 4:26),

said Paul. Don't try to avoid, deny, or repress your anger. Feel it, but do not indulge it. How can we do that? Confess it to God in prayer. Speak it to God aloud, which will help to get it out of your system. Yell about it, scream about it—to God. And do not express it or engage it otherwise because it is at the very heart of sin. It will betray you. It will turn on you and destroy you.

And how in the world are people supposed to do this? Practice. The same way that people learn to play the piano or eat an elephant. Take small bites, small steps, but do so regularly. Practice daily in your prayers.

Jesus continued,

> whoever insults his brother will be liable to the council (v. 22).

The council (*sunedrion*) referred to the Sanhedrin, the high council of the Temple establishment. Did Jesus mean that the Sanhedrin should hear all cases regarding personal insults and offenses? No. Rather, the intention seems to be a more general authorization for synagogues (local worship centers) to take the mediating role of judging such cases. In the same way that all U.S. Courts have less jurisdiction than the Supreme Court, the highest court of appeal, so Jesus said that synagogue courts (church courts) were under the Sanhedrin, which was the highest court of appeal for the Jews.

This simple phrase constitutes the acceptance of a church court system of judicial appeal. It is unlikely that Jesus meant that the highest court in Israel should hear every petty accusation of insult or slander because it would be so very impractical. But rather, He more likely meant that the high court would provide the final appeal, should the lower courts fail to satisfy the litigants.

Central court administration had proven to be a problem for Moses, who had taken the advice of his father-in-law, Jethro, and established a system of appellate courts. That was the model in use, and the model recommended for New Testament churches.

Jesus did two things with this phrase. First, he suggested an appeals court system for the church that would handle, not cases of civil law, but cases of moral law. The jurisdiction of these courts would pertain to breaches of unmitigated anger that overflowed into outbursts of accusations and offenses, what we might call hate speech. The purpose of such church courts was to provide a method for resolving problems before civil laws were broken, and to provide a method for teaching moral responsibility and providing justice at the lowest levels of society.

Jesus knew that a foundation of personal moral responsibility and social justice among the least powerful people was essential for cultural sustainability and economic (*oikos*) development. The pillars of social satisfaction and contentment are personal moral responsibility and the fair or righteous exercise of social justice among all of the people. And this kind of satisfaction does not trickle down from the top, but bubbles up from the bottom, like leaven in the loaf.

7. Beyond The Pale

But I say to you that everyone who is angry with his brother will be liable to judgment; whoever insults his brother will be liable to the council; and whoever says, 'You fool!' will be liable to the hell of fire. So if you are offering your gift at the altar and there remember that your brother has something against you, leave your gift there before the altar and go. First be reconciled to your brother, and then come and offer your gift. Come to terms quickly with your accuser while you are going with him to court, lest your accuser hand you over to the judge, and the judge to the guard, and you be put in prison. Truly, I say to you, you will never get out until you have paid the last penny. —**Matthew 5:22-26**

Verse 22 shows a progression of increasingly unrestrained anger. The verse begins with unexpressed and unjustified anger. It begins as a thought or feeling,

> "whoever is angry with his brother without a cause" (v. 22, Authorized Version).

The consequence of such a thought or feeling is "the judgment" (*ho krisis*). Unjustified anger is unjust and contrary to the spirit and the letter of God's law. To harbor such sentiment is to be guilty of harboring unjust thoughts and liable to God's wrath. The context of this verse is the prohibition against murder, with the implication that unrestrained anger is the cause of murder and liable to the same judgment by God.

Then the Lord provides two examples of how the expression of that anger and its injustice get played out. Anger is like gasoline. It is dangerous to store it up. The expression of anger is like spitting gasoline, which is bad enough because it is a fire hazard. But not only is it a potential hazard, spitting gasoline (anger) is a veritable blow torch because we must remember that the tongue is a fire.

> "And the tongue is a fire, a world of unrighteousness. The tongue is set among our members, staining the whole body, setting on fire the entire course of life, and set on fire by hell" (James 3:6).

The gasoline of anger passes over the fire of the tongue as it gets expressed, and the more that it is expressed the greater the fire. The expression of anger is like spitting fire.

In the first case, the anger is expressed as an insult. The Authorized Version reads,

> "whosoever shall say to his brother, Raca, shall be in danger of the council" (v. 22).

Raca is a Chaldean word that means worthless or empty. We can think of it as calling someone a zero or a nothing. The often overlooked qualifier "without a cause" (v. 21) applies to both examples. In the first example it is not quite an insult, but is more a belittling comment. It is not an actual attack as much as it is a brushing aside. Nonetheless, it always involves the defamation of character because it disregards and devalues the person as a person. Remember that this expression of anger is unjust, without cause. It is a dismissal or rejection of the person as being unworthy of response or acknowledgment without cause. It is the negation of the person's common humanity.

The second stage of the intensification of the expression of anger involves an actual accusation—you fool! The precise word here is less important than the increase of intensity. Here the expression of anger does not merely dismiss the value of the person, but constitutes an outright attack on his character. Again, remember that the accusation is unfounded, without cause and unjust. If the accusation is just, then the expression is righteous, and that's a different situation.

Jesus spat righteous anger at the Pharisees in Matthew 23-24. And Paul called the Corinthians foolish, and rightly so. Both of these expressions were righteous. Some people are foolish and their foolishness needs to be seen for what it is. But that's not what Jesus was talking about here. He was talking about false accusations, about angry, unrighteous, and unjust defamation and name calling.

Jesus once explained that whatever goes into the mouth passes into the stomach and is expelled.

> "But what comes out of the mouth proceeds from the heart, and
> this defiles a person. For out of the heart come evil thoughts,
> murder, adultery, sexual immorality, theft, false witness, slander.
> These are what defile a person" (Matthew 15:17-20).

This angry gas that comes out of the mouth passes over the tongue, which is a fire. And the more gas there is, the more intensely it comes, the greater the pressure, the hotter the fire. This kind of slanderous accusation that is without cause sets ablaze a fire that doesn't go out because it sets the other person on fire as well. It produces insult and offense and incites revenge. Anger induces anger. Like trees burning in a forest fire, the anger leaps from tree to tree. The more people involved, the more trees there are, the hotter it burns.

Jesus was saying that unrighteous anger makes a person liable to God's judgment. That doesn't mean that a person is going to Hell for being angry. There is more to God's judgment than sending people to Hell. God has other consequences in His control. The point is that anger brings people under God's judgment. And at the point of simply being angry the issue is a personal matter of conscience, and it can be dealt with there, God willing.

Public Consequences

But when that anger gets expressed, when it manifests itself into a social situation, then it incurs the judgment of the council, of the church, which is the next instrument of God's justice. If the issue is not dealt with in the conscience, it gets bumped up to the next court of appeal—the council, the jurisdiction of the church. Because the anger has been expressed socially, it must now be dealt with by other people.

It can be handled in a family situation, where the head of the house-hold will deal with it. Or it may require a church court, where adjudication falls to the church elders or the church court. When anger escalates to an actual personal accusation or verbal attack, the attacker is then liable to Hell fire. That doesn't mean that every case of slander results in the person going to Hell. Rather, it means that slander puts Hell on the table as a possible consequence.

This verse must be read in the light of Matthew 18:15-18, where Jesus was describing a system of appeals for justice. When an offense occurs, it should be dealt with by the most immediate and *least* powerful means. Anger should be first a matter of conscience. A person with a well-developed conscience will keep his anger under control. But when anger spills out in conversation, it needs to be dealt with immediately and by the parties directly involved, if possible—the one who causes the offense and the one who is offended. If they can't resolve it, they need to bring it to the elders. It should not remain unresolved, because unresolved anger works like an acid on the fabric of community.

The consequences for such a breach of community also escalate with the intensity of the expression. God can bring various consequences through the conscience. Guilt, depression, frustration, and various kinds of personality disorders can and often do result. At the next level the elders also have many avenues for resolution and various consequences that can bring justice to the sin and restoration to the breach. They can help facilitate repentance and reconciliation, and can impose excommunication in the face of the refusal to cooperate. The final consequence, then, said Jesus, is Hell fire, which most certainly means the consignment to eternal punishment in Hell.

But it doesn't necessarily or always mean that God sends people to Hell for being angry. The immediate result of the failure of the elders or church court to restore the breach of community caused by unrestrained anger would be excommunication of those who cannot forgive and forget, or who refuse to provide the determined restitution.

To allow a person harboring a grudge to continue in fellowship is like bringing a bottle of Jack Daniels to an Alcoholics Anonymous meeting. It is dangerous to everyone involved and should not happen. If excommunication succeeds in its established purpose, the excommunicated person will repent, provide restitution if required, and return to fellowship. If the person who continues to harbor a grudge does not repent, that grudge will be their ultimate ticket into Hell. It is not the anger that brings people to Hell, but the failure to repent. Sin does not keep people from God, the lack of repentance keeps people from God. God does not cause people to go to Hell. Rather, people go to Hell of their own free will, their own decision to reject God and God's forgiveness.

GRUDGE AGAINST

> "So if you are offering your gift at the altar and there remember
> that your brother has something against you, leave your gift there
> before the altar and go. First be reconciled to your brother, and
> then come and offer your gift" (vs. 23-24).

This is very interesting. I suspect that most people understand that if they are holding a grudge without cause against someone, they need to go to that person and ask for their forgiveness. Of course, Jesus' admonition against anger does not include righteous anger, anger with justified cause. If it isn't dealt with at the level of personal conscience or resolved between the parties involved, that kind of anger requires a different remedy, but will always be subject to the agreement of the elders as to whether it is genuinely righteous.

Just because you think you are justifiably angry doesn't mean that your anger is righteous. Nonetheless, if you find that you are angry without due cause, that the fault of the problem is yours, you need to go apologize immediately, and make restitution if necessary.

This, however, is not what Jesus was saying here. Verse 23 isn't about *your* anger with someone else. This verse is about someone else's anger against *you*. You may not be mad at all. You may not even know what the problem is. You may only know that someone is mad at you. And when you make that determination, you need to go to that person and find out what the problem is and rectify it. Whether the fault is yours or his doesn't matter. The anger, the grudge threatens the fellowship.

When the fellowship is in danger all parties must work to root out the problem, bring it to light and bring justice to the situation regardless of who is at fault. It doesn't matter who is at fault. There is always enough blame to share. We must not hold on to the grudge or allow grudges entry into the fellowship. Grudges are like cockroaches, they tend to multiply faster than you can kill them.

MONEY

But there is a more specific lesson taught by this verse that virtually all churches have yet to learn. The context of this verse is the collection of tithes and offerings. And the lesson is that anyone who is angry or harboring a grudge must *not* give any tithes or offerings. Said more positively, all tithes and offerings must be given without the baggage or strings that tend to get attached to anger. Church finances must not be allowed to be used to settle arguments or disagreements, or to manipulate or control the church. If the elders discover that this has happened, that someone is trying to manipulate the church through their tithes and offerings, that money needs to be returned until the underlying anger or conflict is resolved.

A lot of people manipulate churches through their financial contributions. If they don't like something, they withhold their giving, and often encourage others to do the same. They "vote" with their pocketbooks, and Jesus here said that this kind of thing has no place in the church. Alternatively, people sometimes give to specific church projects and withhold their giving from other projects. This should not be allowed to happen.

Those who give to the church are not to be in control of the church finances. Control of the finances has been given to the elders, and the members of the church need to respect that. Only unrestricted gifts should be accepted. Other kinds of directed gifts tend to usurp and undermine the authority of the elders. If you can't trust the elders to serve Christ's cause, then you should get out of the church or get new elders. Jesus is quite specific here that no gifts should be motivated by anger or grudges. Indeed, no gifts should be given by or accepted from an angry or manipulative person.

This, of course, goes against modern church financing, by which people take personal advantage of the U.S. Tax Code regarding charitable giving. But then again, the idea of churches being controlled by a civil tax code at all suggests a breach of the separation of church and state. The purpose of the tax code is to serve the state, not the churches. This state's nose needs to get out of the church tent.

Jesus' point was that brotherly reconciliation is more important than all the church giving in the world. Not only can money not "buy me love," as Paul McCartney sang in 1964, but money can't buy forgiveness or fellowship, either.

> "No one can serve two masters, for either he will hate the one
> and love the other, or he will be devoted to the one and despise
> the other. You cannot serve God and money" (Matthew 6:24).

Most people relate verses 23-24 to communion rather than tithes and offerings, probably because it mentions the altar. The context was Old Testament Judaism because Christianity didn't really get organized until later. People tend to read it as,

> "First be reconciled to your brother, and then come..." (v. 23),

which is a fine generic understanding of the Lord's meaning. It does apply to communion because the reception of communion is a renewal of the covenant between the believer and God, and between believers.

Nonetheless, we should not forget that the actual context has more to do with tithes and offerings than communion.

Have I overemphasized the idea that these verses apply to church courts? No, because Jesus reinforced the judicial nature of these verses in verse 25:

> "Come to terms quickly with your accuser while you are going
> with him to court, lest your accuser hand you over to the judge,
> and the judge to the guard, and you be put in prison."

God's law is the general concern of the Sermon on the Mount. Jesus was not only clarifying the law, but just as He provided the grace necessary to avoid the ultimate consequence of God's law—damnation, He was also showing people how to avoid the temporal consequences of God's law. Jesus was here teaching prevention, teaching people how to stay out of trouble.

MORALITY

Understanding the spirit of the law is essential for conformity to God's law. If you don't understand what it means or the intent of the law, you cannot possibly be in willing compliance to it. Oh, you might find that your actions conform to God's law, but apart from understanding it, that conformity will be more accidental than intentional. Jesus was trying to help us better understand the spirit or intention of God's law. The purpose of that law is to establish justice and equity in the world, to reduce and eventually eliminate sin, and to establish an enduring and sustainable human culture.

Toward that end God works through individual conscience, through churches and through civil governments, all of which provide a kind of appellate court system (a method for judging and evaluating) that serves the interests of justice and equity among human beings. Verse 25 provides a method by which people can avoid getting entangled in the higher courts. The higher the court, the greater the retribution for infractions. Jesus was teaching that it is much easier and less painful to address problems at the lowest and most local levels than to have them adjudicated at higher levels. As such, Christians—everyone really—should endeavor to solve disputes at the lowest possible level of jurisdiction.

Unfortunately, over time (throughout history) the world has grown more infatuated with the higher courts and concerns as people have merged and formed various kinds of cooperative human efforts. The sinful urge for power tends to make people want to solve problems with the maximum power and authority on the basis of the highest courts possible. The urge for power often manifests as the urge to merge businesses, corporations, jurisdictions, etc., and is driven by greed and the lust for power and importance. Merge mania has blossomed in the age of globalization creating the world's largest corporations, which tend to dwarf and run roughshod over individuals and smaller organizations. The problem with gigantic organizations is that the sins of the leaders tend to be magnified by the power and reach of their humongous resources, and generally goes unchecked—particularly when there is no sense of their own sinfulness in the first place.

In addition, the thirst for power and control tends to focus our attention and energies (news and reporting) on the higher courts and larger concerns, national and global concerns. Their sheer size, which commands more resources, more influence, and more social impact, appeals to our own urge for power, which manifests as our desire to be important to the largest number of people possible. And this has created a lack of attention and energy at the local levels. This can be seen by the interest and domination of world and national news, and the lack of attention to local news. In this age of globalization local concerns are seen as being less important.

The foundation of a house is usually unseen, so we don't pay any attention to it until there is a problem. Then foundational or structural issues come to the fore, and they are much more difficult and costly to fix. It's best to keep foundational problems from happening in the first place. Jesus was laying a foundation of personal conscience and morality, upon which other social institutions (church and civil) can be safely established. Where that foundation is strong society will be strong. But where that foundation gives way to sin and corruption the other social institutions that are built on it will follow suit.

And the truth is that these other institutions cannot be fixed until the foundations are fixed. Trying to fix civil institutions (government) apart from first addressing the foundational issues of personal conscience and morality—church and family issues—is a waste of time and resources. Government is by its very nature the exercise of civil power, and when those who exercise that power are themselves morally corrupt the power of government will simply multiply that corruption.

In these verses of the Sermon on the Mount we can see Jesus' concern that we focus our attention and energy on the development and maintenance of the lower, local, immediate relationships. Jesus was teaching about conscience, character, personal integrity, and the intent, spirit, or purpose of God's law. Human culture, human civilization is only as strong as its foundational relationships. Sustainable culture is built from the bottom up, not from the top down. The culture is helped and strengthened by attending to the foundational concerns and relationships—conscience, morality, and our nearest neighbors. The fundamental problem that we are experiencing in the current effort toward globalization is that these foundational concerns and relationships have been increasingly neglected.

CULTURE

Popular culture and its media machine pull people away from the concerns of conscience and personal morality, away from interaction with our nearest neighbors as we get caught up in news, concerns, and relationships with things and people that are far away. Increasingly, we are drawn into national and global news, into corporate culture and mass communication through technology. We have friends all over the world, but don't know the people across the street.

The technology is not bad or evil, but it is being hijacked by sin. Sin covets power and wealth, and neglects conscience and morality. People need to step back, read the Bible, and then look again at our current situation. We need to step back from the culture and media blitz that so dominates and controls our attention in order to be able to see our situation for what it actually is. We get so caught up in our activities, our sitcoms, our news, our cell phones, and Internet services that we can't see anything else. People have limited time and attention, limited abilities, and to fill our time and attention with imaginary or distant concerns leaves no time and attention for real and immediate concerns.

The story of the good Samaritan illustrates this situation. The story is about the problems that develop when our concerns for distant things and our own affinity groups supersede our concern for our nearest neighbors. And Jesus' story of the Samaritan happened in a world without the boost that distant concerns and affinity groups get through modern media.

In the story, both the Priest and the Levite were unmoved by the distress of the man immediately before them. The text doesn't say that they were distracted by other concerns, but they were. It allows us to speculate about the causes of their distraction. Nonetheless, from what we know about pastors and other do-gooders today, we can easily imagine them to have been more concerned about the cause or mission they serve, or the people in their own affinity group, than the poor guy on the road. It is very easy, even natural, for people to slip into this kind of distraction.

Jesus concluded this section of the Sermon on the Mount by showing the consequences of not dealing with these issues as He recommended. He concluded with a comment about failing to settle with the accuser before getting to court.

> "Truly, I say to you, you will never get out until you have paid
> the last penny" (v. 26).

The civil court is an institution of justice. It's not supposed to be an institution of mercy. It is not the job of the civil courts to have mercy. If people want mercy, they need to appeal to the institutions of mercy before their case escalates to civil court. The concern of civil court is justice, recompense, and retribution. By giving these concerns to the civil courts, the Lord has given people an incentive to settle their issues themselves out of court. The best and least expensive settlement in any disagreement will always be the settlement out of court, without lawyers, without court costs.

The church is to be the institution of mercy. And that concern then should encourage people to settle things there, at the moral level, at the personal level, in the church courts if necessary, rather than in civil court at the legal level.

The family is the instrument of instruction. The family is generally where people learn how to be civil, where people learn kindness, manners, morality, and civility, or not. The family is the place where children should learn how to resolve their conflicts and problems with other people. In good measure, that is the purpose of the family. And every effort should be made to provide a godly, biblical, family environment and experience. There is a natural progression to human life and learning, and when life's lessons are not learned when they should be learned—in childhood, they become much more difficult to learn later, and nearly impossible to teach apart from the normal environment in which they occur—childhood.

GRACE

Finally then, or I should say initially, conscience is the instrument of grace. When God's grace is received at the level of personal conscience, the Holy Spirit is dispatched to teach, instruct, and inform the conscience according to God's Word, God's intention, God's Spirit. It is an intensely personal thing. And when that happens, or *as* that happens, many problems are simply alleviated. They are nipped in the bud, often before they even find social expression. When people deal with the Lord at the level of their own personal conscience a foundation of personal morality and responsibility is established that is able to stand firm as the weight of other social relationships and institutions impact our lives.

Jesus also said it this way:

> "One who is faithful in a very little is also faithful in much, and one who is dishonest in a very little is also dishonest in much. If then you have not been faithful in the unrighteous wealth, who will entrust to you the true riches? And if you have not been faithful in that which is another's, who will give you that which is your own? No servant can serve two masters, for either he will hate the one and love the other, or he will be devoted to the one and despise the other. You cannot serve God and money" (Luke 16:10-13).

You cannot serve God and whatever it is that money can buy. It is not that God is opposed to money, but that the concern for money tends to drown out the concern for God.

8. Broken Promise

You have heard that it was said, 'You shall not commit adultery.' But I say to you that everyone who looks at a woman with lustful intent has already committed adultery with her in his heart. If your right eye causes you to sin, tear it out and throw it away. For it is better that you lose one of your members than that your whole body be thrown into hell. And if your right hand causes you to sin, cut it off and throw it away. For it is better that you lose one of your members than that your whole body go into hell. It was also said, 'Whoever divorces his wife, let him give her a certificate of divorce.' But I say to you that everyone who divorces his wife, except on the ground of sexual immorality, makes her commit adultery, and whoever marries a divorced woman commits adultery.
—Matthew 5:27-32

Jesus did in verse 27 exactly what He had done in verse 21. There He applied the consequences of the act of murder to the thought of murder—anger. And here He applied the consequences of adultery to the thought of adultery—lust. None of this is new. The Lord simply clarified and reiterated the Old Testament law. He was not opposed to the law, nor was He expounding a new law here. Rather, His remarks were aimed against the false interpretation of the law that had accumulated over centuries of study, manipulation, and the pride of the Temple establishment. Jesus was not a new legislator of a new law, but was a renewed legislator of the renewed law. It wasn't a new iteration of the law that Jesus brought. It was the fulfillment of the old law, which then established a renewed understanding of the law—old law, new eyes.

The traditional understanding of adultery involves any violation of the marriage bed, or extramarital sex, which is fine as far as it goes. But since Jesus was showing us how the intent of the law had as much to do with our thoughts and motives as our actions, we need to apply this idea here, as well. Extramarital sex is the outward crime. The inner thought or motive involves the breach of the marriage covenant or promise. Extramarital sex is always the fruit of a broken covenant or promise, a broken commitment, a failure of loyalty—loyalty to God if one is not married, loyalty to God and spouse if one is.

So, following Jesus' lead of equating the outward action with the inward motivation, the emphasis here needs to be on the promise or covenant rather than on the sex. This shows that we have learned how to apply the idea that Jesus was teaching here. The way that Jesus dealt with murder and anger is the way He dealt with adultery and lust.

To look lustfully upon a woman or man or anything else is a breach of the Tenth Commandment.

> "You shall not covet your neighbor's house; you shall not covet
> your neighbor's wife, or his male servant, or his female servant, or
> his ox, or his donkey, or anything that is your neighbor's" (Exo-
> dus 20:17).

To covet (*châmad*) is to delight in or want something that belongs to someone else. Wanting what belongs to other people is strictly forbidden.

PROGRESS

But the Tenth Commandment does not forbid social progress or self-improvement. If your neighbor has a great car or a wonderful home, it is not against God's commandments to want a nice car or a home like that of your neighbor. Rather, it forbids you wanting *his* car or *his* home. If you get an idea for a home improvement or expansion from the design of your neighbor's house, that's okay. He had a good idea, and there is nothing wrong with sharing good ideas.

There is nothing wrong with admiring other people, as long as that admiration is for good, godly characteristics, qualities, attitudes, and behaviors. Paul told us to imitate him as he imitated Christ (1 Corinthians 11:1). There is no problem with imitating hair styles, clothing, or characteristics of other people, as long as they are good, righteous, and wholesome. Men and women should want to look good and be good. Christians should want to be attractive instruments of grace, beauty, righteousness, and poise—but not in order to seduce others or to ply their wiles upon people. Rather, we should want to be instruments of grace, beauty, righteousness, and poise in order to give God glory, and to attract others to Christ. That is the right motivation. We should not use these things to manipulate other people, other than to draw them to the grace and glory of Jesus Christ. When our motivations and purposes are not in the service of the Lord, they are sinful. Then again, everything that is not in the service of God's glory is sinful.

COVENANT BREAKING

Nonetheless, Jesus' concern regarding adultery is covenant breaking or promise breaking. God is very concerned about covenant breaking because the violation of any covenant makes the violation of other covenants easier and more likely. Why is this of special concern to the Lord? Because God always relates to people covenantally. The primary connection between God and human beings is covenantal. Of course, Christians have a personal relationship with Jesus Christ, who is the Lord of the renewed covenant between God and humanity.

And God's covenant with humanity is always a matter of personal relationships with individual people because of God's Trinitarian character. To be in relationship with God is always a personal matter, but not a strictly private matter, in the same way that individual identity is personal but not private. Individual identity always exists within a web of personal and social relationships. We are social beings and our personal identities are caught up in our social relationships.

Breaking any one covenant or promise makes future breaches easier. Those who cheat on their spouses are more likely to lie, cheat, and steal in other ways as well. One broken promise paves the way for other broken promises. Promise keeping is a skill that is developed through practice. Skill development requires an idealized vision of that skill as it would exist in perfection so that as people improve in covenant keeping, there is always room for improvement. Our covenant with God provides this function.

EYE SIN

> "If your right eye causes you to sin, tear it out and throw it away. For it is better that you lose one of your members than that your whole body be thrown into hell." (v.29).

There is much confusion about this verse and the next. Should these verses be interpreted literally or figuratively? Are they allusions, parables, or allegories? Did Jesus mean to suggest physical disfigurement as a consequence of failure to be perfect? These kinds of questions are not wrong or bad, but they tend to lead us away from the real meaning of the verse.

And why the right eye? Why not the left? The right eye or hand often serves as a biblical allusion to dominance. For most people the right eye or right hand is the dominant eye or hand. *Right* means that which is dominant, the one most relied upon, the strongest one. The right hand was also the hand by which blessings were conveyed (Genesis 48:14-18, Exodus 29:20, Revelation 5:1-7, etc). Right also implies moral correctness, as in *righteous.*

Note also that the word *thee* in the Authorized Version points to God.

> "And if thy right eye offend thee, pluck it out, and cast it from thee" (v. 29).

While the word *thee* appears twice in English, the Greek uses different words each time. The first instance refers to God and the second instance refers to one's self. The point is that when your eye offends God you are in trouble with God. Offending God is not a good thing. But how can my eye offend God? What does that mean? Does it mean that if I am offended by what I see, I should pluck out my eye? Much of what I see on TV and in movies offends me, so should I be plucking out my eye? No. Does it mean that, if God would be offended by what I see, I should then pluck out my eye? This is closer to the real meaning, but Jesus was not recommending surgery or disfigurement.

The Greek word translated as *eye* (*ophthalmos*) can also mean vision and even envy. The word is not just about an eyeball, but also refers to the act of seeing—perceiving. And just as with Jesus' consideration of the mouth, it's not what goes in that is the problem (Matthew 15:11). The problem is not what we see, but how we interpret and understand what we see.

> "And he said to them, 'Then are you also without understanding? Do you not see that whatever goes into a person from outside cannot defile him, since it enters not his heart but his stomach, and is expelled?' (Thus he declared all foods clean.) And he said, 'What comes out of a person is what defiles him. For from within, out of the heart of man, come evil thoughts, sexual im-

morality, theft, murder, adultery, coveting, wickedness, deceit, sensuality, envy ("an evil eye" in the AV—*ophthalmos*), slander, pride, foolishness. All these evil things come from within, and they defile a person" (Mark 7:18-23).

PROJECTION AND RECEPTION

The context of the word *ophthalmos* was sin. Envy or an evil eye comes from within. The eye, understood as the process of seeing, has two functions, two modes or two poles. The eye is the lens through which light flows, and that flow is both inward and outward. The eye receives light or information, and it also projects light or information (or understanding). To perceive a thing requires seeing it in context. And the context is a mental construction that is projected upon what is seen. Things without context are unseen or unnoticed because we have no way to understand them. We can't see what we don't understand. While we can see it physically, the brain will ignore it mentally when it does not make sense to us, when there are no appropriate categories of understanding by which to file it.

The inward flow of light through the eye to the brain has to do with how we see. It has to do with our physical vision, whether we need glasses. But the outward flow of light through the eye from the brain has to do with how we envision things. It is about our vision in the sense of a plan or purpose or a larger context. It provides the mental context or presuppositions by which we are able to make sense out of things that we see.

The eye not only receives light, it also projects light or understanding in the sense of casting a vision. There is more to seeing than light being received on the back of the eyeball. Seeing also involves a complex process of interpretation and understanding of what is seen so that it fits into a context that makes sense to the seer. This is the eye that Jesus has in mind here. If your vision, your perception of things, your worldview offends God, cut it out, remove it, find a better context, a better worldview. Abandon the offensive vision, and take up God's vision in Scripture.

This is what Jesus was communicating here. The verse is not about eye surgery, and anyone who thinks it is has no depth perception. Such a person suffers from a kind of half-blind, one-eyed, myopic visual deprivation that produces a faulty, half-baked understanding of reality. The last part of this verse reads,

> "For it is better that you lose one of your members than that your
> whole body be thrown into hell." (v. 29).

An eye or worldview that offends God will lead a person into Hell.
However, the problem isn't the errant eyeball, but the offense against
God. It is not the eyeball that needs to be removed, but the offense, the
offending vision or understanding. However, if it is the perception, the
vision, or worldview that offends God, then specific offenses will continue to be produced by that worldview until the perception, vision, or
worldview is abandoned and corrected. The failure to see things right,
to see things as God sees them—not perfectly, but adequately—ultimately leads to damnation. Jesus then applied this same line of thinking
to behavior.

> "And if your right hand causes you to sin, cut it off and throw it
> away. For it is better that you lose one of your members than that
> your whole body go into hell." (v. 30).

In the same way that Jesus spoke of the right eye He also spoke of
the right hand. We must apply the same kind of interpretation and
understanding to this verse. An allusion to the right hand in Scripture is
an allusion to work or activity, what one does with one's dominant
hand. The *hand* in Scripture often implies our strongest skills and abilities.

The meaning is: if what you are doing is offensive to God, cut it
out, stop it, don't do it anymore. In the same way, the issue is God's
offense, not our own. The issue is that our work, our dominant activities
offend God. Offending God is a serious matter, and if it is not resolved it
will result in damnation and Hell. In the same way, this verse is not
about amputation—God is not a sadist who wants to inflict pain and
cripple His people. And to think that these verses should be taken literally belies a serious misperception and misunderstanding of God. It
reveals a serious lack of biblical discernment, a one-handed approach (in
this case) that fails to work out the Trinitarian implications of God's
character and the similar character of His reality—our human reality.

TRINITY

The bottom line for these verses about the right eye and the right
hand offending God is not that Jesus was recommending actual organ or
limb removal, but that He was revealing the seriousness of sin that
results from the failure to embrace the doctrine of the Trinity. Sins of
belief or perception (the right eye) and sins of behavior or commission

(the right hand) are the very sins that lead people to damnation and Hell apart from God's grace and our repentance in Christ.

But it is not sin itself that results in damnation. Rather, it is the denial of the grace and the failure to repent of sin that results in damnation. And these kinds of sins are particularly difficult to repent of because apart from Christ people believe them not to be sins. Repenting of one's worldview is impossible until that worldview is replaced by another. People can't repent of the way they understand things until they have a better way of understanding, which Christ alone provides. Acquiring God's worldview is not a matter of work, effort, or accomplishment, but of gift, grace, and reception.

Nonetheless, these sins of the right eye and the right hand must be treated seriously. They must be eliminated at all costs, even potential bodily disfigurement, and that's the point. But again, this is not an argument for actual self-disfigurement. Disfigurement is never necessary for the elimination of sin, and to think that it is reveals a serious failure to understand God's grace and mercy—and the gospel of Jesus Christ. This is an argument for the humble reception of God's grace as the only solution to this impossible problem of rightly understanding the world, understanding what we see, and what we do about it.

DIVORCE

Jesus then brought this perspective to the issues of marriage and adultery.

> "It was also said, 'Whoever divorces his wife, let him give her a certificate of divorce'" (v. 31).

In order to understand what Jesus was teaching about divorce we need to understand what Moses taught about it.

> "When a man takes a wife and marries her, if then she finds no favor in his eyes because he has found some indecency in her, and he writes her a certificate of divorce and puts it in her hand and sends her out of his house, and she departs out of his house, and if she goes and becomes another man's wife, and the latter man hates her and writes her a certificate of divorce and puts it in her hand and sends her out of his house, or if the latter man dies, who took her to be his wife, then her former husband, who sent her away, may not take her again to be his wife, after she has been defiled, for that is an abomination before the Lord. And you shall

not bring sin upon the land that the Lord your God is giving you
for an inheritance" (Deuteronomy 24:1-4).

Note that Moses did not institute or sanction divorce. He only
acknowledged that it was already in existence and was a common practice. The important thing about Moses' divorce injunctions was that
there must be sufficient grounds for divorce. If we think that law is
established by precedent, we might think that Moses established a precedent here, and mistakenly think that he thereby instituted divorce.

But the law of Moses was not law by precedent, but law by God's
declaration or decree. The establishment of biblical law was not determined by the decisions of a court, but by God's decree. Cases were
decided by courts, but not the content of the law. Such is the historic
nature of kingship. Kings decree laws.

Moses was trying to improve a bad situation. Husbands were
divorcing their wives for the most trivial reasons, and some for no
ostensible reason at all. This situation was unjust and unfair for the
divorced wives. It placed an undue burden upon those women who had
been divorced, and upon the greater society for their post-divorce care
and welfare. Marriage and family are God's instruments of social welfare, and divorce makes them less effective. Divorced wives fall outside
of the traditional structures of social well-being.

Unfaithfulness was rampant at the time. Remember that when
Moses came down from the mountain with the Law in hand, he found
the people dancing before a golden calf in complete and utter violation
of the very First Commandment. We err when we think that Old Testament Israel had been faithful to God's law, but now and then slipped
and incurred God's wrath. Rather, God's law came to a completely heathen and unfaithful people—the Jews—in order to draw them into
increasing faithfulness. And now and then their enduring faithlessness
merited God's wrath. It was not that the general tenor of ancient Israel
was moving from some period of established faithfulness to the loss of
that faithfulness over time. But rather that ancient Israel was moving
from the complete unfaithfulness of humanity apart from God to
increasing faithfulness in fits and starts. This explains Jesus' response to
the Pharisees who inquired of Him about divorce:

> "And Pharisees came up to him and tested him by asking, 'Is it
> lawful to divorce one's wife for any cause?' He answered, 'Have
> you not read that he who created them from the beginning made
> them male and female, and said, "Therefore a man shall leave his

father and his mother and hold fast to his wife, and the two shall become one flesh?" So they are no longer two but one flesh. What therefore God has joined together, let not man separate.' They said to him, 'Why then did Moses command one to give a certificate of divorce and to send her away?' He said to them, 'Because of your hardness of heart Moses allowed you to divorce your wives, but from the beginning it was not so. And I say to you: whoever divorces his wife, except for sexual immorality, and marries another, commits adultery.' The disciples said to him, 'If such is the case of a man with his wife, it is better not to marry.' But he said to them, 'Not everyone can receive this saying, but only those to whom it is given. For there are eunuchs who have been so from birth, and there are eunuchs who have been made eunuchs by men, and there are eunuchs who have made themselves eunuchs for the sake of the kingdom of heaven. Let the one who is able to receive this receive it'" (Matthew 19:3-12).

This matter of divorce has been poorly understood from antiquity forward. For the most part, people still don't get it! The ancient Israelites failed to understand Moses' teaching, and clung haphazardly to their heathen practices in spite of God's law. They didn't make a clean break from their sinfulness and godlessness immediately upon Moses' descent from the mountain. Rather, God's covenant had to be renewed again and again.

The Pagan view of women was that they were chattel, property, that they belonged to their husband like a cow or a goat belonged to the husband. And more often than not Pagan husbandmen approached the raising of their families in the same ways that they bred farm stock. This is a serious error because it denies the humanity of half of the human race, and has been the source of much confusion, consternation, and difficulties. Neither God nor Moses taught this perspective. Rather, both taught against it.

ONE MAN ONE WOMAN

God's plan for the family from the beginning was one man and one woman who were bound in covenant for life (Genesis 2:24). The purpose of the marriage covenant bond was threefold: 1) the glory of God, 2) the health of the those involved and the longevity of the human race, and 3) the happiness of the family (social contentment). But sin interfered, and people put their own unbiblical understanding and their own selfish desires first.

Consequently, unhappy men, thinking that their wives were the source of their unhappiness, divorced and/or abandoned their wives— and God's covenant, hoping to improve their situation. But they didn't improve it, they made things worse for their divorced wives and for the community. So, Moses stepped in and brought a measure of God's justice to this situation by insisting that divorce requests be submitted in writing to the elders for evaluation and adjudication. Divorce was never God's plan, but had been permitted on limited grounds because of the hardness of the hearts of God's people. The source or authority for divorce is not God, but sin.

Part of the confusion about Jesus' teaching on divorce has come from a misunderstanding of Matthew 19:11 where Jesus said,

> "Not everyone can receive this saying, but only those to whom it
> is given."

What saying was Jesus referring to? Too many commentators have suggested that He was referring to the previous verse where the disciples concluded,

> "If such is the case of a man with his wife, it is better not to
> marry" (Matthew 19:10).

Note two things about this conclusion: First, nowhere did Jesus (or Scripture) teach that it is better not to marry (other than particular circumstances of hardship, for instance, 1 Corinthians 7). Second, the disciples seldom understood Jesus correctly. Jesus was not referring to the disciples' misunderstanding of His teaching in verse 10. Rather, He was referring to His own teaching on divorce:

> "Because of your hardness of heart Moses allowed you to divorce
> your wives, but from the beginning it was not so. And I say to
> you: whoever divorces his wife, except for sexual immorality, and
> marries another, commits adultery" (Matthew 19:8-9).

This is the hard saying referred to in Matthew 19:11:

> "All men cannot receive this saying, save they to whom it is
> given."

Avoiding marriage is easy, not hard. The avoidance of marriage fosters irresponsibility and immaturity, and these things are easy. The harder things are responsibility and maturity. And nothing fosters responsibility and maturity better than biblical marriage. We must understand that marriage was not given for our pleasure, but for our good. Eve was not given to Adam because of Adam's loneliness (or horniness), but because of Adam's need for maturity and socialization (Genesis 2:18). Biblical marriage civilizes people. The more difficult thing is to marry and stay married. Being a good husband or wife is a high calling—and that is what Jesus was talking about. That is the saying that not everyone can receive. The truth of this teaching, this saying, must be given to humanity because it does not arise from the natural desires of humanity. Little boys and girls don't want to grow up. They just want to play. Playing makes them happy.

COVENANT LOYALTY

One of the primary purposes of God's laws against adultery is to keep the marriage bed pure, where purity is a function of loyalty to the covenant. Sexual fidelity, loyalty to the covenant, is an important biblical value, and everything that Jesus said about divorce and adultery serves this value. Jesus said that a divorce that leads to remarriage causes adultery. Sexual immorality (fornication, *porneia*) is adultery. And marrying a divorced woman is a kind of adultery. It is not the ideal situation, and God's teaching about marriage is the ideal or perfect situation.

This teaching, this interpretation is very offensive to people today, but what Jesus said was that this "saying" has always been offensive to people. The demand for perfection is always offensive to sinners. Nonetheless, this is God's view about marriage and adultery. Too few people live up to it today, and in all likelihood living up to God's perfection has been a problem throughout history. But the fact that people don't—can't or won't—live up to it doesn't change the fact that it is God's teaching. Perfection is the model in order to always inspire us to better performance, better living.

Does this mean that anyone who violates the marriage covenant is destined for Hell? No. People don't go to Hell because of their sin. People go to Hell because they refuse to repent. Consequently, it is best to view God's teaching about marriage and adultery with a view to the future rather than lamenting about the past.

Okay, so you have sinned. You don't meet God's criteria for perfection. Who does?! But we don't need to delve into people's sexual history to determine that they fall short of God's standard. There are many other aspects of people's lives that don't measure up to God's demands. So, don't get stuck dwelling on God's teaching about divorce. If you are divorced, it's in the past and not something that can be changed. It was wrong regardless of whose fault it was. But there is forgiveness in Christ. So, receive it and move on. The greater sin in this case is not the divorce, but the failure to receive God's forgiveness.

Repent of your old ways and habits and turn your face to the future in Christ. We are new creatures in Christ through regeneration.

> "We are not like Moses, who put a veil over his face so that the sons of Israel could not steadfastly look to the end of the thing being done away. (But their thoughts were blinded; for until the present the same veil remains on the reading of the old covenant, not taken away.) But this veil has been done away in Christ" (2 Corinthians 3:13-14).

In Christ we have new eyes and a new vision for the future. In Christ there is real forgiveness and new life. Hallelujah!

9. Swearing

Again you have heard that it was said to those of old, 'You shall not swear falsely, but shall perform to the Lord what you have sworn.' But I say to you, Do not take an oath at all, either by heaven, for it is the throne of God, or by the earth, for it is his footstool, or by Jerusalem, for it is the city of the great King. And do not take an oath by your head, for you cannot make one hair white or black. Let what you say be simply 'Yes' or 'No;' anything more than this comes from evil.

—Matthew 5:33-37

"And now, O Israel, listen to the statutes and the rules that I am teaching you, and do them, that you may live, and go in and take possession of the land that the Lord, the God of your fathers, is giving you. You shall not add to the word that I command you, nor take from it, that you may keep the commandments of the Lord your God that I command you. Your eyes have seen what the Lord did at Baal-peor, for the Lord your God destroyed from among you all the men who followed the Baal of Peor. But you who held fast to the Lord God are all alive today. See, I have taught you statutes and rules, as the Lord my God commanded me, that you should do them in the land that you are entering to take possession of it. Keep them and do them, for that will be your wisdom and your understanding in the sight of the peoples, who, when they hear all these statutes, will say, 'Surely this great nation is a wise and understanding people.' For what great nation is there that has a god so near to it as the Lord our God is to us, whenever we call upon him? And what great nation is there, that has statutes and rules so righteous as all this law that I set before you today?

Only take care, and keep your soul diligently, lest you forget the things that your eyes have seen, and lest they depart from your heart all the days of your life. Make them known to your children and your children's children—how on the day that you stood before the Lord your God at Horeb, the Lord said to me, 'Gather the people to me, that I may let them hear my words, so that they may learn to fear me all the days that they live on the earth, and that they may teach their children so.' And you came near and stood at the foot of the mountain, while the mountain burned with fire to the heart of heaven, wrapped in darkness, cloud, and gloom. Then the Lord spoke to you out of the midst of the fire. You heard the sound of words, but saw no form; there was only a voice. And he declared to you his covenant, which he commanded you to perform, that is, the Ten Commandments, and he wrote them on two tablets of stone. And the Lord commanded me at that time to teach you statutes and rules, that you might do them in the land that you are going over to possess.

Therefore watch yourselves very carefully. Since you saw no form on the day that the Lord spoke to you at Horeb out of the midst of the fire, beware lest you act corruptly by making a carved image for yourselves, in the form of any figure, the likeness of male or female, the likeness of any animal that is on the earth, the likeness of any winged bird that flies in the air, the likeness of anything that creeps on the ground, the likeness of any fish that is in the water under the earth. And beware lest you raise your eyes to heaven, and when you see the sun and the moon and the stars, all the host of heaven, you be drawn away and bow down to them and serve them, things that the Lord your God has allotted to all the peoples under the whole heaven. But the Lord has taken you and brought you out of the iron furnace, out of Egypt, to be a people of his own inheritance, as you are this day. Furthermore, the Lord was angry Lord with me because of you, and he swore that I should not cross the Jordan, and that I should not enter the good land that the Lord your God is giving you for an inheritance. For I must die in this land; I must not go over the Jordan. But you shall go over and take possession of that good land. Take care, lest you forget the covenant of the Lord your Lord, which he made with you, and make a carved image, the form of anything that the Lord your God has forbidden you. For the Lord your God is a consuming fire, a jealous God" (Deuteronomy 4:1-24).

"You shall not take the name of the Lord your God in vain, for
the Lord will not hold him guiltless who takes his name in vain"
(Exodus 20:7).

Jesus was here clarifying the Third Commandment. He was not
issuing a new law or a new commandment or making any adjustment to
God's initial statement of that commandment. Rather, Jesus was
correcting a misunderstanding that had accumulated over Israel's
history. He was here clarifying the original intent of the Third
Commandment.

Understanding this Commandment requires that we understand
what it means to take the Lord's name in vain. And as is true with all of
God's Commandments, the negative statement of the commandment
forbids one thing, and implies an opposite or positive act of obedience,
as well. If I say to you, "Don't talk to me that way." I also mean that you
should talk to me in the opposite way. So, if I said, "Don't talk to me
disrespectfully." I also mean, "Talk to me respectfully."

Applying this to the case of the Third Commandment, we see that
we are to take the Lord seriously or earnestly, because seriousness,
earnestness, is the opposite of vanity. While Jesus spoke of the name of
the Lord, He meant, not merely God's appellation, but His character.
The biblical name of a thing is a description of its character. To take
someone seriously is to take his name seriously. Don't engage in slander.
Don't say untrue things about God. Don't give God a bad name. This is
what it means to not take God's name in vain.

VANITY

The first definition of vanity has to do with pride. Vanity is a form
of pride. And the opposite of vanity is humility. We are to take the
Lord's name with humility, without pride. All thought, consideration,
and acknowledgment of the Lord is to be done in humility. We are to
come before the Lord humbly, clearly and honestly understanding His
position and role in the world, and ours.

The second definition of vanity suggests valuelessness and futility. A
vain thing has no value and is futile, useless. So, thinking and acting as if
God is without value is a way of taking the name of the Lord in vain.
Taking the name of the Lord in vain includes thinking or saying that
God is a useless or futile idea. This Commandment forbids all irrever-
ence toward God in thought, action, and intent. The positive side of this

Commandment demands that all consideration of God be reverent and respectful.

Reverence and respect are central elements of worship and are woven into liturgical worship services and religious ceremonies. However, this attitude or approach is to be attached to all references to God, in church, at home, at work—wherever, not just at church, not just during worship. Speaking about God should always be done with esteem and deference, period.

Calvin associated this verse with Isaiah 45:22-24:

> "Turn to me and be saved, all the ends of the earth! For I am
> God, and there is no other. By myself I have sworn; from my
> mouth has gone out in righteousness a word that shall not return:
> 'To me every knee shall bow, every tongue shall swear alle-
> giance.' Only in the Lord, it shall be said of me, are righteousness
> and strength; to him shall come and be ashamed all who were in-
> censed against him."

This turning to God involves a swearing of allegiance and is equated to the taking of God's name, which shall not be done in vain. Jesus' point was that it shall not be done without respect and humility. It shall not be done lightly, frivolously, or without effect—without conse-quence. The positive commandment is that all mention of God shall be done with respect and humility, with reverence, seriousness, and effec-tuality.

Along these same lines, Isaiah wrote,

> "For as the rain and the snow come down from heaven and do
> not return there but water the earth, making it bring forth and
> sprout, giving seed to the sower and bread to the eater, so shall
> my word be that goes out from my mouth; it shall not return to
> me empty, but it shall accomplish that which I purpose, and shall
> succeed in the thing for which I sent it" (Isaiah 55:10-11).

God's Word always produces an effect in the world. To take God's name or to swear allegiance to Jesus Christ apart from any effect in one's own life is forbidden. God forbids empty or broken promises, promises that have no consequences.

God's Covenant

So, what is the purpose of God's Word? God's purpose is to bring humanity under His covenant, His promise, and the loving protection He provides. And what is God's most fundamental promise? It is articulated in Deuteronomy 28. God promises blessings for obedience and curses for disobedience. And by shaping His promise in this way, God has guaranteed the involvement of every human being on the planet in His covenant for all time. This is the universal or objective character of God's covenant or promise. It stands apart from all human subjectivity and discrimination. God is no respecter of persons, which means that this covenant promise has been applied to all humanity for all time. No one can escape it because everyone will live in obedience to it or not.

Of course, this is God's Old Testament covenant, which has undergone many administrations through biblical history. The problem with the Old Testament covenant was that it proved to be impossible for people to meet its terms and conditions. And God knew that this would be the case from the beginning, but we didn't. Why is the impossibility of the covenant important? Because it is essential for people to acknowledge the fact of their own inability apart from Christ to live as God demands. The purpose of biblical history was to demonstrate the human inability to live in obedience to God.

God appeared to Moses in ancient Israel and gave them the law, the prophets, the temple, and the culture. But Israel failed to live in obedience to God's covenant, and received God's curses as promised. Israel's biblical history is marked by constant failure and several great catastrophes (punctuated, of course, by blessings and good times as well).

Nonetheless, Israel broke into civil war following the reign of Solomon, and that war never actually ended. The Assyrians destroyed and captured the capital of the Northern Kingdom in 722 B.C. The Babylonians destroyed the Southern Kingdom—Jerusalem and the Temple—in 586 B.C. The Temple was rebuilt, and the Romans destroyed Jerusalem and the Second Temple in 70 A.D. The nation of Israel was wiped from history until the mid-1900s, when Israel was reestablished as a secular nation in Palestine following World War II.

The covenant renewal of the New Testament through Jesus Christ came about because of the covenant obedience of Jesus Christ, even unto death on the cross. This New Covenant is the same as the Old Covenant with one difference: Jesus Christ rendered human covenant obedience possible, but only through God's grace and His dispatching of the Holy Spirit. So, Jesus Christ is the New Covenant administrator. And when people are in Christ or under Christ or in union with Christ through regeneration by the power and presence of the Holy Spirit, their obedience is guaranteed—not immediately, not completely in this life, but truly, adequately. Why? Because it is Christ who redeemed His people and promised to complete in them what God had begun.

The power and strength of the Holy Spirit is such that He works within people, in their minds and hearts, to bring them both the desire and the ability to grow in faithfulness over time. And the Holy Spirit is God through the Trinity, and what God sets out to do, He will accomplish. So, this New Covenant administration will succeed. Covenant obedience will ultimately defeat covenant disobedience in the fullness of time.

As God said through Isaiah, His Word is like rain and snow that water the fields and cause crops to grow. God's Word will accomplish what it set out to do—to bless obedience and curse disobedience. God will fulfill His covenant. Nothing can stop it. Individuals will either live in faithfulness to God by the power and presence of the Holy Spirit through regeneration and reap blessings beyond their wildest imaginations, or they will not, and will reap God's curse, which will bring about their ultimate destruction and damnation. God's promise is that His blessings will increase and eventually dominate the world. Ignoring, denying, or making light of this fact is what Jesus meant by taking God's name in vain.

In times of old, it was said,

"You shall not swear falsely, but shall perform to the Lord what you have sworn" (v. 33).

This swearing is not a matter of cussing, though cussing is evidence of sin and disobedience. Rather, this swearing involves the taking of an oath, or in modern parlance, of confessing or acknowledging God's truth. It means entering into association or affiliation with God. All who are in association or affiliation with God must live in faithful obedience. That was the Old Covenant.

And the Lord provided many ceremonies and cultural practices by which the ancient Jews could identify and affiliate with God and His people. But it didn't work. It lost them their nation, their place in the world. And the Jews became wanderers, with no homeland. This was all part of God's plan.

TRINITARIAN CHARACTER

With the destruction of Israel, Christians came to see that God had not intended to create a special nation of covenanted people, but to take His covenant to the entire world. God hadn't chosen Israel because they were special. God is not a respecter of persons or nations. Rather, God chose Israel in order to demonstrate human inability and to show the human need to rely upon Him. Jesus then demonstrated that the God upon which people must rely is necessarily Trinitarian. God's Trinitarian character could only be demonstrated by sending His Son, Jesus Christ, who would in turn send the Holy Spirit for the regeneration and reformation of humanity in the likeness of God. Jesus' mission was to reestablish man's pre-Fall relationship with God, but in the experience and maturity of forgiveness rather than in Man's pre-Fall state of simple innocence.

The Trinitarian character of God and Man's reflected image of that character are essential to salvation. There is no salvation apart from the engagement of God's Trinitarian character, a character which transforms and reforms sinners from the inside out. God's purpose has always been the reformation of human character through the power and presence of the Holy Spirit. Yes, God is concerned about externals, about behavior and morality, about society and human culture. But these things cannot be changed from the outside in. They can only be changed from the inside out. And God's reaching into humanity to change individual character is accomplished by the character of the Trinity and our created likeness to that character.

So Jesus said,

> "Do not take an oath at all, either by heaven, for it is the throne of God, or by the earth, for it is his footstool, or by Jerusalem, for it is the city of the great King. And do not take an oath by your head, for you cannot make one hair white or black" (vs. 34-36).

Jesus noted that the Jews spent way too much time and energy on external oaths and ceremonies and not nearly enough time or energy on internal obedience of the heart. The oaths and ceremonies had become religious practices and increasingly ritualistic, empty practices that only isolated the Jews from other people. God had called them to be separate from others and to establish a culture of love and obedience that was distinct from the fallen culture of sin and disobedience. But the harder they worked at this task, the more it failed. This failure did not surprise God. Rather, He had anticipated it. He knew that Jesus' advent and the dispensation of the Holy Sprint would be required to fulfill His mission.

Just like inbreeding weakens the gene pool, over time spiritual incest weakened Israel's faithfulness. In a manner of speaking, Israel tamed God over the centuries by institutionalizing her religious practices. It's not that the institutionalization of those religious practices was wrong, but there is a right way to do it and a wrong way to do it. The right way is to keep the focus on individual hearts and minds, and the wrong way is to turn it into a show, an exhibit. Faithfulness had been captured and put on show at the Temple. It became a thing for show and status. People went to the Temple to parade their faithfulness.

When faithfulness becomes a cultural exhibit, it loses its life, its dynamic power to effect hearts and minds. When the heart of a culture is paraded as an institutional exhibit, it is already dead. Exhibits are lifeless artifacts, not dynamic truths and passions that fuel God's cause. Finally, in their cultural isolation (their spiritual inbreeding or focus on themselves) and the institutionalization of their religion, they had nothing to offer, except God's law.

God's law had taken them as far as it could. The more they tried to understand it, the more they gave themselves to live by it, the more they focused on it, the more it showed them their own failures and weaknesses. To focus on law is to focus on institutionalization and to incur the consequences of human shortsightedness and sin. The effort to package God for general consumption, which is what it means to institutionalize Him, demonstrated their own failure and inability, which in turn became the fuel for God's curse. Their effort to live in obedience to God's law became an untenable situation. Apart from Christ, obedience was out of reach because of our innate human inability and sin. God's blessings were simply out of reach. And Israel was left with nothing but God's curses. The law could only convict them—and it did.

THE REMEDY

Jesus understood this situation correctly and gave Himself to its remedy. He did what no one else could do because He was what no one else was—the Son of God. He lived in perfect obedience, and fulfilled God's Old Testament covenant for the world. How was one man's obedience the fulfillment of God's covenant for humanity? Let me illustrate.

When my family and I lived in Evansville, Indiana, we lived across from a keeper of sheep, an old farmer who had a flock of sheep—Leroy Niehaus. One of his sayings or stories went like this: *How can you get a flock of sheep into a truck?* I had no idea. His answer: *Get one in. All you have to do,* he'd say, *is get one in and the rest will follow.* For him it simply illustrated a true thing about sheep, which is also true about people. People, like sheep, are followers.

This is exactly what God did with Christ. I can imagine Jesus asking His Father, *How can these people be saved? How can these crusty, dis-obedient, hard-headed people ever get into the kingdom, Dad?*

And God answered, *Save one. Just get one in, Son. You lead and the rest will follow.* And so He did. But the only one who could actually get in was Himself, the others were too sin encrusted. So, He did what was necessary. He perfectly obeyed God's commandments, and made a propitiatory sacrifice to appease God and purchase His people. And the rest is history. It's not over yet, of course, but it will happen as sure as day follows night. The Lord's sheep will follow Him. They are in the process of following even now.

It's an irresistible process. Nothing can stop it. Does this mean that everyone will eventually be saved? No. But it does mean that everyone who God wants to be saved and everyone who actually wants to be saved will in fact be saved. But some people won't be saved because they don't actually want to be, because they reject God. And that is a very painful reality for us to admit—and for God to abide.

Trying to understand this painful reality is an unfruitful line of thought. It is enough to know that it breaks God's heart, even though it serves His purpose by fulfilling His covenant promise. It fulfills it by providing the negative consequences for disobedience of God's promise. The only positive lesson to be garnered from the fact that not everyone will be saved is that God's covenant Word is completely true. It will not fail to produce what God said it would produce—blessings and curses. The blessings show us what to do, the curses show us what *not* to do. And both are very valuable pieces of information.

OATHS

In these verses of the Sermon on the Mount Jesus was telling us what to do. He said, *Don't take any oaths.* Then He listed various kinds of oaths that people had been taking: swearing by heaven or by earth or by the holy city of Jerusalem, the jewel of the Jewish crown; swearing by your own head (*kephalē*), your own power and authority; and swearing to the best of your ability. He said that such swearing or oath taking won't work. We don't have the power or ability to keep our own promises, apart from Christ.

Again, people were using this swearing, these oaths, as ways of identifying themselves as being faithful to God. People thought that they could belong to the community of the faithful by publicly swearing oaths of obedience to God. But here Jesus said that these kinds of things were only outward actions, words and ceremonies—exhibits—that people mistakenly identified with internal faithfulness.

I will live in obedience to God, I swear it!

Such an oath is an attempt to convince one's self, others, and even God, that I can do something that I am innately unable to do, apart from Christ. His point was that oaths and ceremonies were being used for the sake of appearances. Saying your were faithful was equated with actually being faithful. This is a perpetual problem, new in every generation.

God's first concern is not the outside of the cup. God doesn't need you to take an oath of obedience to Him. God just needs you to actually be obedient. Our behavior is the fruit or evidence of our promise. Our public, verbal promise adds nothing to God's covenant. We did not get under His covenant by making a promise, nor by being baptized, or by taking membership vows. There's nothing wrong with such things— and they do have value, but they do not constitute faithfulness. People can and do make false promises. We are not made faithful by our promise to be faithful. We are made faithful by the blood of Christ and the power of the Holy Spirit. Jesus told a story about this kind of error.

> "A man had two sons. And he went to the first and said, 'Son, go and work in the vineyard today.' And he (the first son) answered, 'I will not,' but afterward he changed his mind and went. And he went to the other son and said the same. And he answered, 'I go, sir,' but did not go. Which of the two did the will of his father?" (Matthew 21:28-31).

Both sons took an oath. They both made a promise. One promised he would not go, but did. And the other promised he would go, but didn't. Both sons lied to their father. Neither son did what he said he would do. Both sons broke their promise because neither was faithful to his own words. And neither promise, neither oath, helped in the least. What mattered was the doing, the going, not the promising.

God gathers His people together for worship, not so that we can make promises to Him, but so that we can hear His word, hear His promise to us. Again, there is nothing wrong with our making oaths and promises to be obedient, but the measure of faithfulness is the behavior, not the promise. And the power to keep the promise is Christ's, not ours. And too often people confuse the promise with the action. People have a tendency to think that the action of promise-making is the action of faithfulness. But it is not! You are not a faithful

Christian because you walked the aisle or because you got baptized or because you joined a church or because you say that you are.

Again, doing these things does make a difference. It raises the ante. Doing these things, making such promises, serves as an acknowledgment that you know about God and His covenant. But these things don't help us keep our promises. These things only make faithlessness all the worse. They turn the failure to comply into willful disobedience.

These things are okay if they provide an incentive to be faithful, to seek the Lord, to repent, conform, reform, whatever you want to call it. They are okay for the faithful, for those who are actually saved. But they are damning for those who think that they are okay because they made the decision or the promise, because they took the oath, because they got baptized or joined the church.

And again, these things—baptism, oath taking, and church membership—are okay. But they are the result of faithfulness, not the cause. Apart from Christ, apart from actual regeneration and obedience to Christ that comes through Christ, they are all the more damning because they say to God, *I'm able to live in obedience to your demands on my own and apart from your interference in my life.*

Such a statement is untrue. We are under God's covenant (Deuteronomy 28) simply because we are human beings, period. It's inherited. It's a function of our birth, of original sin. We are under God's general and eternal covenant because God made the covenant with various representatives of humanity. All who are under God's covenant are representatives of that covenant to humanity. All covenant keepers are God's ambassadors to the world. Nothing we say or promise has put us under the covenant and nothing we say or denounce can get us out from under it. The only words that are important to the covenant are God's words. He speaks, and we listen.

Of course we can—and must—acknowledge that we are under God's covenant because we are. It is important to confess this truth. But to say that we aren't when we are, or to say that we are when we aren't constitutes a lie, and makes us more guilty of deceit than we would be had we said nothing.

INTEGRITY

> "Let what you say be simply 'Yes' or 'No'; anything more than this comes from evil" (v. 37).

The Authorized Version reads,

"But let your communication be, Yea, yea; Nay, nay: for whatsoever is more than these cometh of evil."

The idea here is to mean what you say and say what you mean. When
you say *yes* mean yes. And when you say *no* mean no. This is a plea for
basic honesty and integrity. Hardly anything could be more simple or
more basic, and yet the lack of honesty and integrity is among the most
prevalent problem in society today. We are a nation of liars, cheaters,
and fast talkers—not the only nation, of course. There are many. The
cultural milieu in which we live is so saturated with lying, cheating, and
fast talking that we have come to think that it is normal. It's everywhere
and everyone does it to one extent or another. Our lies and broken
promises harm others, just as the lies and broken promises of others
harm us.

   People justify themselves to themselves by asking, *What does one
little white lie matter?* And more often than not, one little white lie
doesn't matter much—unless you are the one being lied to. We tend to
think that when we lie to others it doesn't matter much, but when others lie to us we tend to think that it matters a lot. But the truth is that if
it doesn't matter much, then it wouldn't make much difference to just
tell the truth, either. If it doesn't matter one way, it doesn't matter the
other.

   So, when people feed us a little white lie, and we discover that a
friend has lied to us, we wonder why he thinks so little of us that he
would lie about such an apparently unimportant thing. And if we don't
discover that it's a lie and believe it ourselves, then the next time the
issue comes up, the person who lied will have to lie again in order to
protect the first lie from being discovered. And round and round she
goes, weaving a web of lies and deceit for no apparent reason, or for
some insignificant reason.

   The more that people engage in lying and cheating, the more
untrustworthy the community or society or nation as a whole becomes.
The problem is that truth and integrity are critical for social progress
and economic development because promise-making and promise-
keeping are the foundational bedrock of human civilization. The reliable
correspondence between what a person says and what a person does
effects every aspect of our lives.

   The banking industry is built upon the trustworthiness of our personal promises. The corruption of promise-keeping erodes the ability to
conduct business—buying, selling, lending, borrowing, etc. Corruption

eats away the economy. The failure to keep a financial promise results in a monetary default of one kind or another. A loan is a promise, and the failure to make payments results in a loss of capital for someone else.

In addition, science and technology require the honest and faithful observation and reporting of experiences and facts. Love and marriage are established on mutual trustworthiness. Indeed, there is no area of life that does not depend upon personal honesty and integrity. And conversely, there is no area of life that is free from the accumulative and corrosive effects of lying and cheating. While one little white lie may not make much difference in the overall scheme of things, a society of liars and cheaters are like a thousand cuts on the body politic, which drain the life blood from the body of a nation.

Again, the idea of swearing has two meanings: cussing and oath taking. Cussing or cursing should be avoided because it offends God either by its lewdness, obscenity, and filthiness or by using the name of the Lord without proper respect. And because sins tend to cluster, because where one sin is displayed others are lurking, cussing amounts to the denouncement of one's own character as being untrustworthy. Cussing is the announcement that you are an unrepentant sinner.

Oath taking, on the other hand—unlike cussing, is not strictly forbidden, but should be avoided whenever possible. Oath taking is not sinful, unless the oath serves to hide the truth or becomes a broken promise. The problem with taking an oath to "tell the whole truth and nothing but the truth so help you God" is two-fold. First, to suggest what you (or anyone) says is the whole truth will always be false because no one, no human being, knows the whole truth. The whole truth must always be perfectly objective and people are mostly subjective. In addition, the suggestion that I'm telling the truth *this time* because I'm swearing to it implies that I was at some previous time not telling the truth. To swear that I'm telling the truth is a confession that I don't always tell the truth.

The Lord was clarifying the teaching that the Third Commandment forbids lying and cheating, and by implication it demands that people be truthful—all the time, not just sometimes, not just under oath.[11] The Third Commandment binds people to God's covenant through honesty and integrity in all circumstances and relationships, and particularly when God is involved. Thus, it primarily means honesty and

---

11 It is true that Rahab lied to those who sought after the Israelites (Joshua 2), but her deception to the king's men honored her covenant to God. This story was not a justification for lying, but a story of primary covenant faithfulness.

fidelity to God in all circumstances. All references to God must be made with honesty, integrity, reverence, honor, and humility. Any other attitude toward God is sinful.

10. Eye of Justice

*You have heard that it was said, 'An eye for an eye and a tooth
for a tooth.' But I say to you, Do not resist the one who is evil.
But if anyone slaps you on the right cheek, turn to him the
other also. And if anyone would sue you and take your tunic,
let him have your cloak as well. And if anyone forces you to go
one mile, go with him two miles. Give to the one who begs
from you, and do not refuse the one who would borrow from
you.*   —Matthew 5:38-42

The teaching about an eye for an eye has a long history of correct
exegesis and an equally long history of misunderstanding. It
originates in Leviticus 24:19-20,

> "If anyone injures his neighbor, as he has done it shall be done to
> him, fracture for fracture, eye for eye, tooth for tooth; whatever
> injury he has given a person shall be given to him."

Keep in mind that establishing justice in the world is a major
biblical theme. The idea was not that the injured person would take up
the cause of his own revenge for injuries sustained. Rather, justice
always requires that judgment and punishment be meted out by courts
and judges, where hearings and investigations can be engaged more
objectively.

The point is that the idea of an eye for an eye and a tooth for a
tooth is not an invitation to take up the cause of personal revenge. This
was not an invitation to take the law into our own hands. It was a guide
for courts and judges, not individuals or families. The Lord forbids the
taking of revenge.

"Beloved, never avenge yourselves, but leave it to the
wrath of God, for it is written, 'Vengeance is mine, I
will repay, says the Lord'" (Romans 12:19).

Paul was citing the Old Testament law and practice. The Old Testament law was given in part in order to stop the practice of revenge
taking. So, it has a long history. Revenge is probably a hard-wired
genetic stimulus response. You poke me, I poke you back. You can see
this behavior in children, especially little boys. Nonetheless, God forbids
it. It leads to fights, family feuds, and wars.

Again, Jesus was correcting an error, the error of using God's law as
an excuse for taking revenge. The law itself was not wrong, but people
had been applying it wrongly. So, He first acknowledged their understanding and practice of the law, that they had indeed heard that it was
said, "An eye for an eye and a tooth for a tooth." It was a righteous and
legal law, but it didn't apply to people personally.

It was intended to be a principle of justice for court use, not a principle for personal revenge taking. The context of this verse is a court
scene, where an Israelite woman's son had been brought to Moses for
adjudication. The Lord was speaking to Moses about the principles of
justice. The exercise of justice requires the engagement of God's Word.

So, how were people supposed to respond to being wronged? The
motivation for revenge is often the desire for righteousness and justice
in the face of insult and injury. People rightly believe that there ought to
be some way to address injustice and personal wrong doing. And there
is—engaging God's Word, living by biblical principles and teachings!

But doing things God's way doesn't lead to immediate satisfaction.
In addition, social corruption, deceit, and extortion tend to pervert justice. And people tend to be impatient. They want justice right away,
and when they don't get it they start figuring out ways to accomplish it
themselves. All of this leads to revenge upon revenge. So, the Lord forbids it all. Justice is in God's hands, not ours.

Of course there are things we can do to engage God's justice. He
has provided courts and judges, churches and elders, police and attor-
neys, but note that none of these things involve taking personal revenge.
To say that justice is in God's hands means that the correct engagement
of God's Word and way will result in justice—not always right away,
but over time God's Word will produce an increasingly just and righteous social order. So, if you are tempted to go the way of an eye for an
eye, Jesus provided an alternative.

Do Not Resist

> "I say to you, 'Do not resist the one who is evil. But if anyone
> slaps you on the right cheek, turn to him the other also'" (v. 39).

This prohibition does not forbid self-defense. If our bodies or our families or homes are in danger, we can—and must—protect ourselves against the various criminal elements who would do us or our loved ones harm. We are not to passively enable thieves, rapists, murders, extortionists, or bullies by calmly sitting by while they reap their havoc.

The situation that Jesus mentioned here was being slapped with an *open hand* (*rhapizō*), not beaten or pummeled. It was an allusion to being offended. Jesus was trying to nip this problem in the bud, before it gets out of hand. Whenever we are offended we are to catch ourselves early in the process. We are to stop the anger from boiling over into uncontrollable rage.

Before you get mad, said Jesus, *turn the other cheek.* The person who slapped you has made a symbolic gesture with an open hand. In fact, at that point, the guy who has slapped you thinks that you have offended him. That's why he slapped you. The slapper thinks that the slapee needs to come to his senses. And maybe he does!

So, if you in fact do need to come to your senses, if your being slapped causes you to acknowledge that you are the person who has done the wrong, then turning the other cheek can serve as an acknowledgment of your error. At that point you might say something like, "Wow! You know that was wrong of me. I deserve more than a slap. And you can help me not to make that mistake again by whacking me on the other cheek in order to help me make a memory so that I don't do it again."

You should also work an apology in there, too. And if you were in the wrong, let that be the end of it. You've given the person you offended a way to satisfy his sense of outrage and his need for justice, which should keep his need for revenge from boiling over. If you deserve it, take your lumps, apologize, forgive, and move on.

But when the person who slapped you has been offended unjustly or pretends to be offended, then by offering him your other cheek you make his guilt for his pretense all the more visible. If you do not deserve to be slapped, but still offer your other cheek, it is like piling coals upon the head of the unjust person who has slapped you.

The turning of your other cheek is not an effort to embarrass him, but to instruct him in the principles and practices of righteousness. By turning the other cheek you demonstrate patience and maturity. That demonstration will either convict you if you are in the wrong, or him if he is in the wrong. Either way, God wins because justice and righteousness benefit from patience and maturity.

Paul spoke to this in Romans 12:19-21:

> "Beloved, never avenge yourselves, but leave it to the wrath of God, for it is written, 'Vengeance is mine, I will repay, says the Lord.' To the contrary, 'if your enemy is hungry, feed him; if he is thirsty, give him something to drink; for by so doing you will heap burning coals on his head.' Do not be overcome by evil, but overcome evil with good."

We are to serve righteousness and goodness in everything that we think, say, and do. Doing what is right, being fair and just with people, even when they treat us unfairly and unjustly is the right thing to do because it serves God's purposes. So, if someone is unjustly offended by you or by something you have done or said, and they slap you physically or symbolically, give them another opportunity to do the same thing, to repeat the injustice. Bear the offense graciously in the hope that your willingness to bear it will reveal the truth of their injustice and contribute to their repentance.

WITNESS

By not engaging the urge to revenge you provide a witness to the power and goodness of Christ, who holds you back. This whole scenario provides a perfect opportunity to witness, to share the love and power of Christ because at the point of being slapped, of being offended, more than words are involved. The person to whom you are witnessing the restraining love of Christ will see that the gospel is more than mere words because it restrains you, and this is a critical element for successful witnessing. The gospel is not an intellectual argument. It is a way of life, a way of living, a lifestyle. Jesus used this tact when He was slapped before the High Priest.

> "If what I said is wrong, bear witness about the wrong; but if what I said is right, why do you strike me?" (John 18:23).

He challenged the High Priest to prove that what He had said was wrong. This was an act of submission to the legally instituted authority of the High Priest, a willingness to abide by the ruling of the High Priest, and to challenge the High Priest to make the case that Jesus was wrong. Why did He do this? Because if Jesus wasn't wrong, the High Priest was morally bound by his office to honor the truth. And the failure of the High Priest to honor the truth, to honor the fact that Jesus was right was a confession of his own corruption, which then annulled the High Priest's authority in the matter. God's truth always trumps human authority.

Jesus was so opposed the ways of the world that He said that it was better to take one on the chin than to get involved with worldly conflict, strife, and lawsuits. Jesus and the apostles were adamant about Christians not getting embroiled in worldly legal obligations like courts, suits, criminality (slander, defamation, theft, extortion, etc.), and debt.

Nor was Jesus saying that Christians should never communicate something offensive. It is not that Christians should intentionally offend people, but that we should make every effort not to offend God. We also need to make every effort not to offend others with what we say and do. But we are not to worry about whether what God says and does will offend people. That's between Him and them. We need to let Him work that out with them directly, personally.

Being offended by God or by God's Word is often part of the process of conversion, as God weans people from the milk of their own thoughts and ideas to the meat of God's thoughts and ideas. *When*—not *if*—people are offended by the gospel, then so be it. Their offense is a function of their own pride, and they need to take it to the Lord in prayer. To remove such an offense would be to give the reins to pride.

OFFENSE

The Lord insisted that Christians go on the offensive. When Peter identified Jesus as the Christ, the Lord responded.

> "And I tell you, you are Peter, and on this rock I will build my
> church, and the gates of hell shall not prevail against it" (Matthew
> 16:18).

The church was to batter down the gates of Hell with the message that Jesus is the Christ. There is no more offensive message than this to the minions of Satan. And Christians are not to shrink from its proclamation.

Yet, we are *not* to resist evil. But why not? How can our not resisting evil serve God's desire for justice? God mandates righteousness and justice, so why are we commanded to not resist what opposes God's righteousness and justice? What about passive resistance? That seemed to work for Gandhi, and Gandhi admitted that he got the idea from the Bible. Hasn't passive resistance had a lot of success? God's long range plan is the elimination of evil in the world. So, why can't we help by doing a little resisting? I mean, if we don't resist it, won't it just get worse?

In order to understand this we need to understand God's strategy for His war against Satan. From the beginning God has insisted on fighting Israel's battles. When we read the Old Testament battle stories we see that God consistently fought for Israel. For instance, the story of David and Goliath illustrates this point. David was offended by Goliath's taunting of Israel because he believed that God was offended by it. So, David was out to defend God's honor. Little did he know that God was out to save David for later service.

When Saul heard of it, he outfitted David in his own battle armor to give him the best possible advantage against Goliath. But Saul's ways were worldly ways. The armor didn't fit and crippled David's ability to move about. And when David discovered this, he abandoned the armor (the ways of the world) and took up what God had taught him—his sling. He had learned and practiced the sling as a boy in the fields as he watched his sheep. He had used it against bears and lions, and determined that it would work against Goliath, as well. It was God's provision.

So David stepped onto the battlefield where Goliath waited for him. Goliath was surprised because David was a boy, and because he appeared to be completely unarmed. David had no defensive armor. And that is the point. He did not fear the evil that Goliath had in mind for him. The word *evil* (*ponēros*) in verse 39 can also be translated as *harm*. Do not resist harm. David was not afraid of being harmed. Had he been afraid, he would have resisted God's leadership, and put on Saul's armor. But Saul's armor (the ways of the world) crippled David's ability to exercise God's gift—his God-given ability to use the sling. Had he worn it, Goliath would have mistaken him for a soldier rather than a mere boy, and simply killed him.

The biblical idea of not resisting evil must be reclaimed today. But it doesn't mean what people think it means. David did not resist Goliath when he stood before him in battle. People usually think that not resisting evil means not fighting against it or not opposing it. But that would mean letting evil run its course unchecked. And God is the God of justice, so that cannot be what it means. Jesus was not undermining God's concern for justice.

Resist Not

The Greek word translated *resist* (*anthistēmi*) literally means to stand apart or stand opposed. So, if we are not to resist a thing, it means that we are not to stand apart from it. We are not to stand opposed to it. Thus, it means that we are to stand with the thing we are resisting, but not in support of it. Rather, the idea is to engage it, to interact with it, to be involved with it.

Jesus' example was turning the other cheek. We are not to turn away from the evil of being slapped. We are not to be afraid of harm, but we are to stand our ground and call upon the righteousness of Christ to protect us from harm. However, the purpose of our engagement is to convert the evil or wrong-thinking with which we are engaged. Evil can be declawed and converted as it comes into contact with Christ's righteousness through us. Not resisting evil means not running away from it, but engaging it in the righteousness of Christ.

In contrast, when we fight evil with worldly words or weapons, it gets stronger because it organizes itself against our attack. If I know that someone is at war with me, I will work to strengthen my defenses. When we declare war on evil, it similarly works to strengthen its defenses against us.

Jesus' alternative to this strategy of aggression against evil (opposing it) was to follow God's lead, to rely on God's providence, God's Words and God's ways. Had David opposed Goliath with the weapons of worldly strength and power—Saul's weapons, Goliath would have squashed him like a bug. So, David did not resist Goliath, but put his fear of the evil and harm that Goliath could do to him aside. David looked the evil that Goliath represented in the eye, without resistance or fear of the evil, without worrying about the harm that might come to him, and trusted God to do with Goliath as God had done with the bear and the lion. God had trained David to become a master of the sling. So, he didn't resist Goliath, he didn't resist engaging Goliath, he didn't resist engaging harm.

It wasn't David who defeated Goliath. It was God. But didn't David stand before Goliath on the battlefield? Yes, of course he did. So how was it God and not David who defeated Goliath? It was God because David refused to be afraid. David also refused Saul's armor, refused to rely on the ways of the world, or to engage the fears of the world. David engaged Goliath with the righteousness of God's providence represented by David's sling. It was God because David put God's honor before his own. Goliath had offended God, and David went in the name of God to

defend God's honor. It was God because David trusted what God had
taught him more than he feared the evil and harm that Goliath represented.

So, how are we to not resist evil? We are not to be afraid that evil
will win the battle. We are to trust in God's ways, to trust in what God
has taught as being the best way to accomplish the ultimate defeat of
Satan and his evil. And what are these ways of God that we are to trust?
The law and the prophets, and now Jesus Christ, crucified and risen. We
are to live as Scripture teaches us to live, in love and obedience to God's
every word. And just as God defeated Goliath by teaching David how to
use the sling, God will defeat Satan and evil in our lives by teaching us
how to live in grace, in righteousness and godliness, in forgiveness and
repentance. These are the weapons of our offense. This is the providence that prepares God's people to fear no evil and to trust God
enough to not resist evil, to not run from it, but to engage it, and trust
that God's righteousness will win the battle.

OVER THE TOP

> "And if anyone would sue you and take your tunic, let him have
> your cloak as well" (v. 40).

Note first that the context of this verse is a court setting. It's not
about someone stealing the shirt off your back. It is about being sued. If
someone sues you, give them what they want, and don't sue them back.
That just contributes to the revenge problem. God does not want us
taking revenge—not physically or emotionally, and not legally, either.
Be willing to lose everything to stay out of court. We actually see this
quite a bit in today's world. People and companies will almost always try
to first settle out of court because they know that a court settlement will
likely be much more costly.

However, this is not an invitation to give everything away to the
bullies and extortionists of the world, and take up a life of poverty. The
point is for Christians to avoid getting caught up in the legal machinery
of the world, even when it proves to be costly to do so. But neither is
this a demand to always avoid the legal machinery of civil court. Rather,
it is a caution to not expect godliness or satisfaction from the world's
courts. They have their uses and purposes. They are institutions of the
Lord. He was simply saying that wrestling a pig is always a messy business. So, don't try it unless you are prepared to get dirty.

"And if anyone forces you to go one mile, go with him two
miles" (v. 41).

Albert Barnes provided a helpful comment on this verse.

"In order that the royal commands might be delivered with safety
and dispatch in different parts of the empire, Cyrus stationed
horsemen at proper intervals on all the great public highways.
One of those delivered the message to another, and intelligence
was thus rapidly and safely communicated. These heralds were
permitted to compel any person, or to press any horse, boat, ship,
or other vehicle that they might need for the quick transmission
of the king's commandments. It was to this custom that our Savior refers. Rather, says he, than resist a public authority requiring
your attendance and aid for a certain distance, go peaceably twice
the distance."[12]

The person who did the conscripting was a messenger of the king,
in service to the king. The idea here is not to resist the secular authorities, but to cooperate with them when conscripted. To resist would
likely embroil the resister in some form of physical retribution or in the
legal machinery of the state that would charge him with some crime for
resisting and either throw him in jail or exact a fine. All of those consequences would likely be greater than simply doing twice as much as
asked. In addition, by cooperating and exceeding the demands of the
conscription, one would put one's self in good graces with the conscrip-
tor.

"Give to the one who begs from you, and do not refuse the one
who would borrow from you" (v. 42).

Are we to take this literally, figuratively, practically—what? If we
take it literally, it could easily put us all in the poorhouse. If we take it
figuratively, we may never engage Christian charity at all. So, we take it
as a general principle. Giving to the needy is good, godly, kind, and
righteous. It is better to err on the side of generosity and give to a con
artist than to fail to help a genuinely needy person. Yet, there are more
genuinely needy people in the world than we have the means to provide
for.

So, unless we exercise some generosity discernment, we could harm
ourselves and our families by giving the farm away. There are people
who do this, who are generous to a fault, who give themselves into the

---

12 *Notes On The Bible*, Matthew 5:41, Albert Barnes, public domain.

poorhouse. The root of this problem is the lack of financial discipline, responsibility, and understanding. Of course there are other people who are stingy to a fault. Scrooge in Dickens' book, *A Christmas Carol*, was such a person. Both extremes regarding charity and lending are wrong. Discernment takes the middle ground by being both generous and responsible.

It is true that we always have the poor with us (Matthew 26:11). But this fact is not a statement of resignation that the Lord just can't fix the problem of poverty. Rather, it is a statement of the reality of the times in which we live, and that poverty is a tenacious reality. There will always be a certain amount of inequity with regard to possessions and incomes. Some have more, some less—and it will always be this way. So, as long as there is poverty we should understand it as providing opportunities to exercise our generosity because generosity does as much for the giver as it does for the receiver—sometimes more, as was the moral of Dicken's story.

CHARITY VERSES PHILANTHROPY

Note also the immediacy of the biblical context. It was a person to person situation. This does not necessarily preclude the various kinds of anonymous giving through various charitable agencies in the corporate world today. They have their place and purpose. But it must be noted that our modern non-profit corporations and institutions that are dedicated to providing for the poor are themselves a lousy substitute for the biblical structure of tithing and alms giving. When generosity is filtered through a corporate entity and made anonymous we are deprived of the immediate and personal contact—and supervision of those gifts—that is part and parcel of biblical charity (love, 1 Corinthians 13), of personally knowing the people who are the recipients of our gifts. That personal contact serves our own sanctification, and theirs. And when it is watered down through the structures of anonymity it serves neither. In addition, the purpose of the corporate giving can become self-serving and ideological, rather than being a genuine concern for the alleviation of poverty.

Jesus extended this principle to include borrowers as well as the needy,

"do not refuse the one who would borrow from you" (v. 42).

And as with the first half of this verse, the literal execution of this principle would likely break the bank. So, again, it is to be done with discretion in order to keep us from the poorhouse ourselves. And, again, that discretion must not be understood as a reason not to exercise generosity.

Paul understood the lesson of these verses:

> "Do not be overcome by evil, but overcome evil with good" (Romans 12:21).

Do not shrink back from (or resist) engagement with evil. Do not fear harm. But meet evil with Christ's truth and righteousness.

11. Evangelizing Adversaries

You have heard that it was said, 'You shall love your neighbor and hate your enemy.' But I say to you, Love your enemies and pray for those who persecute you, so that you may be sons of your Father who is in heaven. For he makes his sun rise on the evil and on the good, and sends rain on the just and on the unjust. For if you love those who love you, what reward do you have? Do not even the tax collectors do the same? And if you greet only your brothers, what more are you doing than others? Do not even the Gentiles do the same? You therefore must be perfect, as your heavenly Father is perfect.

—Matthew 5:43-48

The Lord again reminded His congregation on the mount of the commonly accepted way of understanding God's demand of neighborly love, and again the old way was half true. The true half that had been woven into the Old Testament is represented by Leviticus 19:18:

> "You shall not take vengeance or bear a grudge against the sons
> of your own people, but you shall love your neighbor as yourself:
> I am the Lord."

Over the centuries the idea that love for one's neighbors and friends came to imply hatred of one's enemies. It isn't difficult to see why the ancient Israelites focused this command on themselves to the exclusion of other tribes and peoples. The verse does say that this behavior is to be directed toward "your own people." And it served an important purpose.

However, several problems developed over time. The inward or self-sustaining direction of this concern led to moral stagnation and cul-

tural isolation, which contributed to the corruption of their commitment to God. And these things generated fear and hatred—especially
toward Israel's enemies.

Contrary to popular belief, hatred does have a role to play in biblical
obedience. God insists that His people hate evil. The Psalmist, for
instance wrote,

> "You have loved righteousness and hated wickedness. Therefore
> God, your God, has anointed you with the oil of gladness beyond
> your companions" (Psalm 45:7).[13]

While it is true that the Lord had separated Israel out from the other
nations and peoples, that separation or cultural uniqueness did not provide a reason or excuse to do anything except reject the things about
them and their godless cultures that God hates. God's hatred of evil is
not a license to kill or destroy, yet in the light of Christ we are to
engage the enemies of God with God's Word in the light of Jesus
Christ.

Granted that Leviticus 19:18 mentioned the sons of Israel as a distinct people, but the purpose of that mention was the emphasis of Israel's
cultural mission to create a loving and God-centered social order. The
Old Testament was given to an agrarian people who did not have the
benefits of modern travel and communication, which meant that ninety
nine percent of the time the only people that the ancient Israelites had
contact with were other Israelites. The point of the law was to legislate
neighborly love for others and the forbiddance of vengeance in thought,
word and deed. Note that the forbiddance of vengeance is not the forbiddance of justice. It is, rather, the forbiddance of personal or family
driven vengeance as a means of justice.

Adding what might be considered to be a logical implication to
God's law, action on the basis of the hatred of one's enemies was both
unauthorized and illegitimate. God was quite specific that His law was
to stand as it had been given. Evil is to simply be avoided, and when it
cannot be avoided, it is to be met with Christ's love and righteousness. It
is the function of civil government to legislate against evil.

---

13 See also: Deuteronomy 12:31, 16:22; Ezekiel 35:6, Psalm 139:22; Amos 5:15, 6:8;
    Mattthew 6:24. This is a difficult and dangerous issue. In order to love God we
    must also hate what God hates, but not allow that hatred to manifest in
    vengeance or revenge. The destruction of evil is God's job, the rejection of evil is
    ours—and we must cling to God's definitions of good and evil.

"You shall not add to the word that I command you, nor take
from it, that you may keep the commandments of the Lord your
God that I command you" (Deuteronomy 4:2, etc.).

All additions or deletions of God's Word are strictly forbidden. God
had made a point to forbid this kind of thing because He knows that
people are very prone to add their own thoughts and ideas to it. Again,
note that this does not forbid the application of God's law to new and
previously unknown situations, or the careful extension and/or implications of the well-established principles of God's law. The problem is that
unauthorized hatred or actions against other people quench the Spirit of
evangelism and leads to cultural and moral stagnation. For the most part
ordinary people are to simply avoid what God calls evil. We are to trust
God and avoid sin.

The root idea of the Hebrew word translated as *neighbor* is *flock*.
The idea of neighbor includes all of the people within the orbit of our
lives, those people with whom we have contact, with whom we flock.
The ordinary ancient Israelite would have had very little contact with
anyone outside of his flock or neighborhood because there were few
means for such contact. Travel was difficult, and life generally had a
small social orbit of family and immediate neighbors.

The essential teaching of Leviticus 19:18 is love, concern, and care—
charity—for other people. Just as people do not harm themselves, we are
not to harm others. The general intention of the verse is to refrain from
vengeance and grudges, and the idea of loving our neighbors provides
an example as to how that is to be accomplished.

OLD HABITS

But people, being natural sinners, found what they thought was
wiggle room in God's law, and used it to justify their own deep seated
fears and insecurities. Indeed, fear and hatred are the natural emotions
and condition of people everywhere. And God has always directed people away from our natural primitive condition (original sin) by engaging God's law strictly as it has been given from time immemorial.
Nonetheless, as the ancient Israelites were dancing before the golden calf
of their own imagination when Moses came down from the mountain
with God's law in his hands, so people have always preferred their own
thoughts and ways to the thoughts and ways of God. Overcoming this
problem is the prime directive of Scripture. Overcoming this temptation
requires constant vigilance.

Israel was to be separated as a culture from the rest of humanity in order to institute a culture of godliness. And that meant that they were to be separated unto God. In addition, that separation, their dedication to God, their sanctification, was to serve as a point of contact for the rest of humanity. It was not that Israel was to turn in upon herself and keep God's gifts and customs to themselves, but that Israel was to be a blessing to the nations of the world (Genesis 12:2).

The culture of Israel was to impact the rest of humanity in a positive way on behalf of the Lord. It was to create an inviolable boundary or separation that would protect Israel from the sins and dangers of other people and societies in order to demonstrate that such separation could not accomplish God's purpose. But God wasn't simply protecting Israel from the virus of sin. That virus had already been unleashed upon all of humanity. No one was exempt. Everyone already had it.

Thus, God was developing an antibody (the church), with which He would inoculate the world with the love and obedience to Himself, the Messiah of God. God's people are to take the culture of dedication to the God of the Bible and sanctification in Christ to the world. That is the dominion mandate. And sharing the gospel through evangelism is the means of dominion.

The difficulty has always been establishing and maintaining the culture of God according to the biblical standard in the light of Christ. The Old Testament Temple establishment in Jerusalem failed to accomplish that task. It failed in the light of Christ, who destroyed it in A.D. 70 and simultaneously established the Christian church to carry God's dominion mandate forward in the Spirit of love and service.

DOMINION
When God blessed Adam and Eve He told them to

> "be fruitful and multiply and fill the earth and subdue it and have dominion over the fish of the sea and over the birds of the heavens and over every living thing that moves on the earth" (Genesis 1:28).

God's people were to have dominion, not only over the birds and the fish, but over "every living thing," which included every living (extant) person. This dominion was a matter of exercising God's authority. And the first and foremost place that authority needed to be exercised was and is with humanity, with people. It is not that one group is to dominate another, but that God is to ultimately dominate everyone. In the earliest expression of Israel God was the king, and this is the dominion model. The authority for the dominion mandate is not human authority, but God's authority, which in the world of people is always representative authority.

Of course there is an order to God's authority that centers in Scripture and the church, and issues from duly elected elders and pastors, and cascades throughout the people of God according to biblical instruction. Churches do not have civil authority. Rather, unbelievers and excommunicated church members are to have the freedom to engage their sins as long as civil laws are not broken. Civil law enforcement is a function of civil government. And civil law does not reflect the jurisdiction of the church.

This does not mean that church members are not subject to civil law—they are. It means that civil law does not encroach into areas of church responsibility, into areas of moral instruction. Sin and civil law provide consequences for disobedience. The church then provides moral instruction about the truth of God's Word experientially as people encounter God's curses and consequences for disobedience. Civil government wields the sword for coercion, law enforcement. The church wields the Word for conversion, moral instruction. The church is not to be involved with coercion, nor is civil government to be involved with conversion or moral instruction.

The political realm or public square is the place for public discussion and persuasion regarding social policies and legal interpretation and understanding of the law. And all parties must have access to free public expression about such matters unless that expression teaches or endorses criminality. Criminals and those who violate the public good as defined by the civil authorities and the legal system of the society, cannot be allowed to game the system for their own advantage, or destroy, or undermine civil order.

However, the purpose of the political realm or public square is the discussion and persuasion that may lead to potential social and legal changes. Consequently, the political realm or public square is the place for the free discussion of God's Word and the free exercise of biblical evangelism.

Two Kinds

Of course, there is an oppressive kind of dominion that is better defined as domination or totalitarianism that is based upon fear, hatred, and the power or force to coerce others against their will. And there is another kind of dominion that involves the willing engagement of the love of God and the willing obedience to God's way of life as the basis or foundation for genuine human freedom and self-expression. The first kind is more like an enforced submission to a political and religious order that comes from without. Islamic submission comes to mind, where submission is mandated and imposed by the agencies of civil government through the unity of church and state.

But the second kind of dominion is like the active, personal, and willing engagement of a truth or a cause that people have come to understand and believe to be the best possible truth or cause. This kind of truth or cause does not need to be reinforced by civil government because the person who believes in this cause or truth will personally and freely work for it or toward it regardless of all obstacles.

The impetus for this kind of dominion comes from within as the expression of personal commitment to truth. In the former case the cause is taken up as a burden or duty that is imposed upon others. But in the latter case it is freely taken up as a joy and a passion that is self-imposed. The difference is social or civil coercion versus personal willing compliance.

The love of neighbor as one's self is to be a dominion of this second kind, with the cultus of God's people serving as the engine of that dominion. Such love cannot be legislated by civil government, but it can be encouraged by the church. This is God's endgame, that God's love will ultimately infect all humanity by exposure to the culture of God's people. We should not seek the protection of God's people from the cultures of the world through separatism, but the engagement of the world by God's people through evangelism.

God's love is intended to sweep people off their feet, to disabuse them of their pagan and primitive fears and hatreds, and give them an overwhelming desire for love and self-sacrificial service to Jesus Christ and to one another. This endgame cannot be accomplished by people who hate one another, nor can it be imposed upon people against their will. Rather, it must be embraced personally, willingly, and gladly. If humanity is to be brought together under the banner of God's love, all fear and hatred toward others must be abandoned.

So, Jesus called attention to the methodology of such practice:

> "I say to you, Love your enemies and pray for those who perse-
> cute you" (v. 44).

Most people understand this command to stand against the teaching of the Old Testament, but it doesn't. Rather, it is a clarification of the Old Testament teaching. It is much more clear and direct than the Old Testament was. And Jesus had a much broader and more inclusive understanding of who God's people are than the ancient Israelites did. So, in these things Jesus' instruction does stand apart from common Old Testament interpretation. But it is not a new teaching. Yet, it is also true that inasmuch as Christians have actually heard and practiced Jesus' clarification of the law, they will also stand apart from the practice of the Old Testament Jews through the exercise of grace and mercy toward others.

LOVE

What does it mean to love one's enemies? The Greek word is *agapaō*, a derivative of *agapē* and means to have a benevolent concern for someone. We are to have a benevolent concern for those whom we don't like or who don't like us. We are to want for them what God wants for them—salvation and their active engagement of God's truth and the glad and willing practice of God's way. It doesn't matter whether we like them or not, or whether they like us or not. We are called to love them, not to like them, the difference being that love will help us to want what is best for them, whether they become our personal friends or not.

Our prayers for those who would persecute us are to become the active means for the expression of our love for them. Even while they may consider themselves to be our enemies, we are not to consider them in this regard. Even while they may be engaged in our persecution and in doing us harm, we are not to return such things to them. Rather, we are to seriously and regularly pray for their genuine well-being, where well-being is understood to be God's will for their lives. God has promised blessing for obedience and curses for disobedience (Deuteronomy 28). So, our prayers for God to bless them are also simultaneously prayers for them to live in obedience to God's Word and will, and thus to be worthy of God's blessing.

But having said that, we are not lobbying for a works-righteous faith. Rather, we understand the central lesson of Scripture and human faithfulness can only be accomplished through the power and presence of the Holy Spirit through regeneration. So, the worthiness to be blessed is accomplished by Christ on the cross and is bestowed to us by the grace of God through the Holy Spirit.

Curiously, verse 44 is much longer in the Authorized Version:

> "But I say unto you, Love your enemies, bless them that curse
> you, do good to them that hate you, and pray for them which
> despitefully use you, and persecute you."

The modern versions (and the Greek manuscripts upon which they are based) do not contain two important phrases: "do good to them that hate you, and pray for them which despitefully use you." For reasons too long and involved to go into here, I believe that the Authorized Version is to be preferred. There is much good historical evidence for the acceptance and use of these phrases, which simply provide additional practical application of the general meaning of the verse.

BENEVOLENCE

The point is that love has practical applications. Our benevolence must have feet of clay. It must be more than a mere attitude. It must also break out in the accomplishment of actual good, and not wallow in mere regard for someone's well-being. We are to pray for God's blessings to fall upon those who are actively engaged in slandering, insulting, and doing us harm. Again, our prayer for their blessing is also a prayer that they will come to love and obey the Lord as the means to receive that blessing.

We might be tempted to pray for God to take revenge upon them for us, but that is not what Jesus said. Jesus was putting an end to the desire for vengeance in the human heart. So, when we pray for such people we must not pray for God to take vengeance upon them because such a prayer would only reveal our own desire for vengeance. Consequently, we are to genuinely pray and work for their good.

And why should people do this? What would motivate people to abandon their old habits of fear and hatred? Jesus gave the proper motivation:

> "so that you may be sons of your Father who is in heaven" (v.
> 45).

The idea here is that we are to act like God with regard to God's benevolence because we have been created in the image and likeness of God (Genesis 1:26). To be a follower or disciple is to emulate the Master. Jesus said,

> "A new commandment I give to you, that you love one another:
> just as I have loved you, you also are to love one another. By this

all people will know that you are my disciples, if you have love
for one another" (John 13:34-35).

While obedience to God's Word is not the cause of faithfulness or
salvation, these things are not real apart from personal, willing obedience. Because God is full of truth and integrity we must also exercise
truth and integrity. We will, of course, fall short of perfectly imitating
God in this regard. Nonetheless, we must strive and grow toward such
perfection.

We must endeavor to honor our family name, our Father's name—
God's name and His character. Obviously, we cannot perfectly emulate
God in everything that He is, but there are some of His characteristics
that we are to focus on, and the ones given here are God's graciousness
and mercy. Pointing to these characteristics Christ added,

> "For he makes his sun rise on the evil and on the good, and sends
> rain on the just and on the unjust" (v. 45).

Luke captured this idea when he recorded Jesus' instructions to

> "love your enemies, and do good, and lend, expecting nothing in
> return, and your reward will be great, and you will be sons of the
> Most High, for he is kind to the ungrateful and the evil" (Luke
> 6:35).

Jesus has given these instructions, not merely for our own sanctification and maturity in the faith, but He has given them as a method of
evangelism. God's purpose is the eradication of sin and evil and the ultimate salvation of all extant people. God's purpose is nothing less than
the conversion of the entire world through the ministry of Jesus Christ.

The most difficult people to reach will always be our enemies.
Whether we consider them to be enemies or they consider us to be enemies is immaterial because that consideration is itself the obstacle that
interferes with gospel transmission. This is not a command to deny that
we have enemies or that our enemies are out to do us harm. Nor does it
require us to deny that God Himself has enemies. God's enemies are
many and formidable, and the denial of such facts is both foolish and
dangerous.

Nonetheless, God's strategy is to patch up and eliminate the personal offenses that tend to separate people, that tend to create personal
grudges and enemies, by modeling the grace of forgiveness. That grace,
both the grace that He has shown us and that we are to show others, is
powerful medicine for personal relationships. We are to apply it liber-

ally. The Lord needs to clear away all our personal offenses with one another in order to make the offense of the gospel clear.

We need to forgive each other of the offenses that we can forgive in order to make the offense that we cannot forgive stand out more clearly. The purpose of making the offense of the gospel stand out more clearly among all people is to make clear our need for a forgiveness that we cannot ourselves provide, in order to help us see our need for a Savior. We are to proclaim and extend God's forgiveness, which is also an accusation against sinners, and let Jesus deal with it through His Holy Spirit.

As long as we hold on to our personal grudges—our own fears and frustrations—we tend to think that we are in control. As long as I am angry with you, my anger controls the character of our relationship. Or if you are angry with me, then your anger controls the relationship. How does anger control the relationship? By dominating it. The anger is the dominant emotion in the relationship. It dwarfs all other feelings and concerns. Anger keeps people apart, and when people who are angry with one another do come together, they fight. That's how anger works. And what the Lord is showing us here is that our anger cripples the forward momentum of the gospel. It interferes with the process of evangelism. It destroys our ability to communicate the gospel, and makes us useless to the Lord.

So, our fear and anger must be dealt with, and much of this Sermon on the Mount has dealt with it from a variety of perspectives. If we could simply abandon our fear and anger, then we should. But we can't. It's as if fear and anger take on personas of their own. It's like they have a hold on us as much as we have a hold on them. They tend to control us through domination and intimidation, and interfere with the dominion of the Lord.

The only thing that dissipates our fear and anger, our grudges that blind us and neuter us with regard to gospel propagation, is forgiveness. Forgiveness releases our anger and sets us free. It frees us from the domination and control of fear, anger, and sin. Once people are free from the dominating control of their own fear and anger, their own sin, they are confronted with guilt.

GUILT

Yes, we have been forgiven, but we have not been acquitted. The Lord has *not* declared us not guilty. He had declared us forgiven. And the reason that we need forgiveness is that we are in fact guilty. People who are not guilty do not need forgiveness. To be not guilty is to be sinless. Sinners, on the other hand, are guilty!

So, to give sinners an acquittal rather than forgiveness would be a travesty of justice. It would constitute a lie and an injustice. Our guilt requires forgiveness, which means that the consequences of our sin and guilt are removed. But the fact of our sin and guilt remains in the declaration of our forgiveness. At the point of being forgiven, we should be grateful that the consequences of our sin and guilt have been removed. But the truth is that forgiveness does not remove the guilt.

The gospel itself, the proclamation of forgiveness through Christ's propitiation on the cross, is at the same time an accusation or declaration of sin and guilt. Because the gospel is sufficient for the forgiveness of the whole world, it is also the declaration of the sin and guilt of the whole world. Forgiveness is unnecessary apart from guilt. And because God is the only real God of the whole world,

> "he makes his sun rise on the evil and on the good, and sends rain
> on the just and on the unjust" (v. 45).

God mercifully provides the blessings of life indiscriminately upon both the just and the unjust.

Why would God do that? Because His ultimate purpose is the salvation of the whole world, all extant people. In the war between God and evil, God has already ultimately won. And He will win by destroying evil itself, but not the people who have been captured by evil. They will be converted (some of them), and their conversion, the conversion of those who are evil and opposed to God, will be the most effective weapon against the evil that inhabits so many. The conversion of people who are locked into service to evil through fear and hatred—without actually killing them—is a very attractive phenomena. It's like a surgical procedure that saves people from a life-threatening disease.

SURGICAL EVANGELISM

The Lord uses this procedure for the evangelism of those who have been captured by fear, hatred, and anger. Christians are not to sequester themselves away from such people by holing up in some ghetto or another, but are to be consumed by the Lord's mission to convert those who have been captured by fear and hatred. And how will the Lord convert such people? By loving them and doing good to them in the name of Jesus Christ—through us, through His people.

When Christians treat those who hate God, or who hate them for whatever reasons, with honesty and integrity, and actually do them good, they present God as the genuinely loving, graceful Father that He actually is. To forgive and refuse to hold a grudge against those who mistreat and abuse you unjustly speaks volumes about the reality of God in your life and of the effectiveness of God's program for worldwide evangelism. It makes the gospel more than words, more than an argument or a system of theology by showing the actual effect of the gospel on human sin, by curtailing revenge through forgiveness.

And especially when this is not just the abstract idea of forgiveness of sins by an abstract and remote God off in heaven, but is my actual, present forgiveness of you of your actual, present injustice against me— or your forgiveness of someone else, etc. At the point of actual forgiveness and the abandonment of real grudges between actual people, the gospel becomes a reality, where before it was only an abstract idea.

Jesus illustrated this by asking a question.

> "For if you love those who love you, what reward do you have?
> Do not even the tax collectors do the same? And if you greet only
> your brothers, what more are you doing than others? Do not
> even the Gentiles do the same" (Matthew 5:46-47)?

God claims to love all people. So, Christians must put feet on this claim in order to make it real, in order to demonstrate that it is more than an idealistic sentiment. While the rest of the world might be honored for loving their own, Christians must demonstrate the love that God claims by loving and doing good to those who hate them, regardless of the consequences or response.

High Calling

Is this a Utopian dream? The idea of loving people by giving them whatever they want is a Romantic myth. That's not the way that real love works. Genuine love, biblical love is a matter of being committed to give people what is genuinely good for them, what God wants for them. To substitute my desires or their desires for God's desires will always result in a travesty of justice and a mockery of love. God wants people to be free and independent and not to be slaves to sin. Neither are we to be slaves to our own desires, nor to the desires of others. Human freedom is found by becoming slaves to God's desire because His desire really is for our good. Only God can free us from slavery to sin.

Paul wrote to the Galatians,

> "For you were called to freedom, brothers. Only do not use your
> freedom as an opportunity for the flesh, but through love serve
> one another. For the whole law is fulfilled in one word: 'You
> shall love your neighbor as yourself'" (Galatians 5:13-14).

This is a high calling, but it is not a high calling that is just for pastors or
elders, but it is a high calling for all Christians. And just in case we failed
to understand that Christianity is a high calling, Jesus added,

> "You therefore must be perfect, as your heavenly Father is per-
> fect" (v. 48).

And why would Christ call His people to be perfect when He,
above all others, knows exactly how imperfect people actually are? Isn't
such a command ingenuous? Not at all. God commands His people to
do and to be what they cannot do or be in and of themselves in order to
insure that the fulfillment of His command is accomplished by the
power and presence of His Holy Spirit through regeneration. The high
calling of Christianity is the call to the death of the Old Man and the
birth of the New in the name—the character—of Jesus Christ. This high
calling is only possible when people personally trust and rely upon the
Holy Spirit.

12. Gospel Secrets

Beware of practicing your righteousness before other people in order to be seen by them, for then you will have no reward from your Father who is in heaven. Thus, when you give to the needy, sound no trumpet before you, as the hypocrites do in the synagogues and in the streets, that they may be praised by others. Truly, I say to you, they have received their reward. But when you give to the needy, do not let your left hand know what your right hand is doing, so that your giving may be in secret. And your Father who sees in secret will reward you.　　　　　　　　　　　　　　　　　　　*—Matthew 6:1-4*

Jesus was not simply concerned about moral behavior or performance, and to think that moral behavior was His primary or even His first concern is a widely misunderstood perspective known generally as moralism or Pietism. It is often practiced as a form of works-righteousness, and when it is, it is an error. It mistakes the result for the cause. It does not have to be practiced as works-righteousness, and can be practiced simply as a response of thankfulness and obedience to God's unmerited grace. It often looks the same superficially, but it isn't. Intention is important.

Verse 1 speaks directly to this issue of practicing it as works-righteousness. Jesus provided a caution regarding our motivation for behavior, our motivation for behaving faithfully. The Lord is always very concerned about people having the proper motivation, and not attempting to turn morality into a kind of performance or self-justification. The motivation for performance based behavior will always fall short of Jesus' intent for His disciples as expressed in this Sermon on the Mount. The concern about performance is always a concern about the outside of the cup, about style rather than substance. It is a concern for show and impression, a concern that reveals a misunderstanding about the gospel and God's grace and leads to a worldly ambition, a concern that is to be avoided.

This caution, however, does not mean that we are to avoid Christian morality. Jesus said no such thing. The whole point of the Sermon on the Mount is to direct and encourage Christians to the genuine practice of Christian morality, but to do so for the right reasons, for the right purpose, and in the right ways. In short, that purpose is the service of God's glory. It's not about us, not about our sanctification, though our sanctification is important and will indeed follow a correct engagement of or response to the gospel. Rather, our concern is to be about God, about Jesus Christ, and about His righteousness.

BEWARE

We know this because the first word of verse 1 is *beware* (*prosechō*) or *take heed* in the Authorized Version. It means to pay attention or to be cautious. We are not to avoid Christian morality, but are to pay attention to it and direct our motivations for wanting to be moral people to the worship of Christ alone, and not for performance or attainment. The caution comes because it is very easy and quite common to engage morality in order to become a better person. And, while there is certainly nothing wrong with becoming a better person, there is something wrong with being prideful about it.

Pride creeps into our motivations and our character—especially as we are engaged in self-improvement. And as soon as we begin thinking that we are better than others, we have already crossed the line. Thus, we are to be aware of our motivations. We are to take caution against doing things in order to be seen—for show.

There is something seriously wrong with morality for show. Doing things in order to be seen, in order to be noticed by other people, is what Hollywood stars do, and it is to be completely avoided. Such behavior is not Christian, nor actually moral. It is, rather, selfish, and of no use to God. Does this mean that Hollywood stars cannot be moral people or cannot do good because they are stars? Not at all. Jesus is not cautioning against doing good things or against being moral people. He is cautioning against doing such things for your resume or for your image.

This Sermon on the Mount is about motivation more than behavior. Jesus requires moral behavior, and yet moral behavior without the right motivation—the genuine love and worship of God—is an idolatry of the most dangerous kind. The danger is that it is both the root and the fruit of humanism, which is another name for atheism. And when it does take on a religious character, as in religiously based humanism, it is opposed to the God of Scripture. Doing the right thing for the wrong reason turns out to be nothing more than a personal justification for a misunderstanding about what righteousness actually is. It is clinging to one's own thought and values rather than taking up God's thoughts and values.

The other thing to notice about this verse is that it is less about righteousness, which is the favorite modern translation, and more about money. The context is alms-giving, charity, about providing for the poor and less fortunate. Curiously, while most Hollywood stars are most able to engage in this kind of charity because they are rich, they are least able to engage it as Jesus demands because of their self-centered—and at best, humanistic—motivations. This is not true of every Hollywood star, but it appears to be generally true because it is true about the Hollywood worldview. Of course, it is not limited to Hollywood, either.

TAX DEDUCTIBLE

And here is another modern twist to this issue. Making charitable donations for tax purposes, in order to reduce one's taxes (a function of being seen by the Internal Revenue Service), is the very kind of thing that Jesus cautioned against here. Doing something good for the tax write-off is simply the wrong motivation. Doing it for the tax deduction is doing it before men in order to be seen. It may be possible to cooperate with the IRS in this regard without falling into the sin that Jesus cautions about. It probably can be done for the right reasons, and still be reported to the IRS. But I suspect that actually doing that is quite rare. I hope I'm wrong.

Nonetheless, for Christians, noting that charity can be engaged for the right purposes so that the tax deduction can still be claimed is a very dangerous observation because it temps us to rationalize that, while other people can easily make this error, we—because of our supposed superior morality—are immune to it. Avoiding pride is a tricky business. To get it right, the truth of Christ's righteousness and of one's own regeneration must genuinely exist at the very core of our being without self-deception.

Thinking that Jesus' caution here is just for weak Christians is completely wrong headed. It is for the weak, of course. Who was Jesus speaking to in the Sermon on the Mount? Was He speaking to Jews? Or Christians? Or His disciples? He was speaking to all of them. He was speaking to those who followed Him to the mountain, some were actual believers and some were not. So, Jesus was not simply cautioning the average follower about this temptation and sin (though He was not excluding them). He was cautioning His closest disciples. They were there, and disciples—above everyone else—are always in more danger from self-justification than the average person precisely because they are more moral than the average person. Moving up the sanctification ladder does not remove people from temptation and moral fuzziness. It increases both! The temptations become greater because of their greater responsibilities, and the moral dilemmas become more difficult because of the increased complexities that accompany increased responsibilities.

Listen to these translations of verse 1:

> "When you do good deeds, don't try to show off. If you do, you won't get a reward from your Father in heaven" (Contemporary English Version).

> "Take care not to be doing your charitable giving before men, so as to be seen by them. Otherwise, you have not a reward from your Father in heaven" (English Majority Text Version).

The verse stresses the idea of being moral in order to be rewarded in heaven. At least that seems to be our ordinary modern reading of the verse. And *reward* is the correct translation of the Greek (*misthos*).

Much of the New Testament conveys the idea of being rewarded in heaven for faithfulness—and so we must accept it as being true. It is an acceptable and clearly biblical motivation for Christian faithfulness. Seeking a heavenly reward for faithfulness is preferable to not engaging faithfulness at all. And it is preferable to postpone the reward to the afterlife in order to keep the pride of superiority at bay.

Motivation

That said, it is quite possible, even probable, to infuse the motivation of doing something for the reward with narrow self-interest and pride. But these things are to be avoided, as well. This is why our motivation must be for the service of God's glory and not for our own benefit. Christians are stewards and servants, which means that Christian owners or masters must still maintain a life of service to Christ (Colossians 4:1). Christians are to always be in service to Jesus Christ no matter how much human responsibility they acquire. The whole focus for Christians is to serve God in Christ, not self. Like the ancient Israelites when Moses lifted up the serpent in the desert (Numbers 21:9, John 3:14–15), we are to keep our eyes on the cross, not on one another or on the dangers that beset us. At the same time, it would be utter foolishness to ignore those dangers.

The second verse continues the theme of the first, and provides more detail about how not to be charitable.

> "Thus, when you give to the needy, sound no trumpet before
> you, as the hypocrites do in the synagogues and in the streets,
> that they may be praised by others" (v. 2).

Not only does this verse provide an example about how *not* to do charity, but it also identifies as hypocrites (*hupokritēs*) those who do it the wrong way. To be a hypocrite is to be an actor, someone who pretends to be something s/he is not. Indeed, Christians are to abandon all pretense and focus themselves on what is genuine. As Paul wrote,

> "Finally, brothers, whatever is true, whatever is honorable, what-
> ever is just, whatever is pure, whatever is lovely, whatever is
> commendable, if there is any excellence, if there is anything wor-
> thy of praise, think about these things" (Philippians 4:8).

Faithfulness is the antidote to hypocrisy.

We are not to avoid fellowship or worship because we think that Christians are hypocrites, because we don't want to associate with people like that. People who are concerned about hypocrisy often separate themselves from worship with those they determine to be hypocritical. But such separation is not necessarily biblical or helpful. There are times and occasions when Christians must separate from unbelievers (2 Corinthians 6:17), but the call to separation is never to be an excuse to avoid genuine worship or fellowship. Separation is never an escape from true worship, but always an escape to it.

Hypocrisy is a huge problem among people in the churches and out. And avoidance of worship and fellowship is actually a kind of denial, and does nothing to alleviate the problem. The underlying problem of hypocrisy is faithlessness. At least confessing unbelievers have the integrity to admit their denial of God. Whereas hypocrites pretend to believe, pretend to be faithful, when they are not. And for the most part, they add the denial of their own unbelief and hypocrisy to their problem of faithlessness.

We must also note that hypocrisy and false belief are related because people might not think of themselves as being hypocrites because they have convinced themselves that they are faithful. But such faithfulness conforms to a false gospel. In fact, false belief is the primary problem behind hypocrisy because of the psychological difficulties of understanding one's self to be an actual hypocrite. When confronted with an accusation of hypocrisy people do one of three things: 1) deny it, 2) change their beliefs or 3) change their behaviors. Hypocrisy is incompatible with rational sanity.

This also means that when one person thinks that another person is a hypocrite, the central problem between them usually pertains to different beliefs or belief systems—different worldviews. In all likelihood each person thinks that his behavior is consistent with his beliefs.

Thus, the driving force behind accusations of hypocrisy are actually about differing beliefs, differing perspectives, different assumptions and/or worldviews. Where hypocrisy is alleged there is a lack of common understanding or common faith. Thus, hypocrisy is a common problem, a community problem, a social problem, not simply an individual problem. Accusations of hypocrisy indicate a lack of community or social unity, social cohesiveness, a lack of commonly held moral beliefs and practices.

This means that Jesus was not simply the cause of divisions in and around Jerusalem, the divisions preceded Jesus. Jesus simply pointed out the hypocrisy that was already there, He didn't cause it. Nonetheless, Jesus was a catalyst that clarified and accentuated those divisions. And the divisions then were, as such divisions are now, related to false belief. It wasn't that Jesus introduced or accelerated false beliefs, but that His teaching and ministry clarified them. What is false is seen more clearly as being false when it is seen in the light of truth. The light of truth reveals falsehood to be what it actually is.

"Truly, said Jesus, they have received their reward" (v. 2).

And the reward of hypocrites is the temporary attention they get for pretending to be something they are not. Such attention is necessarily temporary because hypocrisy will be found out in the light of Christ. In opposition to this temporary reward of attention, Jesus promised an eternal reward in heaven. Contrasted here are both the ideas of temporal versus eternal reward, and also an immediate verses a deferred reward. People can have a minor, temporary, meaningless reward now or a major, eternal, meaningful reward later.

Jesus continued, providing one of the least understood verses in Scripture,

> "But when you give to the needy, do not let your left hand know
> what your right hand is doing" (v. 3).

This is simply a continuation of the same idea of not putting attention on yourself, of doing your alms work privately, in secret. We are to be generous to the poor, and to keep that generosity private, secret—between the giver and the receiver only. There are a couple of reasons for this. One is to keep pride away from the giver, and the other is to maintain the dignity of the recipient.

CHARITY & HYPOCRISY

People don't like being on the receiving end of charity, which brings us to another issue of hypocrisy. People don't like receiving charity—handouts. It really is a blow to personal dignity to think that you can't take care of yourself and need the charity of others. This is particularly true of the prideful, but applies to everyone.

At least this has pretty much always been the case, but in the modern world we find that this insight is no longer true. Many people today are looking everywhere for what they can get for nothing. Entitlement mentality has gone mainstream. People today pride themselves on getting government disability or some sort of free support, of winning the lottery, which is now governmentally sanctioned for the tax income it receives from gambling, now that it is regulated.

Note that most of the time, gambling proceeds are justified by governments by dedicating them to charitable concerns—mostly education or elder care. And this attitude on the part of governments and legislators is a function of hypocrisy as much as any other kind of hypocrisy.

Note also that charity by civil government is always insulated or buffered by the fact that the it occludes the identity of the givers by making the charitable expenditures a function of tax spending. Government charity comes, not from a person, but from public funds, which removes the personal relationship from the kindness, turning it into more of a kind of prostitution than an act of love. People engage in government charity to relieve their consciences of guilt, rather than as an act of genuine love and concern.

In some ways this is different from the hypocrisy that Jesus was talking about, and in some ways it is the same for both those who prefer governmental charity and those who receive it. For instance, pretending to be injured when you aren't, and applying for government benefits on that basis involves pretending to be something that you aren't. It's hypocritical. Or pretending that an injury is worse than it actually is still constitutes pretending and, therefore, hypocrisy. Or pretending to be indigent when you are actually only lazy is also a kind of hypocrisy. The fact is that public charity encourages hypocrisy because it temps people to game the system for freebies.

It also involves false belief and false ideas. And the damnable thing about these particular false beliefs is that they are taught and encouraged at every level by the society in which we currently live. This should be very shocking news, but it isn't. In today's world it gets little attention because it has been going on for more than a generation. Taking what you can get from the government, from churches and Christians or other people or groups who are trying to help is understood today to be a smart thing to do.

CORPORATE CHARITY

And this behavior is modeled by the highest echelons of contemporary society! Contemporary businesses and corporations, both profit and non-profit, regularly engage in such practices. How is this done? In many ways: by playing along with tax codes that provide incentives for various behaviors, by maximizing legal tax write-offs, by receiving grants or aid, by padding government contracts or prices charged to or through the government for services, etc. When other societies engage in this kind of behavior we call it corruption. But we think that it's okay for us because it legal. However, it's not that legalizing a thing makes it moral, but legalizing an immoral thing makes the law and the lawmakers immoral.

In addition, the gambling industry provides the lure of getting something for nothing (or for a very small cost, a ticket or whatever). Even churches are involved in this kind of corruption in as much as they encourage gambling or provide charity for people who are scamming them. Things are pretty hypocritical when the government hands out free money and calls it tax rebates or "Cash for Clunkers."[14]

Why is such activity an indication of governmental hypocrisy? Because the government is pretending to be what it isn't. Civil government is involved in things in which it has no right, authority, or jurisdiction. The primary area of involvement for civil government is justice.

---

14 http://en.wikipedia.org/wiki/Car_Allowance_Rebate_System

Mercy belongs to the jurisdiction of the church. Again, the definition of hypocrisy is pretending to be other than you actually are. This distinction of jurisdictions is unknown today because the distinctions between law and grace are denied. People have abandoned the biblical social model.

God is very much opposed to hypocrisy in all of its many forms, personal, social and governmental. Why? Because the Lord knows how easily people can be influenced. He knows how easily we can justify our own behaviors and beliefs. He knows how gullible we are to false teaching and the temptations of sin. The Lord knows our tendencies toward hypocrisy, and has set these several admonitions against it. Our charity is to be done privately,

> "so that your giving may be in secret. And your Father who sees
> in secret will reward you" (v. 4).

At first, this may seem to be at odds with other verses where we are admonished to edify others by being good examples of Christian behavior, so that others can see our example and emulate it. But this verse is no different, really. If we take this admonition literally, we will be generous and tell no one about it. And that is, in fact, the example that we are to provide. If all believers would do the same, there would be much sharing and charity, with little attention drawn to it. And that is the model for the Christian community. We are to hide our charity in order to protect ourselves from pride and our neighbors from indignity. We would want the same kind of confidentiality if we were the recipients of charity. We don't want people knowing that we are unable to provide for ourselves.

HIDDEN CHARITY

These concerns are very much related to the story of the healing of two blind men:

> "And as Jesus passed on from there, two blind men followed him,
> crying aloud, 'Have mercy on us, Son of David.' When he en-
> tered the house, the blind men came to him, and Jesus said to
> them, 'Do you believe that I am able to do this?' They said to
> him, 'Yes, Lord.' Then he touched their eyes, saying, 'According
> to your faith be it done to you.' And their eyes were opened. And
> Jesus sternly warned them, 'See that no one knows about it'"
> (Matthew 9:23-30).

There are several stories like this, where Jesus told people not to say anything about Him or about some miracle He performed. Surely you have wondered, why not? Why would the Lord not want people to talk Him up? The traditional answer is that He was anticipating His crucifixion and resurrection. So, He needed to hold off until everything was ready, which is true, of course. The fulfillment of Scripture needed to unfold according to a particular time table. But that being said, is there any application of this idea for us today?

Yes, there is. The story of the healed blind men in Matthew 9 and the admonitions against hypocrisy in the Sermon on the Mount share the element of privacy. The issue is privacy, not secrecy. The difference is important. Healing, like alms-giving is always intensely personal and private. It is between God and the individuals involved. To publish stories of miracles of healing, or about patterns of charitable giving, turns them into public or political events or stories, into public relations and marketing tools, rather than acts of love and charity. It changes the focus and nature of the events themselves.

The use of healing or charity as political events or photo opportunities involves the use of hypocrisy because the intensely personal and private experience of these things is very different from the public or political use of such things. Turning charity or healing into experiences or stories for public consumption or political use portrays them as what they are not. It turns them into what they are not, which is the definition of hypocrisy. It turns something subjective into something objective, something private into something public. It turns love and charity inside-out. It turns the blessings of God into tools for political or public manipulation. In the same vein Jesus quoted Isaiah.

> "Behold, my servant whom I have chosen, my beloved with whom my soul is well pleased. I will put my Spirit upon him, and he will proclaim justice to the Gentiles. He will not quarrel or cry aloud, nor will anyone hear his voice in the streets; a bruised reed he will not break, and a smoldering wick he will not quench, until he brings justice to victory; and in his name the Gentiles will hope" (Matthew 12:18-21).

The key verse here, which says that the Messiah will not be heard in the streets, is of the same character. It's about the intensely personal and private concerns of salvation, which is a kind of healing. And, inasmuch as salvation becomes a public issue or a political football or a concern to be debated for some political purpose or used politically, it inevitably gets portrayed in the media as being something that it is not. Hypocrisy creeps into Christianity when it takes on a political purpose or use that God didn't give it. When stories of salvation or healing are used as fundraisers, or for marketing purposes, the purpose of salvation and healing are inevitably degraded.

Jesus seems to be saying that the issues of salvation and faithfulness are intimate and private concerns that are primarily between God and His people, and are not to be used for other purposes—political purposes, financial purposes, marketing purposes.

So, on the one hand evangelistic services and conversations are to take place in the public realm for the purpose of glorifying God and identifying or establishing connections with God's people, of sharing the gospel. But on the other hand, the concerns of faithfulness are not to be used by the civil government or its non-governmental associations. Church leaders are free—indeed, they have an obligation—to proclaim the free grace of the gospel and to persuade people of the truth of God's Word and of God's way, to encourage love and charity, and to do so publicly. But civil leaders have the obligation to stay out of those concerns, to allow the church to be what God has ordained it to be—the institution of public mercy.

SEPARATION OF JURISDICTIONS

The church wields the word of hope and encouragement (the gospel), and the state wields the word of fear and punishment (the law). The church and state have different jurisdictions, and their separation is not merely a matter of legality, but is also a matter of spirituality. The state is to be concerned with legalities and law enforcement, and not venture into areas of spirituality. And the church is to be concerned with spirituality, and not venture into areas of legality. People today don't understand this. They don't know what God has called His church to be and do. They think that God's church is supposed to be a kind of voluntary club, a toothless, gutless association of do-gooders.

On the other hand, the church should not be involved in civil jurisdiction, either. But because civil government has expanded into every aspect of modern society, people think that this is what civil government is supposed to do. But, according to God's Word, it's not. The state should be involved in concerns of justice and defense, and not be involved in the concerns of gospel and grace— preaching, teaching and healing. These are spiritual concerns and belong to the jurisdiction of the church.

According to Scripture, and in order to avoid hypocrisy, the state or civil government is to have a very narrowly defined role in society. It is the institution of legal and physical enforcement, which involves legal interpretation, establishment, and defense. These are mentioned because the civil government exercises jurisdiction exclusively in the public realm, where the church has an obligation to publicly exercise its instruments of persuasion regarding God, Scripture, Christ, and the gospel, as well.

The jurisdiction of the church belongs solely to the church. It has no public jurisdiction, but it does have public obligations. Its relationship to the public sphere is one of influence not jurisdiction. The temptation is for civil government to exclude the church from the public realm because the church has no public jurisdiction, and because civil government has the power (the force) to do so. But the fact that the church has no jurisdiction in the public realm does not mean that it has no valid role or obligations in the public sphere.

Indeed, the church and her leaders are obligated to be involved in the public realm through the God-given instruments of gospel promotion—preaching, teaching, and healing. These are the instruments of God's grace and wherever they are engaged, Christ and His church, His body, is engaged. Preaching, teaching and healing are instruments of the church, not the civil government. And when the civil government engages in them, it is in violation of what we commonly call the separation of church and state.

People tend to think of the church as the building on the corner, but nothing could be farther from the gospel truth. Such an idea ghettoizes Christianity and impedes God's mission in the world. The church is the people of God and the church exists wherever God's people are. And wherever God's people are, they are to be actively engaged in God's mission. Nothing could be more harmful or damaging to the mission of Christ's church than to forbid it from exercising its institutions of preaching, teaching, and healing in the public realm. The gospel must have unfettered access to public expression.

The secret of the Sermon on the Mount is that God's mission of salvation is intensely personal and, at the same time, public. It is about God's relationship with individuals, but also about the relationships between individuals. It is about the most intimate kind of healing imaginable—the healing of the heart, the mind, the soul, but also about the healing of various social ills. And while the leading edge of God's mission of soul salvation always reaches into the public square in order to reach unrepentant sinners, the heart of that mission is not fodder for political use or abuse.

Salvation is the mission of the church, not the mission of the state. The mission of the state is justice, not grace. So, just as the church is not to encroach into the jurisdiction of the state regarding civil law, neither is the state to encroach into the jurisdiction of the church regarding spirituality—preaching, teaching, and healing.

And it must be understood that while the church is not a physical entity but a corporate entity, it necessarily overlaps from the spiritual realm into areas of physical being, into the public square. So, while the church functions in the private and personal lives of individuals, individuals in turn function in public, in society.

Again, the instruments of spirituality, of the church, are preaching, teaching, and healing. And these institutions belong to the jurisdiction of the church, not the state.

13. Prayer & Protagonism

And when you pray, you must not be like the hypocrites. For they love to stand and pray in the synagogues and at the street corners, that they may be seen by others. Truly, I say to you, they have received their reward. But when you pray, go into your room and shut the door and pray to your Father who is in secret. And your Father who sees in secret will reward you. And when you pray, do not heap up empty phrases as the Gentiles do, for they think that they will be heard for their many words. Do not be like them, for your Father knows what you need before you ask him. —Matthew 6:5-8

Prayer should be the most personal and intimate thing that we do. Prayer is communication with God. That communication must be sincere. All hypocrisy is to be avoided. Jesus has been saying this same thing in a variety of ways throughout the Sermon on the Mount. This is simply a restatement of verse 1. The issue is personal integrity. Here Jesus applies personal integrity to prayer because prayer is at the heart of faithfulness. While it is true that faithfulness is demonstrated by behavior, it is established by character. Faithfulness is playing our God-given role in life.

But life is not theater. Life is not a play. It is real. It is not something imaginary or abstract, but something actual and concrete. We are not to pretend as if we are playing in a fantasy. We are not to live our lives as if we are engaged in a drama or a dream, as if we can abstract ourselves from our actual, historical, physical, bodily context. We are not to live our lives on the basis of some drama or story that we concoct or imagine for or about ourselves. We are not to live storybook lives. Rather, we are to live our lives on the basis of the story that God has given us, on His story, not ours.

God has placed us in the midst of His story, on His earth, in His timeline. That is where we are. That is our context. We are to live in the midst of His story, not our story. History is real, where our stories are abstract figments of our imaginations. His story is eternal, where ours are temporary. This means that we are to understand ourselves as being the persons and the people that God created us to be, individually and corporately. It means understanding ourselves as creatures of God, as reflecting God's Trinitarian image and engaging the gifts that God has given us. It means not denying these things or inventing some other godless identity for ourselves.

Work It, Don't Play At It

Yet, at the same time, theater imitates life. So, life does have theatrical elements. We do have roles to play. But because they are real roles, roles given by God, we must not play at them. We must not pretend to be something we are not. Rather, we must actually be what we actually are, what God has created us to be. We belong to God, and so we must live for God. We must actually live for God, and not just pretend to live for God. Our life in Christ must be genuine, earnest.

> "You shall love the Lord your God with with all your heart and with all your soul and with all your strength and with all your mind" (Luke 10:27).

There must be no room for doubt or pretense. We must not only be what-you-see-is-what-you-get kind of people, but people must actually see Christ in us. Our imitation of Christ must be genuine imitation. We must not pretend that Christ is in us, but we must be actual representatives of Christ. We must genuinely present Christ. Our lives must provide efficacious testimony on behalf of Christ.

> "You must not be like the hypocrites" (v. 5).

In part, Jesus was testifying that there are indeed religious hypocrites, and that such hypocrites have always been prominent people, people who stand out in a crowd, people who make themselves stand out in a crowd by pretending to be special, pretending to have special status, special rights, special skills, or gifts, or to be part of a special class of people. And so when Jesus forbade us to not be like them at prayer, we can apply His admonition more broadly and understand that we are not to be like them in any way.

We are not to seek or pretend to have any special rights, status, gifts, or class, neither above nor below anyone else. In good measure, this is endemic to the unity that Jesus gave His disciples. Christians do not engage in race, status, or class divisions or behavior, period! Avoiding these kinds of divisions is a discipline of Christian unity. But neither are we to be in conflict with people who make such pretenses. To enter into conflict with such people is to join them in their belief that race, status, or class pretenses are real, and they are not. All such behavior is hypocrisy, and is to simply be abandoned in Christ.

But it cannot simply be abandoned and leave a vacuum. No such vacuum ever actually exists. Nature abhors a vacuum, so something rushes in to fill it, whether air, water, or character. Thus, our abandonment must be an abandonment into Christ. We must imitate Christ in order that Christ may fill our character and our person with His Character and Person. And yet, Christians do not become Christ, though our very identities are forever changed as we grow in the likeness of Christ. All other human character or identity is hypocrisy because it involves pretending to be something that God did not create people to be. Finding ourselves in Christ is finding our personal character and integrity in Christ.

Thus, when we pray we must not pray in order to be seen by others or as if we are being seen by others. Our prayer must not be self-conscious, but must simply be Christ-conscious. Jesus said that those who pray hypocritically, who pray in order to be seen by others already have their reward. The goal or purpose of their prayer—to be seen—has been fulfilled in the seeing. If that's what they want, that's what they get. But such getting is not a blessing. Rather, it comes in place of God's blessing, instead of God's blessing. And again, we must note that this admonition has application beyond prayer. It applies to our love of God and through that to all of life.

HOT AIR

Earlier Jesus warned people after a particularly acidic encounter with religious officials.

> "Watch out; beware of the leaven of the Pharisees and the leaven of Herod" (Mark 8:15).

Leaven is used in bread to make it lighter and more pleasing to eat, which means that Jesus said that the Pharisees and the Romans used hypocrisy to make their teaching lighter and easier to stomach. Hypocrisy turns the weight of truth into pleasant lightness, by filling it with hot air.

Jesus first told us how *not* to pray, how *not* to live as hypocrites. And in the next verse He told us how to pray, how to live with integrity.

> "But when you pray, go into your room and shut the door and
> pray to your Father who is in secret. And your Father who sees in
> secret will reward you" (v. 6).

It is not that our prayer is to be secretive or introspective, but that it is to be private. The Greek word translated as *secret* (*kruptos*) suggests inwardness and privacy. The point is not to do it for show.

Prayer is intensely personal and private. God reads our hearts. He understands our innermost desires—better than we understand ourselves. Nonetheless, we are to express those desires to God, not to inform Him of them, but to align ourselves with His desires. And inasmuch as we align our thoughts and prayers with God's desires, God will indeed bring those desires to fruition, not because they are our desires, but because they are His. God will accomplish His own purposes.

And the secret to getting your prayers answered is to get them in proper alignment with His purposes. God will move mountains to accomplish His own purposes. Nothing can thwart the purposes of God. We are to pray for the accomplishment of God's purposes in our lives, in the lives of our friends and families, in our schools and businesses, in our churches and governments. And by making our prayers align with God's desires we also make ourselves available to the Lord for service. When our desires are in line with God's desires, He will use us to accomplish His purposes.

ALONE & TOGETHER

Verse 6 directs us to pray to God in the privacy of our own rooms, that is, alone. It is not that we are to avoid corporate prayer, but that our corporate prayer must be supported by our private prayer.

From a trinitarian perspective there are three overlapping points of communication in prayer, all of which are essential. Prayer is a three-way communication that includes you (the person who is praying), God Himself, and God's people. The unity of the church, the unity of God's

people, is established through the privacy of our personal prayer, in our
prayer closets.

The reward that God has for those who engage prayer as here
instructed is unity or union with Christ. Christian unity is a fruit of
prayer. Being in unity or in union with someone means to be on the
same page with them, to have the same concerns and agenda. And unity
with Christ means that our personal and individual concerns and agen-
das are the same as Christ's concerns and agenda. We are to align ourselves, our thinking, our hearts and minds, with Him, with His thinking, with His heart, His mind. We are to seek a one-to-one correspondence with the Lord as best as we are able. And the only way to do that
is to align ourselves with Scripture, with the revelation of God.

Christian unity is not a matter of being in political or administrative
alliance with other Christians. That kind of alliance among other Christians takes our eyes off Jesus and puts our attention on one another.
These kinds of alliances produce monotheistic uniformity, not trinitarian unity. These kinds of alliances can only be achieved through com-
promise because of our limited and sinful perspectives, our different
preferences and personalities, and our different callings. Whereas, trinitarian unity issues from the fullness and integrity of God's covenant
because of Christ's sinless perspective and manifests in the diversity of
human character in Christ. Indeed, Christian unity cannot be found in
ourselves, nor in our various statements or documents, not in our various churches, alliances, or denominations, not in our differing analyses,
theologies, or in our politics.

Rather, Christian unity is a function of our prayer closets, of Christ
in our hearts and minds. It is not a fruit of getting together in order to
pray. It's not a matter of posturing or prattling about the importance of
our roles or responsibilities regarding Christian unity. It's not a fruit of
praying in mass rallies for Christian unity. Rather, Christian unity is
demonstrated by going into our own rooms by ourselves and praying to
God in secret, in private, and keeping it to ourselves because that is what
it means for something to be private. Christian unity is found by aligning ourselves, our thoughts and desires, with God's thoughts and desires
as they have been revealed in Scripture.

Christian unity is the unity of the body of Christ. And the unity of
the body is found in the cooperative diversity of its parts. Each part, each
person, each church has a different God-given role to play. Each has a
unique perspective, a different function, a unique purpose, different
gifts. So, how can each of the diverse parts of the body be in unity? Sim-

ple. Their unity is a function of their trinitarian character in Christ. The diversity of Christian character, the diversity of function, is the unity. The whole, though greater than the parts, is still a product of the parts. The unity of the whole depends on the cooperative diversity and the integrity of the parts.

But again, the unity of the body of Christ is not found by seeking outward unity with other Christians. It is found by individual Christians going into their prayer closets alone, and aligning themselves—their own thoughts and desires—to God's thoughts and desires as revealed in the Bible. Unity is the alignment of the subjectivity of the individual with the objectivity of God, as revealed in Scripture.

The toe doesn't need to know what the ear is hearing. Nor does the elbow need to see what the eye sees. The body can't function if the ear is trying to be a toe or the eye an elbow. The body only functions when each part does its own particular job, when each individual is in alignment with God's particular purpose for him or for her.

But who will be in charge of the unity? How will people know if they are in unity with Christ? Well, *Christ* is in charge of the unity. It's His body, not ours. The body doesn't belong to the foot or the knee. If anything, the head is in charge, and Christ alone is the head of the church. So, each part needs to be in proper alignment, not with each other, but with the Head. Alignment—cooperation, obedience, and integrity in the Head—in Christ—is unity.

FINDING UNITY

Our prayers are a form of communication with the Head of the church, and that communication flows three ways: head to part, part to head, and part to part (from Christ to the individual, from the individual to Christ, and from individual to individual). How does this work? First of all, prayer is listening. Before we speak, we must listen to the Head, who speaks through His Word, through the Bible. All prayer begins with reading the Bible, listening to God's Word. There is no other way to know about God's desires, plans, and purposes.

Secondly, prayer is speaking God's desires and purposes back to Him in the privacy of our own rooms, in our own hearts, as our own desires. As we listen for God's desires and purposes in Scripture and pray those desires and purposes back to Him in personal prayer, we become aligned with Him. And over time that alignment improves and we grow in grace.

Thirdly, Christian unity is a fruit of the improvement of our personal alignment to God's desires and purposes in Christ. The better we are in personal alignment with Christ, the more we are in alignment with the rest of Christ's people, who are also becoming better aligned to Christ, who is alone the perfect personal human representative of God's desires and purposes on earth.

Consequently, part to part alignment (uniformity), does not serve the alignment of the parts to Christ, but only to one another. Rather, as the parts are aligned to the Head, they are also set in proper alignment with one another by the Lord. Our alignment with Christ yields unity, whereas our alignment with one another yields uniformity. And we are called to unity, not uniformity.

The purpose of going into our prayer closets alone and aligning ourselves with God's desires, plans, and purposes through Jesus Christ is the establishment of Christian unity. This kind of prayer is both the root and fruit of Christian unity. Our part of Christian unity is personal and subjective, while God's part is public and objective.

No agreements between Christians need to be signed and notarized to achieve Christian unity. No special ceremonies or announcements are required. The name of the church doesn't have to change. Administrative procedures don't have to be merged. Money doesn't have to be sent anywhere in particular. Meetings don't need to be planned or attended. God has already given it in Christ.

> "...keep them in your name, which you have given me, that they may be one, even as we are one" (John 17:11).

> "...that they may all be one, just as you, Father, are in me, and I in you, that they also may be in us, so that the world may believe that you have sent me." (John 17:21).

Notice that the unity between God and Christ is not achieved or accomplished. Rather, by the character of the Trinity it simply is already the case. It is endemic to their trinitarian character. The realization of Christian unity requires nothing and changes nothing. Light does not change the darkness, it dispels it. Christian unity is rather like an assumption or presupposition.

What needs to happen is this:

> "when you pray, go into your room and shut the door and pray to your Father who is in secret. And your Father who sees in secret will reward you" (v. 6).

That reward is unity or union with Christ or Christian unity. This probably sounds too simple, and it is simple. But it's not easy, but neither is it hard. It's none of that because it's not about something we do. It's about something that we *are*, something that God has made us to be and which in Christ we simply are.

We live on the redemption side of the cross. The work has already been done by the Lord. All that is left is the receiving and/or realizing of it. The prayer closet that Jesus spoke of here is the reward or gift. The gift is not inside the closet. Nor is the gift a result of our prayer in the closet, as if we bring it about by praying. The prayer closet is itself the gift of Christian unity because it is in prayer that we are most unified in Christ. It works by drawing all of the various parts of the body of Christ together and properly aligning them with the Head, Jesus Christ. No bells, no whistles, no trumpet fanfare, no press releases.

Rather, the corporate unity of the church of Jesus Christ is simply assumed and obvious to those who are in actual, personal unity with Christ through prayer. If it isn't obvious, return to your personal prayer closet and don't come out until it is. But whatever else you do,

> "do not heap up empty phrases as the Gentiles do, for they think
> that they will be heard for their many words. Do not be like
> them, for your Father knows what you need before you ask him"
> (vs. 7-8).

We don't need more lectures, studies, or reports about the state of Christian unity or how to achieve it. We don't need statistics or stirring rhetoric. We don't need proclamations or statements because we cannot add anything to the reality of trinitarian unity in Christ. Jesus Christ completed it by manifesting as a human being.

BELIEF

We are not to be like the Gentiles, unbelievers, who will not believe it even if God was proven to be completely and perfectly documented. Christian unity is not a matter of documentation. It is a matter of belief. So, believe it. Believe in the efficacy of prayer and the unity of the church in Christ. Believe in the death and resurrection of the body of Christ. Believe in the fellowship of the saints, and in eternal life in Christ. Believe in the truth of Christ because it is true, not because it can be proven.

You can't prove it, and neither can I. So what! The effort to prove Christianity is inside-out, upside-down and arsy varsy. It is not the proof that makes the proposition true. Rather, it is the truth of the proposition that makes the proof valid.

We are not to be like those who need proof. Believers don't need proof of the gospel or proof of the unity of the church in Christ. That's like trying to prove the existence of water to fish, or proving air to birds. And because believers don't need proof, we don't need to prove it to anyone else.

Trying to prove the gospel (or the existence of God or the resurrection of Christ or the truth of the Bible) to unbelievers always seems to begin with the believers accepting the supposed neutrality regarding God (or Christ or the Bible) *of the unbeliever!* But the neutrality or objectivity of the unbeliever regarding God is the very thing that is in dispute.

So, agreeing with unbelievers about their axiom of neutrality or objectivity gives the unbeliever an undefeatable advantage. The unbeliever assumes that God is not absolutely essential for a correct understanding of reality. Believers are defeated the moment they make such an assumption of common ground on the basis of unbelief. Taking a proof to the unbeliever is an admission that the unbeliever stands on neutral, objective ground. But he doesn't. Consequently, that argument is lost by the effort of making a false assumption that unbelief is neutral.

Trying to prove the gospel to unbelievers is a fatally flawed approach to evangelism. Nowhere does the Bible try to prove anything about God. It simply declares God's reality. The attempt to prove God (or Christ or the gospel, etc.) cannot work for the same reason that believers don't need proof in order to believe the gospel. Believers don't believe the gospel because it has been proven to be true. Believers believe because God has asserted Himself into their lives.

The light that shines in the darkness does not prove itself to the darkness, it simply asserts itself into the darkness. And everything changes, yet nothing changes. It is not that proofs establish the validity of the gospel. The gospel does not depend upon the validity of proofs. Rather, all proofs of the gospel are valid *because* the gospel is actually true. The truth of the gospel precedes the validity of the proof, and serves as its foundation. The gospel is not true *because* it can be proven. And this fact, this assumption, must lead in evangelism as well. Preaching is not a matter of proving that the Bible or Christianity is true. Preaching is the announcement of God's truth. It's not an argument, but a proclamation.

Unbelievers claim that it needs to be proven because those who don't believe it can't see it. And what is more, the effort to shove a gospel proof down the throats of unbelieving people doesn't work and cannot work because it is not God's method.

God doesn't shove. God draws people. He pulls them into belief and faithfulness with the light of Christ. God's Word pulls people forward into belief and faithfulness. And He does so individually, personally, in the privacy of their own prayers. That's how God does it, so that's how Christian evangelism is to do it.

God already knows what people need before they ask, and that's a good thing because we don't really know what we need. Yet, our asking is not useless or immaterial. Rather, it is essential for us, but not for God. It is essential for us because it confirms our own understanding when we can ask God for what He wants to give us. When we are able to ask for what God wants to give us, He knows that we understand Him. And we understand Him only by standing under Him.

Love's Proof

God is like a man who loves a woman, or a woman who loves a man. It's not a sexual thing, but a covenantal thing. The man proposes to the woman, knowing that genuine love is irresistible, that his love will not fail to win her. Nonetheless, he asks for her hand in covenant. And her answer is not insignificant or immaterial, though if the love is real she cannot resist it anymore than the sky can resist the sun. Nonetheless, her reply is crucial to him who asks, even though he knows that she cannot resist the beauty, passion, or truth of real love. If such human love cannot be resisted, who can resist an infinite love that has been perfectly customized specially for us by an all-knowing, all-loving, perfect Creator? And even if it were possible to resist God's love, who would want to do so? And why would anyone defend such resistance?

We can no more argue or prove such love as a means of evangelism anymore than a man can argue a woman into falling in love with him. Love is not an argument. It is not a logical proposition, though it is proposed. It is not a formula or a program, though it produces patterns and behaviors. Rather, it is a personal confession, a declaration, an announcement. It is a matter of fact. In the case of God, He decreed it and Jesus announced it. Paul clarified it. The apostles established it. And the saints live it.

Christians are to be like the saints who believe it and live it, not like the Gentiles who don't believe it, or the hypocrites who pretend it.

When the saints actually live it in the context of the church in covenant, they are then doing evangelism God's way. The life of simple but genuine faithfulness is the light of Christ. No other ingredients are necessary. It simply shines because it is what it is.

Gather a handful of neighbors, add water, and a generous helping of the Word. Allow the Spirit to stir gently, and bask in the light of Christ —forever.

14. The Disciple's Prayer

Pray then like this: Our Father...   —*Matthew 6:9a*

The flow or context of these verses is important. We need to note that Jesus has just said that when we pray we are to go into our closet, our room. We are to pray in private, and not engage in prayer hypocritically or ostentatiously, but reverently, genuinely, and seriously. We are not to pray like the hypocrites—in order to be seen, in order to be identified by others as godly. Our prayers are to be intensely personal and private.

Having discussed the importance and centrality of prayer in the lives of believers and as the means and end of Christian unity, Jesus went on to provide a model prayer, an ideal prayer. Christians are not merely to pray this prayer, but are to use it as an example of the structure of Christian prayer.

We call it the Lord's Prayer, but it was not simply that the Lord prayed it. Rather, He gave it to His disciples to pray. Because the prayer asks for forgiveness, and the Lord was perfectly sinless and not in need of forgiveness, it was not something that He prayed for Himself. So, it really should be called the Disciples' Prayer. The name of the prayer is not part of Scripture, but has come down to us as a tradition of the church. It's not important unless it undermines our understanding of the perfection of Christ.

If we pay close attention as we engage this prayer, we will see something very odd in the first word of this prayer. It begins, "Our Father" (v. 9). However, because Jesus has just told people to go into their rooms to pray alone, shouldn't it be *My* Father? If we are to pray alone and in private, why should we address God in the plural, as *our*, rather in the singular—*my*? What does it mean when I call God *our*

Father? To what does the word *our* refer? Whose father is being addressed? *Our* is both plural and inclusive. So, who is included in this *our*?

Clearly, the word *our* here refers to the church. It defines who is a member of the church and who isn't, in that it is inclusive of all church members, all those whose Father actually is God. That particular group is composed of regenerate people. Thus, the church is composed of those people who pray this prayer, which as we learned previously is not only a prayer for Christian unity, but is the very means of Christian unity. Unity is not a function of beliefs, interpretation, or doctrine, nor of administration, as if all Christians must belong to one centrally administered organization. Not at all!

UNITY

Rather, Christian unity is a function of trinitarian prayer. Christian unity is established upon prayer and is the fruit of prayer. Christian unity issues from common prayer, so where Christian unity does not exist, the fault is a lack of common prayer. But Christian unity is not a product of prayer, as if we can create Christian unity by praying for it. Christian unity is not something that *we* must create. It is not a function of human effort. It is not something that we can do, or that we need to do. Rather, Christian unity is God-given. It is God's church. He created it. He defined it. He unified it. He upholds it. Not us!

Christian unity is the basis of prayer. It is implied, assumed, inferred, and implicit in the very first word of this prayer—*our*. By saying *our*, we understand ourselves to be in the group that is being referred to. To simply address God as *our* Father is to identify Him as *your* Father, but not yours alone. Rather, it also identifies all who are actual children of God as our brothers and sisters. Christian unity is familial unity. Family members don't all think alike or look alike. They don't have the same skills, the same interests, or gifts. What they have in common is ancestry, a common story, a common inheritance, and a common hope.

The unique aspect of Christianity is not belief in God, nor belief in the Bible, nor belief in Jesus Christ as the Son of God. Even Satan believes in God and the Bible and knows—even understands and believes—that Jesus Christ is the Son of God. But Satan does not share in the inheritance or hope of God. God has written him out of His will. Thus, Christian unity is a function of Christian inheritance. However, it must be stated that Christian inheritance is a matter of grace, not race. Inheritance is given on the basis of God's grace, and is not based on any aspects of human race. God is not a respecter of persons! God has rede-fined the institution of family to be His family. And it is by grace alone that Christians are members of God's family and partakers of Christ's inheritance as His people.

Christian unity is not a matter of signing a document or joining a local church. It is not a legality, but a spirituality. Of course, there are some legal concerns regarding Christian unity, but it is not dependent upon them. Rather, it is the other way around. The legality is dependent upon the reality of the spirituality. Christian unity is not a particular position regarding biblical doctrine, though biblical doctrine is very important. Christian unity is not a matter of belonging to the right church, though church membership is very important.

Christian unity is an attitude, an orientation, a preference, a com-mitment, a presupposition. What does this mean? Christian unity is an attitude, like the position of aircraft relative to a frame of reference (the horizon). The attitude of the believer, like the attitude of an aircraft, depends upon its frame of reference—and for believers that frame of ref-erence is God.

Christian unity is an orientation, that is, an awareness of self with regard to one's position, time, place, and personal relationships. The ori-entation of believers is the awareness of their position in God (Christ, and/or the church), the awareness of time and history, and the awareness of their personal relationship with Jesus Christ.

Christian unity is a preference, a predisposition that favors the Father, the Son, and the Holy Spirit—the Trinity. Believers prefer to love and be loved by God. Believers prefer to read and study Scripture. Believers prefer prayer to other activities. They prefer Christian fellow-ship to other kinds of commingling.

Christian unity is a commitment, much like a marriage. In fact, it is a lot like marriage. Christian unity is covenantal, it is the commitment to remain together in covenant, come what may. It is a spiritual covenant, and not merely a legal contract. And it is a covenant with God and not simply a covenant between Christians. Rather, it is God's covenant with us and not our covenant with Him. The covenant is His. He is the originator of it, not we ourselves. It is His covenant and He keeps it. It is not dependent upon our whims or desires or beliefs or whatever. Christians are in unity because we are in covenant with God through Christ.

And finally, Christian unity is a presupposition. It is something that is assumed by every Christian. Christian unity is not based on what

Christians do or think. It is not a function of faithfulness. And even if it is, who are ordinary Christians to decide whether or not someone else is being faithful? Faithfulness is God's call, not ours—though elders do have various church oversight responsibilities that are not accorded to other Christians. And much intramural bickering among Christians could be avoided if they would abide by the biblical structures of eldership. Christian unity must be assumed to be true on the basis of the integrity of God, not on the basis of human interpretation, belief, or behavior.

Thus, to pray *our Father* is to confess Christian unity with all who are in Christian unity according to God's covenant. It is to acknowledge one's own attitude toward God. It is to profess an orientation regarding God through a personal relationship with Jesus Christ. It is to exercise a preference for godly and biblical thinking and things. It is to honor a commitment to God's covenant and to all who are in God's covenant by the will of God. And it involves a presupposition that the order of authority in the Bible is actually and completely true.

To pray *our* is to pray *my*, but not in the sense of being exclusively mine. Rather, when I say *our* I put myself on the inside of a group—in this case: the church of Jesus Christ. To say *our* is to place *my* identity in the church. To say *our* is to say that I am God's possession, and that He is my Father.

Of course, there is more to this prayer than the first word, but like the first step of a journey or the direction of a trajectory, the beginning is the key to the success of a venture. An arrow that starts out wrong cannot hit the intended target. And so Jesus instructed Christians to go into their rooms by themselves and pray alone, saying, "Our Father" (v. 9). Doing this is a testimony to the Trinity because it relies upon the Holy Spirit to forge the unity of the Church by uniting Christians in attitude, orientation, preference, commitment, and presuppositions—and to do so in a plurality of persons and perspectives.

TRINITARIAN PRAYER

And God is not merely ours as individual Christians, but is ours corporately through the body of Christ, the church. In addition, He is not merely ours corporately, but is our *Father*, as well. God is father to us, and the word *father* does not simply describe a person of parentage, but a relationship of kinship, a close connection marked by common interests or similarity of nature and character. Our father may or may not be our friend, but he is always our father. The relationship of father (parent) does not end, though it changes through time. Even after we have all died, my father is still my father, your mother is still your mother, sons are still sons, and daughters are still daughters. These relationships are eternal.

The Old Testament also regarded God as being our father, but not much. The word *father* is seldom found to refer to God. But it is found in one very important place:

> "For to us a child is born, to us a son is given; and the government shall be upon his shoulder, and his name shall be called Wonderful Counselor, Mighty God, Everlasting Father, Prince of Peace" (Isaiah 9:6).

The Hebrew word for *father* also means patrimony or principal. So, here it refers to that which is always and eternally the most important. A friend from State College, Garry Sutley, used to say, "The main thing is to keep the main thing the main thing." Isaiah said that the child who would one day be born to "us" (to those in covenant with God) was, is, and will always be the main thing. God is Father to his children, always has been, and always will be.

But Old Testament Jews didn't refer to God as father. Because patriarchy and lineage was very important to Old Testament Jews, they thought a lot about the idea of fathers and fatherhood, but not like this. They always tied it to actual blood lineage. Sure, God was a kind of father, but He didn't beget Adam. He created Adam. So, God was understood to be Adam's father, and ours, but in the sense that Einstein is the father of the theory of relativity, or the theory of relativity is the father of the atom bomb.

It wasn't until Jesus was born in fulfillment of Isaiah's prophecy, and then the widespread dispensation of the Holy Spirit upon "all flesh" (Acts 2:17) that the fullness of the Trinity came into play. Of course, the Trinity is a term that describes an eternal being, an eternal reality, so we must not speak in terms of His coming into being. He (the Trinity) did not come into being, but has always existed. Nonetheless, the revelation of God as the Trinity has been historically progressive, and became a much more prominent feature of history through the birth of Christ and His church.

So, as Christians were regenerated or born again in Christ, they began to refer to God as Father. God is the Father of Christian regeneration. And because Jesus commanded Christians to include themselves in the "our" (the corporate character) of the Christian church, they began to do as Jesus had done, to refer to God as Father. Jesus was the only begotten or naturally born son of God, but we are also children of God,

"not of perishable seed but of imperishable, through the living
and abiding word of God" (1 Peter 1:23)

and

"by the washing of regeneration and renewal of the Holy Spirit"
(Titus 3:5).

This is the only grounds by which we can and must refer to God as Father.

It is not that we can pray to God as Father only after we have been born again, but that our prayer to God as Father is the very means of spiritual birth or regeneration. Being born again isn't a public event, it is a private event. It is between you and God through Jesus Christ, who is the Holy Spirit. And yet, this does not mean that we can bring our own spiritual rebirth about by simply praying. It only means that praying alone is the venue of such rebirth in the same way that ordinary birth is a singularly personal and individual event that issues from our relationship with one's mother. In addition, birth also requires corporate involvement between a mother and a father.

Jesus not only gives us instruction about what to do in life, but He also gives us instruction about what not to do. And the Pharisees often provided Him with examples. Consider the following.

"Then Jesus said to the crowds and to his disciples, 'The scribes
and the Pharisees sit on Moses' seat, so practice and observe whatever they tell you—but not what they do. For they preach, but do
not practice. They tie up heavy burdens, hard to bear, and lay
them on people's shoulders, but they themselves are not willing
to move them with their finger. They do all their deeds to be
seen by others. For they make their phylacteries broad and their
fringes long, and they love the place of honor at feasts and the
best seats in the synagogues and greetings in the marketplaces
and being called rabbi by others. But you are not to be called
rabbi, for you have one teacher, and you are all brothers. And call
no man your father on earth, for you have one Father, who is in
heaven. Neither be called instructors, for you have one instructor,
the Christ" (Matthew 23:1-10).

PRACTICE

Note that Jesus said that His hearers should practice some of what
the Pharisees were teaching, but not what they were practicing. Note
that Jesus said here that He was not opposed to everything related to the
Pharisees, but was much opposed to the practice of the Pharisees.
According to tradition, the Pharisees carried on the beliefs, practices,
and traditions of the ancient Assideans.[15]

The Assideans maintained the practice of the Mosaic Law against
the invasion of Greek customs. When the Maccabees struggled against
Antiochus IV (Epiphanes), the Assideans naturally joined their cause (1
Maccabees 2:42, 43). However, not all of the Maccabees were Assideans.
According to 1 Maccabees 7:13, the Scribes and the Assideans sought to
make peace with the Syrians, while the other followers of the Maccabees
suspected deceit. That this suspicion was well founded may be inferred
from the fact that Alcimus, who had been made High Priest by
Demetrius I (1 Maccabees 7:9), slew sixty Assideans in one day (1 Maccabees 7:16). According to 2 Maccabees 14:3, the same Alcimus "willfully defiled himself," and later on he testified before Demetrius:

> "They among the Jews that are called Assideans, of whom Judas
> Machabeus is captain, nourish wars, and raise seditions, and will
> not suffer the realm to be in peace" (2 Maccabees 14:6).

Scholars believe that the Assideans were identical with the later Pharisees
in terms of beliefs, practices, and traditions.

So, was Jesus arguing for or against the Pharisees? It appears that he
was arguing both for them in terms of their doctrine—at least part of it,
but against them in terms of their practice or their application of it. The
issue for Jesus appears to be their integrity, the fact that they taught one
thing but practiced another.

If I understand this rightly, it means that Jesus believed that the
Pharisees had some right doctrine, but some wrong practice. He appears
to be auguring for Christians to take up the teachings of law by the
Pharisees and then actually practice it, rather than negating the doctrine
by not actually practicing it. Calvin commented on this verse that Christ

> "enjoins believers to attend to their words (the Pharisees), and not
> to their actions; as if he had said, that there is no reason why the

---

15 Hebrew, *chasidim*, saints; Greek, *Asidaioi*, men endowed with grace (Psalm 39:5;
148:14).

bad examples of pastors should hinder the children of God from holiness of life."[16]

But at the same time, not everything taught by the Pharisees was kosher. Calvin also said,

> "that, while the Sadducees and Essenes preferred the literal interpretation of Scripture, the Pharisees followed a different manner of teaching, which had been handed down, as it were, to them by their ancestors, which was, to make subtle inquiries into the mystical meaning of Scripture. This was also the reason why they received their name; for they are called Pherusim, that is, expounders. And though they had debased the whole of Scripture by their false opinions, yet, as they plumed themselves on that popular method of instruction, their authority was highly esteemed in explaining the worship of God and the rule of holy life."[17]

Calvin concluded by saying that Christians should "attend to their (the Pharisees') lips rather than to their hands."

It is important to understand what Jesus taught about the Pharisees in order that we may not be like them. As long as the Pharisees taught what God's Word, the Torah, actually said, they were fine. But when they began expounding upon it or speculating about it, adding details, mystical interpretations, or other extra-biblical ideas, they were off base. And furthermore, those extra details, interpretations, and ideas seemed to lead them into a kind of hyper-separatism.

They didn't realize that their own justifications for their hyper-separatism were issuing, not from God's pure Word, but from their own speculations about it. While they thought that their justifications (explanations) provided reasons for their hyper-separatism, Jesus said that their unbiblical commitment to hyper-separatism was in fact driving their speculative analysis of Scripture.

ANTITHESIS

It was important to differentiate between God's Word and the encroaching godless Greek culture of Jesus' day—or the dominant godless culture of our own. But the right way to do that is not to justify that separation by our own (or history's) speculations, but to maintain a clear focus on God's Word. Paul carried on this antithesis against Greek wis-

---

16 *Calvin's Commentaries*, Matthew 23:2, public domain.
17 Ibid.

dom and culture because the tendency to speculate proved to be quite tenacious. It reared its godless head before the ink of the New Testament was dry.

It has taken a long time for the church to learn that the kind of separation taught in Scripture does not forbid cultural interaction between God's people and people from the world's cultures. Rather, it forbids forgetting or blurring the distinctions between God's law and human law. It forbids accommodation or the blending of God's Word with other human or cultural ideas and calling such a blend godly. It forbids, not religious toleration, but religious accommodation.

Unfortunately, this is a difficult distinction to make intellectually because it is not an intellectual distinction. It is a spiritual distinction that can only be made from the repentant side of personal regeneration. It requires ears to hear and eyes to see (Deuteronomy 29:4, Matthew 13:16). This distinction creates an opposition or antithesis between worldliness and biblical godliness.

God's antithesis to the world requires careful observation of important differences between all sorts of things in order to resist the natural and very ordinary urge to depend upon our own experience and understanding, individually and/or culturally. This tendency is especially seen in the area of religion and spirituality, where people tend to think that it's okay to pick and choose various elements from various religious and spiritual teachings and/or traditions to create their own custom-made religion, and then think that the result is God-given. This is not a new phenomenon that has arisen because of modern society. It was also a huge problem in Old Testament Israel, as people continued to worship false gods in high places, a phrase of particular significance in our own day.

There are two sources that lead to the problem of false gods: 1) extra biblical ideas, and 2) biblical speculation. The first comes from the various false gods and false religions of the world. The cure for this problem is provided by the Old Testament itself, which reveals the monotheistic character of God and distinguishes the only real God from the many false gods of the world.

The second stage of the biblical remedy for this problem comes from the New Testament, which reveals the Trinitarian character of God in Jesus Christ. The full revelation of God's character is not merely monotheistic but Trinitarian. The revelation of God's Trinitarian character involves the outpouring or dispensation of the Holy Spirit upon all flesh, first and foremost upon Jesus Christ, and then upon Christ's followers.

The Pharisees stumbled because of the monotheism of the Old Testament and could not (would not) accept the Trinitarianism of the New Testament. The Pharisees based their religious ideas on the Old Testament, but apart from the Holy Spirit their speculations went beyond what Scripture actually said. They went beyond presenting God's Word, and instead went to their own interpretations of God's Word. They expanded it beyond its biblical limitations. On the positive side, it was an effort toward Trinitarian integration, because the seeds of the Trinity are in the Old Testament. But it produced intellectual (human) speculation because the Pharisees lacked the regeneration of the Holy Spirit. We know this because they did not recognize Jesus Christ. Regeneration depends upon the manifestation and direction of Christ alone, and they denied Christ.

Today, Christians are pretty clear about false gods and mostly understand the doctrine of *sola Christos* or Christ alone.[18] Liberal Christians still struggle with this issue, and tend to revert to pantheism to one degree or another through their focus on plurality and diversity.

Ongoing

The error of the Pharisees also continues to be a problem for the church today in that various Christians expound and expand the teachings of the New Testament beyond what Scripture actually says. The manifestations of the problem are many. Some Christians fall into various charismatic or mystical excesses. Others fall into various fundamentalist or legalistic excesses. And I believe that Jesus' instructions to not be like the Pharisees pertains to the errors of fundamentalism and legalism.

By directing us to call God *Father*, Jesus insisted on the trinitarian reality of regeneration in the lives of His people because of the necessity of the power and presence of the Holy Spirit to keep us from this error. Apart from the doctrine of monotheism people tend to the errors of pantheism. And apart from the doctrine of the Trinity people tend to the errors of fundamentalism or legalism.

But in Christ alone people are born again into the reality of God's Trinitarian world. In Christ alone people can avoid the errors of pantheism, the errors of mysticism, the errors of fundamentalism, and legalism.

---

18 See *Colossians—Christos Singularis*, Phillip A. Ross, Pilgrim Platform, Marietta, Ohio, 2010.

In Christ alone is there unity from these errors in the truth of Scripture, the truth of God, who is Father, Son, and Holy Spirit.

15. Art In Heaven

*Pray then like this: "Our Father in heaven, hallowed be your
name. Your kingdom come, your will be done, on earth as it is
in heaven."* —Matthew 6:9-10

Ask a Christian under three feet tall where God is and he will
likely tell you that God lives in heaven. And yet, just as often
will say that God lives in his heart. Press the issue and ask him to
decide which it is—in heaven or in his heart? And he will shrug his
shoulders and look at the ground. He doesn't know how to answer the
question, but he knows that both answers are true. We can't blame him
for not knowing. It's a hard question to answer because he's right, both
answers are true.

So, what do we mean when we say that God is in heaven? The
Greek word (*ouranos*) literally means sky or the idea of elevation. It
shouldn't surprise us that the Greek definition doesn't help. People in
ancient times didn't really know what the Bible means by the word
heaven any more than people do today. We get the idea that heaven is a
place of bliss, delight, and peace, like being in the mountains on a warm
summer day and gazing across a meadow at the horizon from some sort
of high perch. The vista is grand and glorious, and deafeningly quiet. It is
a quiet like city dwellers seldom hear.

God lives there, in the warmth of the sun, in the beauty of the circumstance, in the gazing off in the distance, and at the horizon. Sometimes we say that heaven must exist in another dimension. The Old Testament doesn't really help, either.

"In the beginning, God created the heavens and the earth" (Genesis 1:1).

165

The Hebrew word translated as *heavens* comes from an unused root that means to be lofty. It simply suggests the sky, as in that which is aloft. It alludes to the visible arch of blueness in which the clouds move, and sometimes the higher ether where the stars reside. It indicates something distant from me and from the earth.

It is almost as if whatever heaven is (or heavens are) it is that which distinguishes one thing from another, that which distinguishes the earth from its context—the universe. In the creation of heaven and earth by God we find a Trinitarian context. First there is God, then heaven and finally earth. From the eternally existent, wholly objective, and tran-scendent God came into being the temporal existence of a wholly sub-jective and immanent world. In a sense, heaven is not *of* the earth. It is that which lies outside of and apart from the earth. It is distant, aloof and aloft. It is where God lives.

And yet, our little boy knows that God also lives in his heart. He knows that that which is eternally existent, wholly objective and tran-scendent also resides in his own temporal, wholly subjective, and imma-nent heart. How can the bigness of God fit into the smallness of a human heart? In this dilemma we are seeing the Trinitarian character of the world that God made, the world in which we live. There are two descriptions of the ultimate character of the world and of the things in the world. One description is subjective, and one is objective, one is immanent and one is transcendent, one is temporal and the other eter-nal. Each pair of opposites points to the same unbridgeable difference.

So, how are these two opposites or ultimates related? How can they be held together in the same reality? I don't know. But God holds them together in such a way that the world actually exists. God also gave the means by which His world can be understood and known. That means is His Word.

"And God said…" (Genesis 1:3).

Whatever God said became real. It is not that words in general hold the world together, but that God's Word (or God's Covenant) actually holds the world together. God has the ultimate, objective perspective, and we don't. But the point is that through God's Word in our hearts (in our lives), through regeneration in Christ, we participate in God's ultimate reality, which is the body of Christ. We are in It, yet It is in us, too.

Please forgive me for waxing eloquent and even a bit mystical, but this thing that we are talking about—heaven—is a complex, Trinitarian reality. It is ultimately a mystery, of course. We can understand some of it, but not all of it. Heaven is somehow both here and not here, both immanent and transcendent. But the main thing is that heaven is real. It's not a substance or an essence in the Greek sense, nor an abstraction in some philosophical sense. It is not simply an idea in our minds. Rather, heaven is an actual, complex, multifaceted, and fully-orbed reality that is both fully present and yet not fully present at the same time. This reality—heaven—is "where" God exists. But He doesn't exist in a part of it, He exists in the all of it, and beyond it. God is omnipresent—everywhere at the same time, and beyond everywhere.

HALLOW

> "Our Father in heaven, hallowed be your name" (v. 9).

The hallowed evening of tradition that we celebrate on October 31 is a perversion of the church's intent for the holiday. The word *Halloween* is the only other contemporary usage of the word *hallowed that* I know of. Unfortunately, perverted traditions and wild imaginations have ruined the meaning of the word. The Greek word (*hagiazō*) means to make holy, to consecrate, or sanctify. To hallow something is to solemnly dedicate it or set it apart for a high or sacred purpose. It does not mean that we are to turn God's name into a talisman or some kind of magic word that opens secret doors.

And yet we are we to hallow God's name. The biblical use of the word *name (onoma)* suggests God's character and authority, not simply His designation. God's character and authority are hallowed because God is worthy of honor and respect. To honor and respect someone is to take them seriously. To honor and respect the law is to obey it. To honor and respect God is to honor and respect His Word and His Trinitarian character. It means nothing less than living in love and obedience to Scripture, in the best possible way that would be the most pleasing to God.

I suspect that the reason that the word *hallow* is in such little use and ill-repute today is that there is not much hallowing of God's name that we can point to in our own lives or in society. How can we hallow God's name? How can we honor and respect God's character and authority? Someone asked John the same question. Here's what he said:

> "By this we shall know that we are of the truth and reassure our heart before him; for whenever our heart condemns us, God is greater than our heart, and he knows everything. Beloved, if our heart does not condemn us, we have confidence before God; and

whatever we ask we receive from him, because we keep his commandments and do what pleases him. And this is his commandment, that we believe in the name of his Son Jesus Christ and
love one another, just as he has commanded us. Whoever keeps
his commandments abides in God, and God in him. And by this
we know that he abides in us, by the Spirit whom he has given
us" (1 John 3:19-24).

Doing this hallows God's name. But there is a funny thing about
this hallowing of God's name: we can't do it accidentally. It can only be
done on purpose—intentionally. That means that we can't do it unless
and until we understand it. And yet we can only come to an understanding of it by doing it. So, in one sense the doing comes first, and in
another sense the understanding comes first. But how can they both
come first? Well, because the doing and the knowing are not two different things but one thing.

The doing and the understanding are the same thing. They are a
single, yet complex and dynamic process—like a perpetual motion
machine. The doing produces the knowing, and the additional knowing
then produces more doing, which produces more knowing, which produces more doing, etc. The one grows the other and the other grows
the one. You can start in one and grow into the other, or the other way
around. But you cannot have one without the other. The doing and the
knowing of God always go hand-in-hand, and to neglect either one is
to fail at both.

> "Our Father, who is in Heaven, Hallowed be Your name. Your
> kingdom come, your will be done, on earth as it is in heaven" (vs.
> 9-10).

Verse 10 follows verse 9, and that means that there is a logical and
necessary connection between them. The hallowing of God's name
brings His kingdom near, on earth as it is in heaven. What kingdom?
God's kingdom. There are three significant things to note about God's
kingdom. First, it is God's and not ours. Second, it is a kingdom, not a
group, club, republic, or democracy. And third, God rules there, not
you, me, or someone else.

The Greek word translated *kingdom* (*basileia*) properly means roy-
alty, abstractly it means rule, and concretely it suggests a realm. Only
literally or figuratively does it mean a kingdom or reign. But however it
is translated, it means that God's rule or kingdom draws near as a necessary element of the hallowing of God's name. To honor and respect

God is to honor and respect (obey) God's rule, God's authority, on earth as it is in heaven. Furthermore, God's rule applies to all jurisdictions—personal, family, church, and civil. There is no jurisdiction that is not governed by God.

But because God is Trinitarian in character, He respects both the ontological trinity of God's being and the economical trinity of God's activity in history. By praying, "your kingdom come" (v. 9) we are anticipating, not simply the end times, but the progressive coming or unfolding of the kingdom of God, the expansion, and perfection of Christ's church.

The ministry of Jesus began in earnest after John the Baptist was arrested. After John was arrested Jesus began to preach the message of God's kingdom:

> "The time is fulfilled, and the kingdom of God is at hand; repent
> and believe in the gospel" (Mark 1:15).

The kingdom of God is that into which the world is being saved. We are being saved from sin, out of sin, and into the kingdom of God, into the church. The kingdom and the church are not the same. The church is within the kingdom. So, being in the church includes being in the kingdom.

The gospel calls to people everywhere, without distinction or partiality (Romans 2:11), to willingly submit to God's authority. When the disciples asked Jesus why He spoke in parables, He told them that while the kingdom is a reality to those near Him, those in relationship with Him, it is a mystery to those without that relationship (Mark 4:11).

Perceiving the kingdom of God is outside the natural powers of human observation (Luke 17:20) because it is spiritually discerned (John 3:3, 1 Corinthians 2:14). People can't see it unless God shows it to them, even though God's kingdom grows as more people are brought into relationship with Jesus Christ. Eventually God's kingdom will be universal in that every knee (Isaiah 45:23, Philippians 2:10) will bow to the authority of God in Christ (Matthew 25:31-34, Philippians 2:9-11, 2 Timothy 4:1, 2 Timothy 4:18).

God's Will

"Your kingdom come, your will be done" (v. 10).

What is God's will? It is an important question. If we are to participate in the accomplishment of God's will on earth, we need to know

and understand what His will is? Jesus understood that He was involved
in the accomplishment of God's will. As Jesus came closer to the crucifixion event He prayed,

> "Father, if you are willing, remove this cup from me. Neverthe-
> less, not my will, but yours, be done" (Luke 22:42).

Jesus differentiated between God's will and human will. Jesus was
not a masochist. He dreaded the cross as any person would. But He submitted to it from a human standpoint because He understood it to be a
necessary part of God's will. And in this submission Jesus modeled
human faithfulness to God.

So, how do people come to know God's will? The answer is both
simple and complex. The simple part comes from understanding that the
Bible is God's last will and testament, the whole Bible. Think of it like
when someone dies and the family gathers together for the reading of
the will of the deceased. That's part of what we do at worship. We read
God's will—Scripture—in order to understand how He wants His inheritance to be distributed among His children. Scripture is God's will in
two testaments.

In a sense, Christ's death on the cross triggered the activation of
God's will. It comes into force when the person dies. In addition, Christ
functions as both the estate attorney and the central heir as God's only
begotten or natural Son. Of course, God has lots of other adopted children, like us, who receive part of the inheritance through Christ.

Understanding God's will in this way is a very fruitful way to think
about it. While it doesn't always answer all of the detailed questions
about what we should do in this or that circumstance, it does provide
the central truth about God's will, which is the inheritance of God's
kingdom or salvation through faith by grace alone. It is *God's* kingdom
and it must be administered as God has willed it. Our particular role or
function in God's will is a subset of God's will for His people generally.
Understanding and submitting to God's will for His people generally
illuminates the particular details of God's will for our individual lives.
The particulars become clearer as we engage and submit to God's will
for His people in general.

Mission

> "Your kingdom come, your will be done, on earth as it is in
> heaven" (v. 10).

The last phrase of verse 10 tells us that God's mission is not simply to evacuate Christians to heaven, though that may be part of God's mission. But that part is something that God does and which those who are evacuated have no control over. The other part, the mission that God has given His church is the Christianization of the earth, which is the purpose of evangelism. God's kingdom, God's rule, God's authority is coming to earth and will not be complete until it is on earth as it is in heaven. And it is undisputed in heaven. Satan has been cast out and God reigns uncontested. This is where we are going. This is what is coming to earth. This is God's task for the church.

This mission is not just God's mission, but God gave it to Christ, and Christ has given it to His people. While most Christians accept this mission and engage in evangelism in one way or another, most Christians don't really understand how we are to accomplish this mission, apart from witnessing in a random, helter-skelter way. While every Christian values missions, few have any idea about how to go about it biblically.

The biblical method of evangelism is overflow, not overreach. The love of Christ and the truth of the gospel must bubble up from within, starting within our own hearts and minds. Similarly, it must begin from within the church so that it overflows the church and affects, first our own families and then our nearest neighbors and friends. Evangelism must not reach over or ignore our own families and our nearest neighbors and friends in order to preach and teach in the farthest corners of the world. Rather, evangelism is designed to be contagious, contiguous, and coterminous.

Biblical evangelism is not simply sending people *out*, it is bringing people *in*. There must be an undertow to the outgoing wave of evangelism that sucks people into the life of the church. The flow of evangelistic energy is not to be directed out or away from the church, but is to be directed into the church. Not:

> church –> mission –> people

but:

> church <-- mission <-- people.

We are called to make disciples by trinitarian baptism[19] and teaching obedience to Christ. While Matthew 28:18-20 focuses on disciplining the nations, it assumes the existence of a discipled church. Unfortunately in our day, we must recover discipleship in the church before we can export it. We cannot export what we do not have. Christians should not take discipleship and teaching beyond the walls of the church until they have mastered it inside the walls of the church. It must overflow the church.

It is not that there are no serious disciples in the churches, but that there are too few. Every church member should be discipled and taught obedience to Christ. Each Christian should have a teacher, and each Christian should be a teacher to form an unbroken chain of learning and teaching. Unfortunately, such relationships are greatly feared and thought to be either cultic or based on works-righteousness. But when they are done right, which means biblically, they are neither cultic nor works-based.

FAMILY DISCIPLESHIP/EDUCATION

The recovery of Christian discipleship and obedience to Christ begins in the family because the parent-child relationship is a natural discipleship relationship that is readily available and begging for engagement. The need today is for Christian parents to disciple and teach Christian obedience to their own children. And, of course, they must know it before they can teach it.

This is where we are loosing the culture war. The social forces of worldliness in our day have for the most part broken the natural parent-child bonds by the time children are in the third or fourth grades. Dependence upon public education has gutted the sense of personal responsibility that God has given to parents for the discipleship and teaching of their children by creating an institution that undermines parental and Christian authority in the name of progress.

We must reclaim the Christian educational mission by taking personal responsibility for the discipleship and teaching of obedience to Christ to our own children. The public schools aren't doing it, and Sunday Schools can't do it. An hour or two a week cannot withstand the barrage of worldliness from schools and from the entertainment industry. The central theater for Christian discipleship and teaching has always been the home. Contemporary Christians have lost sight of this

---

19 See *Essays On Church—Ordinary Christianity for the World*, Phillip A. Ross, Pilgrim Platform, Marietta, Ohio, 2020, "Baptism."

fact. Christian homes must once again become seedbeds of Christian culture. Too much of the world has flooded into Christian homes and washed away the heart of discipleship and teaching. It has been doing it for generations, but most Christians don't have the courage to acknowledge it.

This is not an argument against education outside the home, nor the suggestion that home schooling is the only biblical model. To reassert Christ into the culture will require that all models and means of education be engaged. Rather, this is an argument for Christian discipleship inside the home as the antidote to godless education and entertainment. Too many families think that entertainment rather than education is the central activity of a family. But such an idea is not biblical, it is commercial and represents an abandonment of biblical values at the heart of the family enterprise.

But we don't need to go overboard and smother our children with rules and fears. Rather, we need to teach them to think biblically in order to release the power and creativity of Christian character that is being hampered by various forms of addiction and sin in the name of education and entertainment. This is not an argument for the elimination of entertainment, but for the reclamation, inculcation, and propagation of biblical values as the central purpose and activity of the family. This is an argument for Christian culture, which is the mission of Christ's church in the world.

We need to think of Christian discipleship as a work of art within the family, as a kind of Christian performance art accomplished by the Holy Spirit through the development of Christian character to the glory of God. In our day the greatest mission need is often in our own family, the Christian family, our own children and grandchildren, and our own churches.

Unfortunately, this field is not ripe for harvest, but is overrun with neglect and worldly weeds. But, while the family fields today are not ripe for harvest, they are ripe for the plowing and planting of the gospel seed. This is the central need of our day. And the need is great, and the time is now.

> "Our Father, who is in Heaven, Hallowed be Your name. Your kingdom come, Your will be done, on earth as it is in Heaven" (v. 9-10).

16. As We Forgive

Give us this day our daily bread, and forgive us our debts, as we also have forgiven our debtors. And lead us not into temptation, but deliver us from evil. —*Matthew 6:11-13*

Also read Exodus 16.

Here Jesus taught His disciples to pray, "Give us..." (v. 11). Everything that was said about the first word of this prayer, "Our..." (Matthew 6:9) applies here to the word *us*. By using the word *us* we place ourselves into Christ's church, into the structure and authority of His church. We place ourselves in relationship with Jesus Christ and with His people. By saying *us* we confess that we belong to Jesus Christ, and that our very identity as individuals is caught up with His people. I am who I am because He is who He is. And what is more, I cannot know who I am apart from knowing who He is.

We are not to pray, Give *me*. The recipient of the requested gift is not an individual but a group—*us*. The gift cannot be adequately received by an individual. To receive it individually constitutes a desecration of the gift because it is not given to *me*. It is given to *us*. And because it is given to *us* it must be received as *our*. The gift is corporate. It belongs to the body of Christ, to the church.

"Give us this day..." (v. 11).

Here we find an allusion to manna (Exodus 16), the daily provision of the Lord for Israel in the desert. The manna came every day and was only good for a day, except for Friday's allotment which would last through Saturday so that the ancient Israelites could keep the ancient

Sabbath. The Israelites ate manna for forty years. No wonder they complained.

By praying "this day" (v. 11) we keep ourselves from looking too far ahead. We are directed to be particularly attentive to the present and not get overly distracted by the past or the future. James agreed.

> "Come now, you who say, 'Today or tomorrow we will go into such and such a town and spend a year there and trade and make a profit'—yet you do not know what tomorrow will bring. What is your life? For you are a mist that appears for a little time and then vanishes. Instead you ought to say, 'If the Lord wills, we will live and do this or that.' As it is, you boast in your arrogance. All such boasting is evil" (James 4:13-16).

This is not an injunction to avoid planning, but a caution to keep our plans in the proper context. And that context is that God guides our lives, not we ourselves. Just as God holds the world together, moment by moment, day by day, year by year, God guides our lives according to His plan, not ours. People are so tempted to forget or ignore this that we are to remind ourselves of it daily. Every day we are to look to God for His providence and care. And we are not to get distracted from the immediate moment by focusing on the future. We don't know the future, apart from what God has revealed in Scripture. The more attention we give to the future, the less we have for the present. And life happens in the present.

MANNA

"Give us this day our daily…" (v. 11).

The word *daily* occurs twenty-two times in the New Testament, but it is rendered by this particular Greek word (*epiousios*) only in this prayer. The word is of questionable origin and doesn't literally mean *daily*. A more literal translation might be *sufficient* or *needful*, but we do in fact have daily needs. So, *daily* is not a wrong translation. The idea is for God to provide what is needed for the day, or what is sufficient for the day.

As an allusion to God's manna, it suggests basic food sufficiency for one cycle of wakefulness, in that manna was supplied daily in sufficient quantity for all of God's people. Manna does not suggest abundance or extravagance. And yet neither was it a minimal supply. People could eat enough to be full.

Manna also was given, not to mere individuals, but to God's people as a whole. While everyone was fed it is unlikely that everyone gathered exactly the same amount. As with other things, some people undoubtedly gathered more than others because they were bigger, stronger, or more able. Some needed more, some less. Yet, nothing in the manna instructions forbade the sharing of the gathered manna, one with another. The only limitation was that it could not be stored, except for the Sabbath.

"Give us this day our daily bread" (v. 11).

We are asking for bread, but does that only or even necessarily mean food for the stomach? The word usually means food in a context like this, not just one kind of food but food generally. Note also that we are asking for our daily bread, or our needful sustenance. It is a request for what we need to sustain us daily. We are asking for our corporate needs to be met. What corporate needs? Who are we? We are Christ's church. We are asking for the Lord to provide for Christ's church what she needs in order to sustain her day by day.

Certainly food, meat and potatoes, are part of that provision, but Christ's church requires more than meat and potatoes. We also require spiritual sustenance—grace, love, fellowship, direction, teaching, wisdom, etc. It is silly to argue that spiritual sustenance is more important than meat and potatoes, just as it is silly to argue that meat and potatoes are more important than spiritual sustenance. Both are necessary, and both are included in this prayer. *Lord, feed our bellies and our hearts—daily. Lord, give us what we need to grow.*

> "And he gave the apostles, the prophets, the evangelists, the shepherds and teachers, to equip the saints for the work of ministry, for building up the body of Christ, until we all attain to the unity of the faith and of the knowledge of the Son of God, to mature manhood, to the measure of the stature of the fullness of Christ, so that we may no longer be children, tossed to and fro by the waves and carried about by every wind of doctrine, by human cunning, by craftiness in deceitful schemes. Rather, speaking the truth in love, we are to grow up in every way into him who is the head, into Christ, from whom the whole body, joined and held together by every joint with which it is equipped, when each part is working properly, makes the body grow so that it builds itself up in love" (Ephesians 4:11-15).

Lord, make it so. Jesus knows that

"Man shall not live by bread alone, but by every word that comes
from the mouth of God" (Matthew 4:4).

Every word. Not just the New Testament, nor just the red letters of
Jesus. This was not a new teaching, but an old teaching. Jesus was
quoting Deuteronomy.

> "And you shall remember the whole way that the Lord your God
> has led you these forty years in the wilderness, that he might
> humble you, testing you to know what was in your heart,
> whether you would keep his commandments or not. And he
> humbled you and let you hunger and fed you with manna, which
> you did not know, nor did your fathers know, that he might
> make you know that man does not live by bread alone, but man
> lives by every word that comes from the mouth of the Lord"
> (Deuteronomy 8:2-3).

So, the prayer for bread is a prayer, not for bread alone, but for every
word that comes from the mouth of the Lord. Daily. This prayer for
bread is a prayer for daily Bible study because that is where the words of
the Lord are found. To pray this prayer is to pray for enough food to
keep us from the distractions of hunger so that we can adequately
concentrate on God's Word and derive the spiritual sustenance we need.
But not just for ourselves, for the body of Christ, the church. Lord, give
us.... Consequently, our Bible study is not simply for ourselves, though
we should benefit from it personally. Rather, our Bible study is to be
food for the body of Christ, for God's people.

Fathers are to insure that their own families have sufficient food for
growth, both meat and potatoes, but also Bible study. Christians should
also be concerned that their neighbors don't starve, either. Of course, in
Christ those neighbors become brothers and sisters who also feed on our
common fellowship in Christ. All those actually in Christ are family.

We cannot ignore the implication that the bread of this prayer may
also suggest communion, the bread of Christ. Paul called the bread of
communion

"a participation in the body of Christ" (1 Corinthians 10:16).

Every aspect of this symbolic bread points to the body of Christ, the
church. And communion is the central symbol of the church. So, this
prayer also asks for the provision of communion for the church. It could
be daily communion, but doesn't need to be. Remember that the word
translated as *daily* can also be translated as *needful* or *sufficient*. This

allusion could suggest our need for regular communion and not simply its daily celebration, unless we understand communion in its ordinary meaning rather than in its sacramental meaning. Ordinarily *communion* means the intimate sharing of thoughts and feelings. So, in this light, we are praying for daily communion with God in our thoughts and feelings, and with one another.

DEBTS

The next verse adds an interesting petition to the prayer:

> "Give us this day our daily bread, and forgive us our debts" (vs. 11-12).

The phrase is neither the beginning nor the end of a sentence. It is a plea for God's mercy and forgiveness. Though different versions of the Lord's Prayer use debts, trespasses, or sins,[20] all of the Bibles I consulted translate it as *debts* because the Greek word (*opheilēma*) means something owed, whether money, dues, a moral obligation, or as the result of an offense. This idea of a debt that was owed was explained by Jesus in a parable.

> "Therefore the kingdom of heaven may be compared to a king who wished to settle accounts with his servants. When he began to settle, one was brought to him who owed him ten thousand talents. And since he could not pay, his master ordered him to be sold, with his wife and children and all that he had, and payment to be made. So the servant fell on his knees, imploring him, 'Have patience with me, and I will pay you everything.' And out of pity for him, the master of that servant released him and forgave him the debt. But when that same servant went out, he found one of his fellow servants who owed him a hundred denarii, and seizing him, he began to choke him, saying, 'Pay what you owe.' So his fellow servant fell down and pleaded with him, 'Have patience with me, and I will pay you.' He refused and went and put him in prison until he should pay the debt. When his fellow servants saw what had taken place, they were greatly distressed, and they went and reported to their master all that had taken place. Then his master summoned him and said to him, 'You wicked servant! I forgave you all that debt because you pleaded with me. And should not you have had mercy on your fellow servant, as I had mercy on you?' And in anger his master delivered him to the jailers, until he should pay all his debt. So also my heavenly Father

---

20 I like to use "offenses." Forgive us our offenses as we forgive those who offend us.

will do to every one of you, if you do not forgive your brother
from your heart" (Matthew 18:23-35).

This parable concludes the same way that this petition concludes:

"and forgive us our debts, as we also have forgiven our debtors"
(v. 12).

If we took Jesus literally at His word we'd all end up in the poorhouse
because we couldn't collect our bills. Or would we? Was Jesus teaching
a vow of poverty here? No, neither of these views is true. Jesus was not
leading people to the poorhouse, nor was He recommending a vow of
poverty.

The lesson of the parable is that God has forgiven us a debt that we
could never pay. A debt that is completely unpayable may as well be
infinite. The debt threatened the steward's family, who could have been
sold as indentured servants in order to retire the debt. As long as that
debt was owed, it was an unbearable burden that only served to oppress
and depress the debtor, and threatened the existence of his family. Such a
debt makes all work feel meaningless because no matter how hard you
work, the debt remains. It takes the joy and enthusiasm out of work and
turns it into oppression and drudgery, and threatens the family.

But when the debt was forgiven the steward was greatly relieved.
His family was preserved and his work could once again be fruitful
toward the betterment of his family. Debts can threaten and destroy
families. And the forgiveness of the debt in the parable demonstrates that
there are some things that are more important than money, that the
existence, integrity, and viability of one family was worth more than ten
thousand talents, which was a sum that would have been completely out
of reach at the time. The lesson was that family trumps money. This was
the lesson that the king wanted the steward to learn.

But when the steward required the debts owed to him by his fellow
servants, he failed to apply the lesson, which meant that he hadn't actually learned it. The steward was ready to ruin the families of his fellow
servants over money. It doesn't really matter how much money was
involved. All we really know is that it was a much smaller debt than had
been forgiven him. The parable concludes with the king, having heard
of the lack of forgiveness by his steward, throwing the steward in prison.
For the unforgiving steward, family did not trump money, which
opened the door for a different lesson. The parable did not teach the
superiority of family over money, nor of money over family. Rather, the

final lesson was the superiority of learning and practicing forgiveness, the superiority of following God's lead, over both money and family.

Grace

The gospel of grace—God's forgiveness—trumps everything. It is significant, however, that the reception of God's grace was not sufficient in the parable. The steward received the forgiveness of his debt with joy. His family and his own work had been preserved by the forgiving grace of the king. It had been a real debt. It had been real forgiveness, and real grace. And it had actually been received. But it was not sufficient.

But wait a minute! We know that Christ's grace is sufficient. So, what's wrong here?

The problem was in the receiving of the lesson of the forgiveness by the steward. Rather than learning the lesson, the steward wanted to profit from the gift of forgiveness that had been given to him by not passing the forgiveness along. By keeping it for himself, he thought that he could not only get out of debt, but he could turn a buck. Now that he was out from under his own debt, any money he made would have been his own. He saw an opportunity, not for the expansion of the gospel of grace, but for his own enrichment. And that was the problem! He had used the Master's forgiveness for his own purposes.

The forgiveness of debts comes only inasmuch as we forgive our debtors (Matthew 6:12). We must pass along the gift of forgiveness and God's gospel of grace. It must permeate all of our relationships and manifest in our own behavior. It must produce gospel fruit. Receiving it is only half of the gospel, and salvation involves the whole gospel. Christians must get the gospel—receive the gift. And in order to get it right, we must also pass it forward to those who don't deserve it. Thus, faithful Christianity means getting the gospel right, and then getting the gospel out. We must receive it and extend it to others. Receiving it is not sufficient.

To ask God to

> "forgive us our debts, as we also have forgiven our debtors" (v. 12)

captures both of these essential factors. God's forgiveness of our debts and receiving God's grace are the same things. And the condition of only forgiving us inasmuch as we forgive others insures that we pass God's grace forward as best we can. Failure to pass it forward amounts to the confession that it is not actually in one's possession, that one has nothing to pass forward, and by implication, that God's grace has not actually or fully been received.

TEMPTATION

> "And lead us not into temptation, but deliver us from evil" (v. 13).

Here we are praying for God's leadership in our lives, and for that leadership to spare us from temptation. The Greek word (*peirasmos*) only means temptation by implication. It literally means to put something to the test. The test that this prayer seeks to avoid is the testing of our ability to resist the temptations of the world. And why should we want to avoid such a test?

Two reasons: First, Jesus tells us here to pray for such avoidance. It's a matter of our obedience. And second, we know that in and of ourselves we will fail such a test. Of course, we can survive such temptation by the presence and power of the Holy Spirit through regeneration, when our degree of sanctification trumps the power of the temptation. Ultimately, of course, the Lord will steer us through all temptations and obstacles. Over time the Lord will temper us to the degree that we will no longer be tempted by such allurements—eventually, in the fullness of the Kingdom.

We also know that God is not evil. So, God does not use temptation for evil purposes. But does God use temptation for His own purposes, in order to test, prove, and/or strengthen His people? Some people claim that God does not tempt people at all, but that is not a biblically defensible idea. Mark said that when "Jesus was led up by the Spirit into the wilderness" He was "tempted by the devil" (Matthew 4:1). Technically, we can say that the devil did the actual tempting, but we cannot avoid the fact that the Spirit, who is God by the reality of the Trinity, led Him into it.

Jesus' wilderness temptations proved His righteousness. But it was not that Christ's righteousness was a theory that needed to be tested to see if it was true. It was, rather, that His wilderness temptations established the public fact of His righteousness. Paul said that

> "No temptation has overtaken you that is not common to man. God is faithful, and he will not let you be tempted beyond your ability, but with the temptation he will also provide the way of escape, that you may be able to endure it" (1 Corinthians 10:13).

Christians will in fact be tempted in the same ways that everyone is tempted. But because God is faithful to His promises, and Christians know God's faithfulness to be true, God will attach a way of escape (*ekbasis*) to the temptations of His people. Christians will not be defeated or captured by the temptation, but will be able to endure it, and learn from it. In fact, the point of this verse is the teaching of perseverance, which is not the avoidance of the struggle of temptation, but the successful conquering of it by the power of endurance.

We cannot avoid temptation. It is a necessary part of our human experience, and a necessary part of our sanctification, our growth in grace. Temptation strengthens us by revealing our weaknesses and because our flesh is no different than anyone else's flesh in that it cannot conquer or endure the temptation, and is forced to either submit to the sin of the temptation or depend upon God's Holy Spirit to provide sufficient endurance. The one way leads to sin and the other way leads to sanctification. And this is the point of this section of the Lord's Prayer.

When we pray for God to

> "lead us not into temptation, but deliver us from evil" (v. 13),

we are praying that God will preserve us from succumbing to the sin of our temptations by the power and presence of His Holy Spirit. Not that God will keep us from all temptation, but that He will so use and accompany us in our temptations so as to drive us to greater dependence upon His Holy Spirit. However, we are not asking God to bring us more temptations so that we can grow even more sanctified. Rather, we are asking God to use the ordinary temptations that come our way as opportunities to increase our dependence upon Him.

And why do we need to go through such temptations? Couldn't God just zap us into conformity? Sure He can. But it would be of no benefit to us for Him to do so. God exposes us to temptations for our benefit and His glory. For whatever reasons, life is filled with temptations. So, as long as the world is configured as it is, temptations are real and cannot be avoided. We may not like this situation. But we did not create it—God did. And to complain about the world that God created is the sin of Romans 9:20:

> "But who are you, O man, to answer back to God? Will what is
> molded say to its molder, 'Why have you made me like this?'"

Such a question, such an attitude reveals the height of presumption, audacity, and unmitigated effrontery.

It leads to an evil from which there is no escape. It is the evil from which we pray for God to deliver us. *O Lord, deliver us from this evil.* Some translations, like the American Standard Version, translate this phrase as "deliver us from the evil one." There are huge textual issues with this verse as we shall see. Nonetheless, the acknowledgment of the definite article in the Greek makes it a specific evil or a personified evil and not merely a generic evil. The concern is the evil of Romans 9, the evil of people judging God or His love or His justice or anything about God, as if human beings are in a position to evaluate God's work of creation. We are in no position to judge God about anything! Rather, God is in the position to judge us about everything. Asking such a question shows that we have it backwards.

All of the modern translations conclude this prayer at this point. However, the *Textus Receptus* or *Received Text* of the Authorized Version contains an additional ending for the prayer.

> "For thine is the kingdom, and the power, and the glory, for
> ever. Amen" (v. 13).

Modern scholars believe this ending to be a late addition to the original text and therefore not authentic. So, they exclude it from their translations, or put it in as a footnote, as if it does not belong to the Word of God.

However, because this ending is included in the overwhelmingly vast majority of the actual Greek manuscripts that have survived, there is good reason to believe that it has been a part of the biblical canon that was in common use among the ancient churches and has come to us through history as a legitimate part of the canon.

The only reason to exclude it is the elevation of modern scholarship over traditional faithfulness. Scholarship is a very valuable tool, but it must not be allowed to trump the faithful witness of the church. This issue is a matter of the Word of God versus the traditions of men, the Word of God versus the traditions of scholarship, the tradition of the church versus the scholarship of the academy.

I don't know about you, but I will side with the church—but not against the academy, except where the academy stands against the church. I will side with the church as she faithfully uses the skills of the academy to further her cause. And I will reject the academy rather than the church when it challenges the clear Word of God.

17. Treasured Treasures

For if you forgive others their trespasses, your heavenly Father will also forgive you, but if you do not forgive others their trespasses, neither will your Father forgive your trespasses. And when you fast, do not look gloomy like the hypocrites, for they disfigure their faces that their fasting may be seen by others. Truly, I say to you, they have received their reward. But when you fast, anoint your head and wash your face, that your fasting may not be seen by others but by your Father who is in secret. And your Father who sees in secret will reward you. Do not lay up for yourselves treasures on earth, where moth and rust destroy and where thieves break in and steal, but lay up for yourselves treasures in heaven, where neither moth nor rust destroys and where thieves do not break in and steal. For where your treasure is, there your heart will be also.

—Matthew 6:14-21

We are tempted to think that verses 14 and 15 simply repeat the admonition of verse 12,

"and forgive us our debts, as we also have forgiven our debtors."

But verses 14 and 15 use a different word—*trespasses* (*paraptōma*) rather than *debts* (*opheilēma*). *Trespasses* suggests a slip-up, lapse, or deviation from some standard. It could be an unintentional slip or a willful transgression of some kind.

These verses have universal application in that God knows that people offend one another daily, that resentment and indignation are common companions, not just among pagans and unbelievers, but among Christians. People are easily offended, suspicious of others, and

184

all too willing to see others in the worst possible light. There are undoubtedly a million reasons for behaving this way. We have no problem justifying such behavior on our own part and then criticizing others for acting similarly.

However, the Lord's solution to this problem is not for us to stop offending others, but to stop being offended by others. We are not responsible for the behavior of other people. We are responsible for our own behavior.

POLITICAL CORRECTNESS

This admonition is quite appropriate and timely for our world today, in that our world is awash in what is known as political correctness. What is political correctness? It is the avoidance of expressions or actions that can be perceived to exclude, marginalize, or insult people who are socially disadvantaged or discriminated against. The problem with this definition is that it relies on some very subjective measures and is open to politicization. And more than merely open to it, the fear of political incorrectness dulls common sense and puts everyone on pins and needles because of the fear of saying something offensive. And because people's beliefs and values are all over the map, and because people are easily offended, there is no way to say anything of any substance without offending someone. The problem is that political correctness requires people to live on the basis of other people's values and sensitivities.

Indeed, the idea of trying to be politically correct hamstrings honesty and integrity by making people say what they don't believe by taking upon themselves political perspectives that contradict what they themselves do believe in order to keep from offending others. For Christians, it always means abandoning common sense and biblical values.

The problem with political correctness is that it is nonpartisan, which means that we must take care not to offend any political sensitivities or beliefs whatsoever because every political view can claim to be socially disadvantaged and discriminated against. Republicans discriminate against Democrats. And Democrats against Republicans. Independents discriminate against them both. Socialists discriminate against capitalists, and capitalists against socialists. The only way to not discriminate against some social or political group or another is to say nothing, but even that discriminates against political activists who think that everyone should get involved in politics. Indeed, the very idea of political correctness mitigates against free speech and the First Amendment. Free speech and political correctness are diametrically opposed.

Christ alone has solved this delicate political problem by demanding that everyone stop being offended by others and practice forgiveness—*carte blanche*, across the board. We must grant forgiveness generously and graciously, to those who do not deserve it, as God has done for us through Christ. The only possible solution to this conflict between political correctness and the First Amendment right of free speech is for each person to refuse to be offended by others, by forgiving others for committing what they perceive as an offense against them. The solution is not controlling the speech of others, but controlling our own reactions, our own anger.

Until we can grant gracious forgiveness to those who offend us, we cannot interact with them in a civil manner. As long as we believe that we have no control over being offended by someone else, we are being manipulated by our sin. Yes, it is sin, and we must call it what it is. It is a sin to be offended by another person. Why? Because Jesus said here that God will forgive us only inasmuch as we forgive others. God forgives us of our sins, so we must be forgiving of the sins of others. And when we fail to forgive others, God refuses to forgive us, and our sin remains.

This, however, does not give us or anyone else license to be insensitive, offensive jerks and then blame others for not forgiving us. As Christians we must do all we can to believe and promote the cause, values, and virtues of Christianity. While we must not be concerned about offending other people, we must be very concerned about not offending God. And when we take care not to offend God we will believe and promote the cause, values, and virtues of Jesus Christ, which grant the maximum possible freedom to all people. We should not worry about offending Republicans or Democrats, socialists, or capitalists, etc. Rather, we must work to not offend God.

CIVILITY

As it is, people bend over backwards in order not to offend one another, and they fail miserably at it. But when people bend over backwards to keep from offending God, they will grow in faithfulness by extending mercy, forgiveness, and service to other people, as Scripture insists. Indeed, civility is a mark of faithfulness to the God of Scripture, and incivility is a mark of unfaithfulness.

The growing crisis of civility in the public square is a sign of faithlessness in the public square. Christ is the power of civilization. Christianity, not the Enlightenment, has provided the social processes whereby Western societies have achieved a superior stage of social organization and economic development.[21]

And yet, people have worked hard to remove all vestiges of Christianity from public education, public discussion, public institutions only to find that those same efforts have undermined public civility. The loss of public civility has followed in the wake of the loss of Christianity as a social virtue. Indeed, there is only one remedy for the crisis in public civility, and that is faithfulness to Jesus Christ, the Lord of the public square. Civility is not simply a problem that can be solved, or even adequately addressed, by individuals. Because it is a social problem, it requires a social solution.

"But," someone will complain, *"I have already forgiven so-and-so, and he continues to offend me. And he does it on purpose!"*

So, lest we think that we can simply make the offer of forgiveness and be done with it, Jesus also directed us to forgive even if the offense is committed seventy times seven times (Matthew 18:22). This mention of extending forgiveness seventy times seven provides the reason and opportunity for the parable of the unforgiving steward, which we looked at in the previous chapter.

Rather than looking for the exception to the forgiveness rule so that we can justify our withholding of forgiveness, we need to realize that just as God's grace is given freely to all, yet not all accept it, so our forgiveness must likewise be given freely to all. The purpose for us to grant forgiveness is not merely the well-being of others, it is also for our own well-being. We don't forgive others simply because it is good for them to be forgiven. Rather, we forgive others because it is good for us to do so. Whether or not the other person accepts our forgiveness is immaterial to this commandment.

The critical element here is not the acceptance of our forgiveness by others, but our giving of it. Just as with God's grace, people are free in their own minds to accept or reject it. And the rejection of God's forgiveness does not reflect on the character of God. God is gracious because He has provided sufficient forgiveness for all. The fact that God is rejected by some in no way diminishes the goodness of God or the efficacy of His gift. It is simply a measure of the hard-headedness of

---

21 *The Rise of Christianity: A Sociologist Reconsiders History,* by Rodney Stark, Princeton University Press, 1996.

sinners. Jesus calls us to disregard the accusations and offenses of other people and simply extend forgiveness, as we ourselves have received it.

We need to quiet the human responses and thoughts that fill our minds so that we can be more attentive to God's thoughts and His biblical admonitions because neglecting God's Word offends God. The reception of God's forgiveness through Christ allows us to engage God's thoughts and admonitions with the sure and certain hope of becoming the people that God has both created and called us to be. Apart from Christ there is no hope of ever satisfying God, and in Christ there is no doubt that we will attain to the stature of the fullness of Christ Himself—not now, but in the fullness of the kingdom of God in glory. In Christ we are free to engage God's Word and Way in order to grow in sanctification and maturity toward this end without the fear of failure that tends to paralyze action. In Christ we are free to engage in the disciplines of discipleship.

There may be times and occasions to withhold forgiveness from unrepentant people. But such a thing is not for individuals to decide. Scripture provides the ways and means to handle such situations (Matthew 18:15-18, etc.). And the thing to notice about God's ways and means is that they are social. They are not the product of an individual, but of elders and churches in consultation. No individual should withhold mercy and forgiveness from another unless explicitly instructed to do so by their own elders and/or church. If people would simply abide by this simple rule, the whole world would take a giant step forward in the love and blessings of God. If any discipline of discipleship needs to be engaged in our time, it is this.

Discipline

The Lord speaks next of another important discipline—fasting. I am going to use fasting as a specific example of Christian discipline in general, and apply what Jesus said about fasting to all of the various disciplines of discipleship because that appears to be what He intends. We will think of fasting as a case study regarding Christian discipline.

Jesus has been cautioning disciples against vanity, pride, and ostentation in many places in this Sermon on the Mount. For instance, He has argued that prayer should be done in private, in the closet (Matthew 6:6). And alms giving should be done in such a way that one's right hand does not know what his left hand is doing (Matthew 6:3). The idea is to practice these things away from public attention, in private, and not for the purpose of drawing attention to one's self.

When Christians fast they are to do so in such a way that no one notices. To look gloomy or disfigure ourselves in any way, or to call attention to ourselves is here forbidden because using Christian discipleship for self-attention is defined by Jesus here as hypocritical. Hypocrites call attention to themselves. They use spirituality for self-advancement rather than service to others. So, said Jesus,

> "when you fast, anoint your head and wash your face" (v. 17).

This is not a call for an anointing ceremony, but a simple injunction to maintain your ordinary habits of personal care and cleanliness in order to not call any attention to yourself. Your fast has nothing to do with anyone except you and God.

And here, if it is correct to apply this idea to the practices of discipleship generally, then we should not call attention to any of our discipleship practices whatsoever. What practices? The various disciplines that result in sanctification or maturity in Christ. We should not call attention to our practice of the fruits of the Spirit

> "...love, joy, peace, patience, kindness, goodness, faithfulness, gentleness, self-control" (Galatians 5:22-23).

We are to simply engage them without calling attention to them, or to the fact that we are engaging them. And neither are we to call attention to our abandonment of our various commitments to the flesh.

> "...sexual immorality, impurity, sensuality, idolatry, sorcery, enmity, strife, jealousy, fits of anger, rivalries, dissensions, divisions, envy, drunkenness, orgies, and things like these" (Galatians 5:19-21).

Neither are we to engage in self-evaluation on the basis of our practice or avoidance of any of these things. We are simply to do what is right and avoid what is wrong. We are not to look to the church or Sunday School or society for brownie points or stars or credit for being the people that God has called us to be. To look for or receive such rewards is an exercise of vanity and hypocrisy. God has not called His people to be extraordinary examples or paragons of morality. He has called us to be ordinary people who live in the midst of ordinary life.

ORDINARY

But don't mistake being ordinary for being mediocre. The unity that Christ has called for cannot be achieved by extra-ordinary people, but neither can it be achieved by mediocre people. In Christ we all lack special distinction, rank and/or status—good or bad, positive or negative, male or female, slave or free. In addition, we are to disregard any efforts to acknowledge or attribute any such distinction, rank, race, or status that others try to apply to us.

> "There is neither Jew nor Greek, there is neither slave nor free,
> there is no male and female, for you are all one in Christ Jesus"
> (Galatians 3:28).

This means that Christian unity requires the abandonment of all special distinction, rank, race, or status, apart from simply abiding in Christ. It means ignoring all worldly attributes of rank or degree, whether superior or inferior, royal, or common. None of it means anything in Christ. Such distinctions are simply abandoned in Christ, abandoned *for* Christ. They are elements, traits, or characteristics of the Old Man, who is dead and buried by baptism (Romans 6:4, Colossians 2:12).

And yet, aiming at being an ordinary Christian is not an abandonment of concern for faithfulness or personal excellence, but the embrace of both as service to Christ. Rather, being an ordinary Christian is the very definition of personal excellence because Christians live in loving and willing service that provides the evidence of Christ's excellence in the world, and Christ is the only perfect person who has ever lived. Indeed, being a Christian is a high calling, but because all Christians share this high calling, it is ordinary.

Being a Christian means being who and what God has called us to be, and doing so with both excellence and humility. It is a function of being an ordinary person, an ordinary Christian, and living in the excellence of Christ in the midst of the ordinary circumstances where God has placed us. God has gifted each of us individually and particularly for our own individual, ordinary circumstances. So, the effort to run away from our lives or our circumstances constitutes the abandonment and/or ignoring of God's purpose and gifting. Doing anything other than blooming where we have been planted amounts to the dereliction of duty and the refusal of God's gifts.

MONEY

Jesus then turned His attention to wealth and investments.

> "Do not lay up for yourselves treasures on earth, where moth and
> rust destroy and where thieves break in and steal, but lay up for

yourselves treasures in heaven, where neither moth nor rust destroys and where thieves do not break in and steal" (Matthew 6:19-20).

Understanding this requires that our understanding of the general idea of these two verses be grasped and then read back into the verse in order to properly define the word *thēsaurizō*, which has been translated as *lay up*.

What the word does not mean is to store up, as in putting our money in a chest. Quite the opposite! It is by putting our money into a chest, putting it into storage, that it becomes subject to moth, rust, and theft. We know that Jesus was not talking about hoarding money or resources because He pointed out the dangers of such storage, and specifically directed people to not do this very thing.

In the next verse, Jesus directed His people to lay up their treasures in heaven. However, this does not mean that we send our money box to God in heaven. Such an idea is absurd. Jesus was not talking about putting money into a box or collecting or saving or amassing money at all.

Was He talking about money? Yes, but not exclusively. So, before we talk about *treasure* (*thēsauros*) as an analogy, we need to deal with the literal meaning of the word. Jesus was not telling people to save money, but to invest it. This was the lesson of the parable of the talents (Matthew 25:14-30).

Remember the story. The master was going on a trip and gave each of three stewards five talents, two talents, and one talent respectively. Two of the stewards invested the money and made interest for the master. But the irresponsible steward who had only one talent, buried it for fear of losing it, and returned it to the master. But the master was furious that he had not invested it, and cast the worthless steward out. The lesson is that the Lord wants a return on His investments.

Applying this lesson to our treasure in heaven we find that Jesus was instructing His people, not to save money in a box, but to invest it in heavenly things, things that forward the kingdom of heaven, things that will increase heaven, things which produce a heavenly interest. With this understanding we look back at verse 19 and see that Jesus was not talking about saving at all, but investing. Saving and investing are similar yet different, and the difference is capitalism. Capitalists invest, they don't merely save.

There are several ways that we could parse this idea. For instance, don't simply invest in bricks and mortar, but in godly ideas. Or don't invest in things that do not appreciate in value over time, like heaven does. Or don't invest in the old world that is passing away, but in the new world that is coming.

MAMMON

The reason for obeying this command is summed up in verse 21:

> "For where your treasure is, there your heart will be also."

People love money, make no mistake about it. And money can be an obstacle to faithfulness when it rivals the love of God. Jesus was teaching about the incompatibility of the two masters. Money is not a problem unless it becomes a master (Matthew 6:24). The two masters that Jesus contrasted were not God and money, but God and *mammon* (*mammōnas*). Matthew used a Chaldean word, not the usual Greek word for money. And he used it to make a point.

We can better understand what Jesus was talking about if we look at other uses of this Chaldean word. In Luke 16:9 Jesus referred to the "mammon of unrighteousness," as if mammon and unrighteousness had something in common. In Luke 16:11 He repeated this idea:

> "If therefore ye have not been faithful in the unrighteous mam-
> mon, who will commit to your trust the true riches?"

Contrasted here are unrighteous mammon and true riches. Most of the time the word *money* is used in the New Testament it is the Greek word (*argurion*) that can also be translated as *pieces of silver*. The point is that *mammon* did not indicate simply money, but a particular kind of money, or a particular approach to money, even a particular view of economics.

Chaldea is another word for Babylon, so Jesus' use of this Chaldean word suggested the Babylonian approach or understanding of money, and the unrighteousness that was at the heart of Babylon. And since Babylon is most famous for its Tower of Babel, which could only have been a product of centralized governmental bureaucracy and taxation, let me suggest that Jesus was here discouraging the uses of Babylonian economics.[22]

---

22 *The Politics of Guilt and Pity*, by R. J. Rushdoony, Ross House Books, 1995,
    "Usury and Cosmic Impersonalism."

God was so singularly opposed to the Babel project that He put a quick and effective end to it (Genesis 10-11). Jesus knew this story. He knew the Scriptures, and the central struggles delineated in Scripture. And the perennial struggle against Babel and its godless and wicked ways, ways that were no doubt institutionalized through a particular use of and social approach to money. Why is money so important? Because it is the engine of civilization. Societies without money are simply not civilized.

Jesus' use of the term "unrighteous mammon" in Luke 16 suggests money that has been ill gotten, the profits of corruption and vice, or unrighteous taxation. Jesus had much to say about unrighteous tax collectors, publicans (*telōnēs*), or tax farmers, who oppressed ordinary people by over taxing them. This was a common theme for Jesus.

Of course, Jesus was not opposed to taxation *per se*, He was opposed to the abuse of taxation. Nor was Jesus opposed to the use of money, He was opposed to the abuse of money. Jesus was not opposed to wealth or business or profits or interest. He was opposed to the abuse of these things. When these things interfere with God's ways, God's purposes, God's concerns, when wealth or money is gained unrighteously or by unrighteous or immoral means, it is tainted with mammon.

And yet, such corruption was so much a part of the culture of the ancient Middle East that Jesus did not recommend fighting against those who had unrighteous power or money. Rather, He recommended that His people learn to deal with it, to befriend those engaged in unrighteous mammon, but not to further their cause, not to help them be corrupt. Take their money if they gave it, sure! But don't use it as they would use it. Rather, receive what is unrighteous and use it for the furtherance of righteousness. As Paul said,

> "Do not be overcome by evil, but overcome evil with good" (Romans 12:21).

Jesus further directed Christians to

> "make friends for yourselves by means of unrighteous wealth (*mammon*), so that when it fails they may receive you into the eternal dwellings" (Luke 16:9).

Jesus knew that people cannot get away from financial graft and corruption. It is woven into our social structures. Nonetheless, Christians are not to engage in unrighteous financial dealings or practices. But when the profits of such practices are freely given, we are to receive them and use them for good.

This does not mean receiving stolen goods or encouraging shady deals—not at all! It means being *in* the world but not *of* the world, living in the midst of corruption, but not practicing it. When Christians actively practice worldliness they become as tainted by worldliness as anyone else. While we must live in it—we have no choice, we must not be *of* it. It must not define who we are.

HEART

"For where your treasure is, there your heart will be also" (v. 21).

If your treasure, your wealth, your money is caught up in unrighteousness, so will your heart be. We cannot earn our living unrighteously and at the same time serve God righteously. The most common and most powerful source of godlessness is the love of money. And it is the love that makes the money unrighteous because money is not an appropriate object of love. The love of money both personifies money and depersonalizes love. It results in the wrong understanding and use of money and the wrong understanding and use of love.

An implication of this is that an effective way to recover from faith-lessness is, not to worry about the state of your heart, but to focus on the state of your finances. Jesus said that our hearts will follow where our pocketbooks lead. Wherever our money is, wherever we invest our money, or our time, or our interests, is where our hearts will follow. The converse is also true, but Jesus put it this particular way.

And this is simply common sense. *Think about it*, said Jesus. *Where your money is, your hearts will follow.* So, if you want to love God, invest in Him, invest in the things He likes. If you want a revival or a reformation, if we want people to turn to the Lord, we need to fund the things that will bring revival and reformation. Conversely, if God's people don't fund these things, who will? If we want an increase of righteousness, we need to encourage the things that teach and promote righteousness.

Jesus said that our hearts will be with our treasure. And while we can legitimately argue that Jesus was talking about the things that we value in a general way, it cannot be disputed that the Greek word (*thēsauros*) means wealth. How we handle money is a good indicator of our values. *So,* said Jesus, *invest your money in things that promote and* encourage the growth and expansion of the kingdom of God on earth as it is in heaven.

18. Eye Light

*The eye is the lamp of the body. So, if your eye is healthy, your
whole body will be full of light, but if your eye is bad, your
whole body will be full of darkness. If then the light in you is
darkness, how great is the darkness!*   *—Matthew 6:22-23*

How is an eye like a lamp? First, does *eye* (*ophthalmos*) mean
eyeball? Yes, it can. The Greek word also implies vision, as in
the act of seeing as opposed to the organ of sight. And figuratively it can even suggest envy, from the idea of casting a jealous or
furtive side glance. It can be used to describe someone looking enviously
or jealously at someone or something. To eye a thing is to look long-
ingly at it, which is more of a facial expression than a process of seeing.
We'll come back to this idea.

Second, does the Greek word *luchnos* mean lamp or light? Again, it
can mean both. It often refers to a portable lamp or a candle. It indicates
a means of illumination.

Now notice that verse 22 is not a comparison between an eye and a
light. Rather, it is a direct statement.

"The eye is the lamp of the body" (v. 22).

It seems to suggest a comparison between an eye and a lamp, but it does
not actually compare them. It equates them. The Authorized Version
says it this way:

"The light of the body is the eye."

Logically, the phrase tells us that the eye, or the way the body sees,
its vision or perspective, and the "light of the body" (whatever that
means!) are equivalent. The context is odd in that both before and after

196

these verses about eyes and light are texts pertaining to money and wealth. Some commentators have suggested that we have a collection of unrelated texts. But I'm going to dismiss that idea in favor of maintaining that the Bible was put together in a way that makes sense, that there is a purpose for the order of the verses. If Jesus' sermon here was simply a collection of stories and sayings, there would be no reason for these particular verses (22-23) to be in this particular place. But God doesn't do things for no reason. So, we will assume that there is a good reason for them to be here, and that these verses about vision illuminate the larger theme that Jesus was talking about regarding discipleship and money.

In order to do that we are going to take these verses literally—not in a wooden sense, but in the sense that they simply mean what they say. Rather than adjusting the meaning of the words to conform to our understanding, we will adjust our understanding to conform to the meaning of the words. We'll begin by looking at the bodily organ known as the eye.

INWARD/OUTWARD

What do we know about the eye? The eye has transparent tissue (lens) through which light passes and strikes photo sensing cells at the back of the eyeball, which communicate electrical impulses to the brain. That is as much of the physical apparatus that we need to know to make the point that light enters the eye. The direction of the light flow is into the eye. That's how we see. Reflected light from objects comes into the eye and the brain interprets the electrical impulses as being whatever objects we have defined them to be. The eye sees by taking in light.

When we put this idea back into Jesus' phrase in verse 22, "The eye is the lamp of the body," we have a difficulty because Jesus was not using the eye in this literal, biological, functional way, where light comes into the eye. Rather, Jesus said that the eye is a lamp or light. The difference is that the eye takes light in and a lamp projects light out. The direction of the flow of the light is opposite of what we would expect from a literal understanding of eye. But we don't want to deny this ordinary function of the eye because it may yet be related to Jesus' point. So, let's keep in mind the idea that the eye receives light, but set it aside for the moment.

We turn now to the Greek word translated as lamp or light (*luchnos*). This word describes a small source of light that is distinguished from the sun, moon, and stars. Think of a lamp or candle. Its purpose and most distinguishing feature is that it illuminates. Light shines out from it. The direction of light flow for a lamp is outward and away from the source, unlike the eye, wherein light flows inward.

We are left with the question, how can an eye, which receives light, be like a lamp, which projects light? This dichotomy is at the center of the point that Jesus is making. What the eye and the lamp have in common is that they are both central to the process of sight or vision.

PERCEPTION

Visual perception is the ability to interpret information and surroundings from visible light in such a way as to discern or distinguish objects or patterns. In order to discern or distinguish objects or patterns in our visual field we need to have in place a contextual web of relevant conceptual analysis—language and understanding. Without a relevant context for understanding a thing or a pattern, people will be blind to it, even when it is in plain sight. We need to know what we are looking at or looking for in order to actually see it.

If people don't know or don't understand what they are looking for (or looking at), they won't be able to see it. They won't know what to differentiate it from so that it stands out as a particular thing or object in their field of vision. This phenomenon operates like an optical illusion or camouflage.

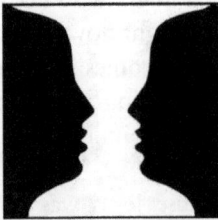

1	2	3	4	5	6	7	8	9	10
11	12	13	14	15	16	17	18	19	20
21	22	23	24	25	26	27	28	29	30
31	32	33	34	35	36	37	38	39	40
41	42	43	44	45	46	47	48	49	50
51	52	53	54	55	56	57	58	59	60
61	62	63	64	65	66	67	68	69	70
71	72	73	74	75	76	77	78	79	80
81	82	83	84	85	86	87	88	89	90
91	92	93	94	95	96	97	98	99	100

There are various kinds of optical illusions that trick the eye into seeing what is not there, or not seeing what is actually there. Like the picture of the woman's face and the vase (left, above), people don't see two images until they know that there are two images to see. Once we know that we can shift our perception between them.

Or think of columns of numbers. To find patterns in the numbers we must know some basic math—addition, subtraction, multiplication, and division. If we don't know math, we won't see any patterns that may exist. And the more math we know the more patterns we will be able to see. And conversely, the less math we know the fewer patterns we will see. Our knowledge of math reveals the patterns that otherwise are not seen. Our knowledge projects various patterns on the columns of numbers.

This idea comes into play here because Jesus spoke quite a bit about blindness, about the necessity of having eyes to see. Nicodemus asked Jesus what He was teaching.

> "Jesus answered him, 'Truly, truly, I say to you, unless one is
> born again he cannot see the kingdom of God.' Nicodemus said
> to him, 'How can a man be born when he is old? Can he enter a
> second time into his mother's womb and be born?' Jesus an-
> swered, 'Truly, truly, I say to you, unless one is born of water and
> the Spirit, he cannot enter the kingdom of God'" (John 3:3-5).

Jesus suggested that Nicodemus could not *see* the kingdom of God because he was not born again. Whereupon Nicodemus admitted that he had no idea what Jesus was talking about. And Jesus concluded by stating the obvious, the necessity of regeneration. The point was that Nicodemus couldn't see what Jesus was pointing out, and Jesus couldn't show it to him apart from Nicodemus' regeneration. Nicodemus needed new eyes, a different conceptual framework that would illuminate the kingdom of God.

In another telling exchange with some Pharisees, Jesus said,

> "'For judgment I came into this world, that those who do not see
> may see, and those who see may become blind.' Some of the
> Pharisees near him heard these things, and said to him, 'Are we
> also blind?' Jesus said to them, 'If you were blind, you would have
> no guilt; but now that you say, "We see," your guilt remains'"
> (John 9:39-41).

Here Jesus said that his mission was to make the blind see and the sighted blind. How odd is that? How does that work? How can some people see a thing and some not see it?

To understand this, we need to put Jesus Christ in context. Jesus Christ, who manifested the reality of the long-awaited Jewish Messiah, is Himself the key to unlocking or understanding the Bible. Scripture is only properly understood by the regenerate in the light of Christ through trinitarian eyes. Apart from these things God is not revealed in the Bible.

VEIL

Remember that Paul accused the Jews of not being able to understand God's biblical law because God had imposed upon them a veil that hid the true meaning of the law from them.[23]

> "Yes, to this day whenever Moses is read a veil lies over their hearts" (2 Corinthians 3:15).

This veil blinded the Jews to the truth of their own Scriptures, and that blindness resulted in many difficulties, much social disease, and various abnormalities. Apart from Christ they could not be who God had created them to be because the manifestation of Jesus Christ is the necessary context for the biblical reality.

The source of the Jewish difficulties—the veil that darkened the understanding of the Jews—is the theology of monotheism, the belief that only one God exists. Please listen carefully so that you don't misunderstand or misconstrue what I'm saying. Pure monotheism is dominated by a concept of the universality of God found in the Abrahamic traditions, usually identified as Judaism, Christianity, and Islam. But this is inaccurate because it fails to differentiate Christianity as Trinitarian, which is a kind of monotheism, but so different that neither Judaism nor Islam recognize it as being monotheistic. The point is that monotheism apart from Christ is false, that both Islam and Judaism fail to understand God as Trinitarian, and therefore fail to understand the most unique thing that defines God. To miss the Trinitarianism of God is to miss God entirely!

The idea of monotheism has also been identified as the Platonic concept of God as put forward by Pseudo-Dionysius the Areopagite, who was a "Christian" Neoplatonist who wrote in the late fifth or early sixth century. He transposed in a thoroughly original way the whole of Pagan Neoplatonism from Plotinus to Proclus (of the Platonic Academy in Athens) into a distinctively new and original Christian context.[24]

Christianity and Platonism were thus philosophically identified as being equivalent. This is problematic because it equates this Platonic and Pagan idea of monotheism with the biblical idea of monotheism apart from Christ, which means apart from the Trinity. Platonic philosophy failed to conceive of or understand Trinitarianism, and therefore failed to understand its own classic philosophical problem of the one and the

---

23 See *Varsy Arsy—Proclaiming the Gospel in First Corinthians*, Phillip A. Ross, Pilgrim Platform, Marietta, Ohio, 2009, pgs. 58-59, etc.

24 http://plato.stanford.edu/entries/pseudo-dionysius-areopagite/

many. Islam found itself delighted with Platonic philosophy because it understands itself as being perfectly rational and denies Christ's divinity. So, the understanding of monotheism in Greek terms satisfied the Islamic understanding of monotheism. Judaism also rejects Trinitarianism for the same reason. And yet this Greek understanding of monotheism has been applied to Christianity for thousands of years by academics as if it is the only or the best way to describe or understand Christianity. But it categorically fails to do justice to the Trinity.

I'm suggesting two things here: First, that the Old Testament idea of monotheism is the source for monotheistic ideas found in the various world cultures. Old Testament ideas about God found their way into various cultures across the globe because the universal character of God is true, and because all humanity and culture issued from Adam, and following the Flood, from Noah. And second, that this Old Testament idea of monotheism actually is the same as the Greek idea of God. And third, this Old Testament, Greek idea of monotheism has been imposed upon New Testament Christianity in contradistinction to the revelation of Jesus Christ that is necessary for the genuinely biblical understanding of God as Trinitarian. Trinitarianism cannot be understood apart from believing that Jesus Christ is actually the Son of God, as being divine.

Therefore, all non-Christian understandings of monotheism are fundamentally Greek in character. The scholars have always allowed Plato and Aristotle to define God, rather than Scripture because they have always assumed the fundamentality of Greek categories of thought. Another way to say this is that Platonic monotheism is responsible for errantly coloring Christian theology with this Pagan view of monotheism and occluding the revelation of the Trinity very early in Christian history. The Greek philosophical categories are dualistic and not Trinitarian, and are therefore inadequate to the revelation of the Trinitarian reality of the only actual God who exists. The Trinitarian God cannot be adequately identified with the dualistic categories of philosophical investigation.

It should also be noted that some forms of Hinduism are also philosophically monotheistic in the same way that Judaism and Islam are philosophically monotheistic, because none of them see Scripture in the light of Christ. Again, in all likelihood, the Jewish roots of monotheism predate the Greek and Hindu versions, and if the biblical history is correct, it seeded them both. It could not be otherwise because the finer elements or aspects of the Trinity did not and could not come into view until the manifestation of Jesus Christ as God's Messiah.

The reality of the Trinity can only be seen against the historical backdrop of biblical monotheism because the Trinity actually is a kind of monotheism. Christian monotheism is Trinitarian. The one are three, the three is one. In Christ, and only in Christ, is God manifest as Father, Son, and Holy Spirit. For the most part the Trinitarian aspects of God have been historically explained with the categories of Greek philosophy —substance, essence, Christ's dual nature, etc. And the overwhelming conclusion of the philosophers has been that the Trinity defies explanation and is a mystery, which are both true.

However, studies by recent theologians have penetrated the shroud of this mystery by denying the wisdom of classic Greek academics and paying closer attention to the biblical texts in the light of Christ.[25] It's not so much that the Greek philosophical categories are wrong, but that they are inadequate to the reality of God. Greek dualistic categories paint their adherents into ultimately opposing corners that leave many biblical texts inadequately explained or simply denied. Greek dualism produces dichotomous thinking in the face of holistic or unified biblical themes.

CHRISTIAN CONTEXT

How did we come to the Trinity in this discussion? We were talking about Jesus' comment that the

"eye is the lamp of the body" (v. 22).

We noted that visual perception means that light comes into the eye, but that the idea of a lamp means that light goes out from the lamp. And yet, Jesus equated the eye and the lamp. Jesus holds together the idea that light comes into the eye with the idea that light goes out from the eye, like light from a lamp. He tells us that both are true.

People don't understand this and so they deny the richness of the text by choosing to understand that Jesus was talking about the function of the eyeball, when He was actually talking about the church, the *body* of Christ. We can see this when we compare the Authorized Version translation of this verse with the English Standard Version translation and notice that the word order has been reversed.

"The light of the body is the eye" (AV).

---

25 See the work of Cornelius Van Til (www.vantil.info), *The one and the many: Studies in the philosophy of order and ultimacy*, by R.J. Rushdoony, Ross House Books, 1971, and various works by Peter Leithart and Ralph Smith.

"The eye is the lamp of the body" (ESV).

Subject and object in the respective sentences are reversed. In the Authorized Version the light of the body is the subject, while in the English Standard Version the eye is the subject. The subject of a sentence is the main thing under discussion. So, these two versions depict Jesus as talking about different subjects. Is this really true? And if so, what does it mean?

It is also of significance that the Greek word translated as *body* is *sōma*, and not *sarx*. As you know, the word *body* can be understood in various ways. It can mean the flesh and blood of an individual, or it can mean many people cooperating together as a group, like a corporate body. In our discussion of Christ's body in 1 Corinthians 11, we determined that Paul's use of the word *sōma* rather than *sarx* in the communion liturgy was significant.[26] While we don't want to play down the importance of Christ's individual body (*sarx*) that was given as a sacrificial propitiation for human sin, neither do we want to ignore the implications of Christ's corporate body (*sōma*) or the body of Christian believers regarding the covenantal celebration of the Lord's Supper. Through communion the *sarx* (body) of the Lord becomes the *sōma* (body) of the church.

The *body* of verse 22 refers to the *sōma* of the church by the power and presence of the Holy Spirit through regeneration and the mystery of the Lord's Supper. This suggests that the light of the body that Jesus was talking about is the vision of the church.

"The light of the body is the eye" (AV).

Grant that Jesus meant that the vision of the church is the eye. What eye? Remember, the eye both receives (takes light in) and projects (shines light out). The eye is the organ of sight, the organ of perception. The eye sees objects for analysis. But the mind must also understand in order for the eye to be able to see what is in front of it. Without understanding, without a contextual web of conceptual understanding, what is sometimes called worldview, the eye can't recognize what it sees. And not recognizing a thing, it fails to see it. Without the proper context and categories of understanding, what the eye sees is simply ignored because the mind cannot make anything of it.

---

26 See the discussion of "Body" in *Arsy Varsy—Reclaiming the Gospel in First Corinthians*, by Phillip A. Ross, Pilgrim Platform, 2008, p. 211.

Was Jesus saying that the vision of the church is the means by which to see? Was He saying that the vision of the church is the means by which the world can be properly understood? I believe He was. He was not simply talking about me and my eyeball, or you and yours, but about us and ability to perceive reality.

What does it mean to talk about *our* eye as being *single*? Jesus continued,

> "The light of the body is the eye: if therefore thine eye be single,
> thy whole body shall be full of light" (v. 22—AV).

He drew a conclusion: *if therefore.* He was saying that if or when this is the case—that the light of the body is the eye, then the eye must certainly be... what? The Authorized Version reads "single." The English Standard Version reads "healthy." The Greek word is *haplous*, and means folded together or mixed into a single thing. And figuratively it means clear, without confusion or parts. When the separate ingredients of a cake get mixed and baked, they become one thing—the cake.

Given all of this, then, it seems that Jesus was saying that when we perceive His vision of the church, of the body of Christ, the vision He was presenting in this Sermon on the Mount, there is clarity and unity in what is seen. The various elements of this Sermon on the Mount become one vision of the church. When the mind is informed by the Holy Spirit through regeneration it projects a unified understanding of the world as defined by God through Scripture upon what it sees, and thereby—and only thereby—can we see the world as God has defined it. The eye is single, the vision is unified, the understanding is comprehensive, and the whole body of believers is so filled with the light of Christ that they radiate God's truth, goodness, and beauty.

Darkness

> "But if your eye is bad, your whole body will be full of darkness.
> If then the light in you is darkness, how great is the darkness!" (v.
> 23).

If our eye... whose eye? *Ours*, both ours as individuals and ours corporately as the body of Christ. If our eye is *bad* (*ponēros*), or evil, wicked, diseased, or hurtful, then that's another story. *Ponēros* does not mean evil or wicked in terms of character, but evil and wicked in terms of its effect or influence. So, He was talking about our eye or vision having a bad effect or influence. When the vision of the church is not complete, whole, or Trinitarian, it fails to communicate God's will for His people. And when that is the case, there is darkness, not light.

When we don't see God's truth, goodness, and beauty expressed in the church, as the church and through the church, in the fullness of the Trinitarian reality, our eye or vision is bad. It is bad when God's truth, goodness, and beauty are not there, or when we fail to see them—either way. When we can't see things properly (as defined by God), when we fail to see the Trinity, darkness fills our whole body. It is not that we just can't see well, it is that we—individually and corporately—are full of darkness, which means that there is no light in us at all. This is an all or nothing deal. If we see the Trinity, He brings light to everything we think, say, and do because God applies to everything. And if we don't see the Trinity, He brings darkness to everything because God applies to nothing. There is no middle ground regarding Jesus' teaching of the singularity of the eye, the unity of the vision of the body of Christ, the Trinitarian reality of God.

The vision of the church is either full of light or it is full of darkness. Either the light overflows or the darkness overflows from the body of Christ. The church plays the role in society that the eye plays in the body. It leads and directs. All information comes through it, or is understood in its terms. Like it or not, realize it or not, the church steers society, either in the light of Christ or in the dark. It always has, and it always will. That is the function of the church.

WORLDVIEW

So, do these verses pertain to how we as individuals see the world? Yes, we are to see the world in the light of Christ. Do these verses pertain to how the church is seen by the world? Yes, the church is to be seen and understood in the light of Christ. Do these verses pertain to how the church views itself and its mission? Yes. Do these verses pertain to how the world is to see or understand the church and her mission? Yes, in the light of Christ the church is unified or single, and her mission to the world is to be unified and whole in its purpose. All of these things, these various perspectives, are true at the same time and all together. This is what Jesus was talking about here.

The implications of this understanding of the singularity of the eye or vision of the church from a Trinitarian perspective are both deep and wide. Jesus was saying that in order to see the truth of Scripture we must bring faith to the text. We must believe that the Bible is completely true and trustworthy, that God actually created the world in six days, that

Mary actually was a virgin, that Christ was an actual Person who lived and died on a cross at Calvary, and that He actually rose from the dead, etc.

While all of these truths are plainly set forth in the Bible, people without faith cannot see them rightly. Why not? Because people must bring faith to Scripture. Faith enlightens the Scriptures and reveals the Trinitarian God. Apart from faith, apart from the regeneration that brings it, these biblical truths are hidden in plain sight.

This insight that Jesus taught in these two verses was not randomly placed here. Rather, it is foundational to His teachings in His Sermon on the Mount. Some scholars have doubted whether the Sermon on the Mount was intended to have application for Christians this side of Jesus' return because it demands a morality that seems impossible. We have determined here that it is to be applied among all who have ears to hear and eyes to see. And it cannot be applied by those who don't see or understand it. So, if *you* understand what Jesus is talking about, it is for you—right now! But if someone doesn't understand it, how could they ever apply it?

Jesus' words are indeed for us who are alive right now. They are for Christ's people now and always. And while it may be impossible for us to live up to them on our own merits, it is not impossible for God, who gives His people faith through regeneration. Our job is to be faithful to whatever little knowledge and understanding of God's Word that we have, to live in obedience to what we understand, with the full and certain hope that as more people live in the light of Christ, more light will shine forth from Christ's church.

19. Too Little Anxious Faith

*No one can serve two masters, for either he will hate the one
and love the other, or he will be devoted to the one and despise
the other. You cannot serve God and money. Therefore I tell
you, do not be anxious about your life, what you will eat or
what you will drink, nor about your body, what you will put
on. Is not life more than food, and the body more than
clothing? Look at the birds of the air: they neither sow nor reap
nor gather into barns, and yet your heavenly Father feeds them.
Are you not of more value than they? And which of you by
being anxious can add a single hour to his span of life? And
why are you anxious about clothing? Consider the lilies of the
field, how they grow: they neither toil nor spin, yet I tell you,
even Solomon in all his glory was not arrayed like one of these.
But if God so clothes the grass of the field, which today is alive
and tomorrow is thrown into the oven, will he not much more
clothe you, O you of little faith?*   —Matthew 6:24-30

It is impossible for two ultimate authorities to rule in our lives at the
same time. The two masters (*kurios*) that Jesus mentioned here
should be translated as *lords*. Of the 748 times this word is used in
the New Testament (Authorized Version), 728 of them are translated as
lord. Of course, the use of the word *lord* does not always point to Jesus
Christ, but it usually does. So such a consideration should not be ruled
out. In this case, Jesus was using the master/slave relationship to illustrate
a point about the God/person relationship. And this means that whatever sense we make of the verse must point to God.

The idea of authority necessarily points out the hierarchical character of authority. Authority must ultimately issue from a single source,

and where there are competing authorities or sources, the ultimate power of all authority is undermined. The definition and character of authority always necessarily require complete allegiance or obedience, otherwise it is not ultimately authoritative. At its root, authority is the power to enforce. So, to have two masters or lords—two gods—is to have two different agencies of enforcement in conflict. The idea of ultimate authority is necessarily totalitarian. In order to be authoritative, one must command the others. Paul's question about Belial applies:

> "What accord has Christ with Belial? Or what portion does a believer share with an unbeliever" (2 Corinthians 6:15)?

The only thing that limits authority is its area of jurisdiction. Jurisdiction is the area or sphere in which an authority has legitimate operation or power to enforce its decisions. And the jurisdiction of a master over a slave is total, as is the jurisdiction of the Lord (*kurios*). And that is the point Jesus was making. Ultimate authority and power must issue from a single source. The nature of humanity, both individually and corporately, requires and depends upon authority. All knowledge, wisdom, power, and government issue from the idea of authority, and authority requires submission and not mere agreement.

The Bible insists on two things regarding authority. First, that all authority belongs to God, that God is the author of all authority. And second, that human authority, a kind of sub-authority under God, be divided into various limited areas in order to counteract the errors and dangers of human sin. The more authority sinful people have, the more they tend to take advantage of their authority for themselves, for their own purposes, which tends to subvert justice and righteousness in favor of personal bias. Only God has ultimate authority, and God has given all authority to Jesus Christ (Matthew 28:18, etc.). So, only Christ has ultimate authority or universal jurisdiction. All other jurisdictions are limited.

CONSCIENCE

And what are these limited areas of jurisdiction? The first one is conscience. Under Christ and in submission to the authority of Jesus Christ is the authority or jurisdiction of personal conscience. This is described in chapter 20, *Of Christian Liberty, and Liberty of Conscience* of the *Westminster Confession of Faith*. It pertains to personal beliefs and behaviors in the light of Christ. In Christ there is real freedom, but it is not the ultimate freedom to do or think whatever we want. We are not God. Rather, it is the freedom, the obligation of conscience, to know, understand, and abide by the Law of Christ (1 Corinthians 9:21, Galatians 6:2). Rejection of the Law of Christ means that the prior law of Moses has jurisdiction (Acts 13:38-39) in matters of conscience. Why does it revert to Mosaic law? Because Moses was the previous covenant Head of humanity.

Conformity to one's conscience is first and foremost personal. People must be free to engage and exercise matters of personal conscience as an expression of freedom under God. This freedom is self-evident and unalienable. It was given by God as a part of our creation. And the first determination of conscience involves one's own membership in Christ's church.

Here we are talking about Christ's universal, invisible, triumphant, and eschatalogical church, not His particular, visible, militant, and historic churches. Membership in this universal church is a matter of conscience or correct motivation. We might also call it a personal relationship with Jesus Christ. And, of course, only God can read our true motivations. And He does! Membership in this church does not depend upon elders or courts, but upon one's own personal, subjective, private confession of sin and faith in Christ. It cannot be faked because God can read our true motivations, and no one on earth has access to these church records. They are kept by God.

But that does not mean that we cannot observe the fruit of conscience. Indeed, it is impossible for people to hide it. Oh, some people are able to disguise it for a while, but truth always wins out and reveals itself (Matthew 7:16). Our seed, whether faithful or not, eventually blooms and produces fruit for all to see. Conscience always produces consequences in the world.

FAMILY, CHURCH, STATE

The other areas of human authority or jurisdiction are: family, church, and civil government (state). Each area of authority or jurisdiction is unique and independent, except at the immediate boundaries between them. At those boundary areas there is some overlap or porosity, where one jurisdiction may have to cooperate with another in order to insure that God's will is done. Families and churches, that is heads of households and elders must cooperate regarding various issues and concerns—for instance, baptism and communion. The family cannot simply insist that the church either baptize or serve communion to any of its members. Nor can the church invade the family and instigate these sacraments apart from active and willing participation by the head of the household. Nor can the church project its various responsibilities upon the state, or abdicate them. Nor can the state usurp or presume upon itself the authority, mission, or jurisdiction of the church. The separations must be maintained through cooperation under God.

The founders of the United States did indeed have the right idea about the separation of the jurisdictions of the church and the state, but failing to constitutionally incorporate the ultimate jurisdiction of Jesus Christ, to whom all authority has been given, their efforts and hopes for civil government have not had the requisite authority, stamina, or clarity to withstand the corrosive acids of sin. By fixing the ultimate authority of the Constitution in an amorphous, deistic, and inadequately crafted idea of god (non-trinitarian), alluding to, but essentially apart from, the Bible, the apex of ultimate authority in the United States has remained unclear. Over time what little clarity it had has diminished as it has suffered the vicissitudes of sin. That is to say that the idea of one master has not reigned supreme according to the highest civil law of the United States.

Consequently, this concern about two masters in verse 24 has in fact haunted American history and has served to undermine all authority in these United States since its inception. I mean that the balance of power in the United States has always been a function of power, influence, and politics, and has intentionally excluded the Christ of Scripture.

As long as we are one nation under God, and the god whom we are under remains a matter of personal interpretation because it is not clearly stated, the authority of civil government is not an ultimate authority but a relative authority, a political authority. And it is relative to the first jurisdiction below that of God Himself—conscience, or as most people prefer to call it personal opinion. As long as civil government fails to clearly name and abide by the authority and jurisdiction of Jesus Christ according to Scripture, it must necessarily abide by the authority and jurisdiction of personal conscience, or perhaps a collection or aggregate of such personal perspectives (political parties). In such a case, civil government becomes a matter of votes and power politics, with all of the various problems associated thereunto.

The only way that our government can work is for the various jurisdictions of authority to honor and maintain their biblical limits, which has not been the case in the United States for generations. This means that any honest, objective public discussion of this issue (Christ's role in civil government, or two masters) will be at best incredibly difficult because those who have significant public voice today have very unbiblical ideas about authority, jurisdiction, and power. And to attempt to force the perspective I am here presenting into the existing categories of understanding or the system of legal practice that currently exists can only twist and distort these biblical ideas beyond their biblical definitions and applications. What is required to even consider what I am suggesting here is a completely different mindset and worldview, different assumptions about the nature of reality, different from the reigning secularism that currently dominates American values and politics, different even than most interpretations of Christianity.

Two Masters

When Jesus said that no one can serve two masters He also meant that everyone can actually serve only one master, only one Lord. One source of ultimate authority will necessarily prevail. And while this verse does not say it here, Matthew meant that the one and only Lord is Jesus Christ. He then told us why this is necessary:

> "for either he will hate the one and love the other, or he will be
> devoted to the one and despise the other" (v. 24).

The division of ultimate loyalties (authority or jurisdiction) always breeds divisiveness and hate because both masters cannot be completely and entirely honored at the same time. Divided loyalties force the birth of hate and the children of hate:

> "quarreling, jealousy, anger, hostility, slander, gossip, conceit, and
> disorder" (2 Corinthians 12:20).

At the ultimate level this is manifest as Satan's rebellion against the authority of God. And it doesn't matter how Satan manifests himself because all failure to honor God's ultimate authority contributes to Satan's cause by undermining God's authority, because it undermines the idea of ultimate loyalty.

To understand what Jesus actually said regarding two masters requires us to look at the literal meaning of the words, *one* and *other* in verse 24. Jesus said that

> "he will hate the one (*heis*) and love the other" (*heteros*).

The *one* (*heis*) is a reference, not only to one of the two masters, but in particular to the one that is dominant—the One, the one that actually represents the idea of oneness or ultimate unity. It is a reference to God.

The *other* (*heteros*) is defined as different from the one. *Hetero* is the opposite of *homo*, which means *same*. And the opposite of *same* is *different*.

When two masters vie for the loyalty of one slave, the conflict produces both love and hate. Because the master/slave relationship means ultimate and complete loyalty, the slave does not have a middle ground between the two masters. A slave cannot be loyal to both, and justifies his loyalty for one or the other by hating the one he does not love. The choice to hate the *one* (*heis*) requires loving the *other* (*heteros*). The association between *hate* and *one* and *love* and *other* in this verse are significant. It suggests that divided loyalties produce the hatred of oneness and the love of otherness, or hating God and loving that which has no reference to God, to loving otherness.

Why does this issue resolve into ultimate categories? Two reasons. First, the two masters (*kurios*) under consideration are gods according to the illustration. In addition, the primary definition of the Hebrew word *ba'al* in the Old Testament is master, and *ba'al* is identified as a false god. This conflict between the true God and false gods is a common Old Testament theme to which this idea refers. Second, the idea of a master/slave relationship implies ultimate human loyalties, or complete submission and obedience.

Consequently, the introduction of a competing authority here suggests the introduction of a false god. *And,* said Jesus, *when such a false god is introduced, the person will naturally find the idea intriguing —interesting.* He will be attracted to it. In other words, he will love it, where love is defined as a natural attraction. And because his attraction has shifted from the *one* to the *other*, and because the issue is ultimate loyalty, he will simultaneously hate his first master (the *one*), as he shifts loyalty to the *other* as a way of justifying the change of loyalty.

We can think of loyalty as a kind of rock that we have in our possession. Loyalty is always defined as all or nothing because relative loyalty is not loyalty. In Jesus' story the first character's ultimate loyalty was to God, the Creator of the Universe and everything in it. He gave his loyalty-rock to God as an expression of his love and devotion to Him. But when an *other* was introduced, he found himself naturally attracted to this *other*, and took his loyalty-rock from God (hate Him) and gave it to the *other* (love him). Only one master can hold a loyalty-rock because loyalty means all or nothing, and there is only one ultimate rock. Humanity, both individually and corporately, cannot abide two masters, two ultimate loyalties, to ultimate authorities, two gods (or more). Then cementing the idea of the introduction of a false god into the hearts and minds of men, Jesus concluded this verse by saying,

"You cannot serve God and money"(or mammon, v. 24).

This was discussed a couple of chapters ago, where we saw that the idea of mammon amounts to a false or untrustworthy kind of money, or a false approach to money, even a false view of economics.[27] Mammon was a synonym for Babylon and the errors of Babylon. We cannot serve the God of Scripture and the values of Babylon. In the Bible Babylon always represents that which is opposed (*heteros*) to God. And that is Jesus' point.

DON'T WORRY

Verse 25 begins with a conclusion, "Therefore...." The conclusion regarding what Jesus had said about praying (Matthew 6:9), forgiving (Matthew 6:14-15), fasting (Matthew 6:16-17), saving or money (Matthew 6:19-21), the singularity of the light of the body (Matthew 6:22-23) and the importance of having only one Lord (Matthew 6:24) is not to worry. The Authorized Version renders v. 25,

"Take no thought for your life."

Don't think about these things. Then He listed the things not to worry about: food and drink, clothing, and length of life. Calvin suggested that this was a healthcare plan, that Jesus' purpose was to reduce the health problems that result from excessive worry, or what we call stress. Whatever health problems you have, stress makes them worse.

> "Therefore I tell you, do not be anxious about your life, what you
> will eat or what you will drink, nor about your body, what you
> will put on. Is not life more than food, and the body more than
> clothing? Look at the birds of the air: they neither sow nor reap
> nor gather into barns, and yet your heavenly Father feeds them.
> Are you not of more value than they? And which of you by be-
> ing anxious can add a single hour to his span of life? And why are
> you anxious about clothing? Consider the lilies of the field, how
> they grow: they neither toil nor spin, yet I tell you, even
> Solomon in all his glory was not arrayed like one of these. But if
> God so clothes the grass of the field, which today is alive and to-
> morrow is thrown into the oven, will he not much more clothe
> you?" (vs. 25-30).

---

27 See "Mammon," page 192.

Calvin also suggested that we not take this idea literally and abandon all worry, but that we engage care or worry moderately. I think he was wrong in this. This is not what Jesus was saying. But I also understand the truth of what Calvin was saying. He knew that people worry. He also knew that without worry or care it seems that nothing would ever get done. Worry is often the cause of planning. Here's some of what Calvin said,

> "Hence it is easy to learn, how far we ought to be anxious about food. Each of us ought to labor, as far as his calling requires and the Lord commands; and each of us ought to be led by his own wants to call upon God. Such anxiety holds an intermediate place between indolent carelessness and the unnecessary torments by which unbelievers kill themselves. But if we give proper attention to the words of Christ, we shall find, that he does not forbid every kind of care, but only what arises from distrust."[28]

A better translation of the Greek word rendered *worry* or *care* (*merimnaō*) might be *distraction*. Jesus' point was that we should not get distracted by the most basic things of life: food and drink, clothing, or length of life. Jesus didn't mean that it might be okay to get a little distracted by them now and then. He meant that we should not get distracted by them at all.

> "Which of you by being anxious can add a single hour to his span of life?" (v. 27).

But Calvin was also right. We should neither neglect doing the things that are necessary for life, nor should we worry ourselves sick about them. The contrast here is not between a little worry and a lot of worry, but between worry and action. Jesus was telling us that God has so arranged the world that we simply need to be who God has created us to be, and the basics will take care of themselves. The issue here is not with the basic things taking care of themselves, but with our being who God has created us to be. When the birds do what birds do, when lilies do what lilies do, when grass does what grass does, all is well. So, people just need to do what God created people to do, which does not involve sin, and the basics will take care of themselves.

This is not a call for a *laissez-faire* attitude of *que sera sera*, whatever will be will be. It is not a call to drift aimlessly through life looking to our random circumstances to provide for our needs. Jesus was not a

---

28 *Calvin's Commentaries*, Matthew 6:25, public domain.

Hippie, bumming life at His Father's expense. No! This is a call to faithfulness, a call to discover our own God-given gifts and talents in Christ
and to engage them fully toward the fulfillment of God's purposes.
When people engage the gifts and talents that God has given them, and
use them for God's purposes, not our own, our basic needs will be so
taken care of that they will be of no concern. It would be like a rich
person worrying about his next meal.

However, for this to happen as God has planned it means that
everyone needs to get on board and do their part. Jesus was not simply
teaching life skills to individuals. He was teaching life skills to His
Church, to communities, to humanity. When He said,

> "Which of you (*humōn*) ...?" (v. 27)

it was the plural you. *Which of y'all by being anxious can add a single
hour to his span of life? None of you can do that, but all of you must do
this: be not anxious.*

Keep in mind that this is only half a thought so far. Jesus was not
finished with this idea about worrying. There are two parts to it. First,
He tells us what not to do—that's where we are now. And second, He
will tell us what to do. That comes soon (v. 33). We are not there yet.
But before we get to the second part, we need to finish the first part.

Matthew closed verse 30 with the Greek word—*oligopistos*. It is
translated as an exclamation:

> "O you of little faith" (v. 30).

The Greek word is actually composed of two words: *oligo*—few
and *pistos*—faith. We best know *oligo* when it is used in the English
word *oligarchy*, or rule by a few. In the same way, Jesus was saying faith
by a few. It is an odd expression and the word seems to be out of
context. So, the translators thought it must be an exclamation of frustration, as if to say, *Boy! You guys are sure small minded* or *little believers*
or *puny Christians!* As if to suggest that small-mindedness leads to
worry. And while that is true, there is more to this exclamation than
that.

The exclamation was undoubtedly a kind of criticism, but it also
suggested a correction. The problem was that too few people were practicing Christianity, and Jesus' exclamation pointed to this fact. While we
can argue that Jesus was criticizing the size of the faith in the community, that each Christian needed to be more faithful. We can also argue
that He was criticizing the size of the community of the faith.

In order for Christianity to work as the engine of science, technology, and capitalism for society at large there needs to be sufficient numbers of people practicing Christianity. Christianity produces an increase of individual and corporate honesty and integrity that are necessary for social development or progress. Sufficient numbers of people need to be actively and faithfully practicing their God-given gifts and talents in the righteousness of Jesus Christ. Jesus may have been pointing to the fact of what we call critical mass regarding the development of Christianity and its fruit—science, technology, and economic development. The critical mass argument has application to both individuals and groups, and requires both personal and corporate honesty and integrity at the minimum.

CRITICAL MASS

While salvation comes by grace alone, Christian growth and maturity come by work. I don't mean that we can force growth and maturity in grace by working at it, which would simply be works-righteousness. But rather I mean that God leads His people into work that is ideally suited for them through their gifts (1 Corinthians 12) and for the accomplishment of His purposes. So, the Lord Himself is actually the engine of Christian growth and maturity.

While this growth and maturity come about through His inspiration, they come about through our (human) perspiration, our effort. In addition, growth comes in fits and starts. The way that Christian growth works is that for long periods of time it seems like nothing is happening, and then suddenly we learn or "get" (understand) something significant, and our understanding takes a giant step forward. A critical mass is reached and suddenly we are forced to reorganize ourselves and our work habits (jobs) around some new insight or breakthrough. Science goes through a similar process. A scientific theory holds sway until a critical mass of unexplained phenomena mount up. At some point those unexplained phenomena suggest a better theory, and the whole of science is reorganized around the better theory.

The same kind of thing happens in churches. At a certain point a kind of critical mass is reached and the church lurches forward in one way or another, regarding growth in terms of membership or understanding. This pattern of reaching a critical mass that then requires some sort of restructuring happens all the time in various kinds of communities—governments, businesses, schools, etc.

It was in this way that Jesus' lamentation about the smallness of the belief of the disciples and/or the smallness of the believing community was also an anticipation and a longing for a kind of critical mass to be reached. He seems to have thought it was close at hand. He often said that the kingdom of God was at hand. He may have uttered this idea as a kind of call to spur on the disciples to continue their struggle to understand what He was talking about, and to engage the disciplines of discipleship and evangelism with greater commitment in the hope and for the glory of the coming kingdom.

Indeed, His exclamation, *O you of little faith (oligopistos)*, was at least three things. It served at least three purposes. First, it provided a call for intensified personal commitment and discipleship. Second, it provided a call to evangelism to grow the community or kingdom. And third, it was an expression of frustration because so many people misunderstood Him.[29] It wasn't until after His crucifixion and resurrection, and the dispensation of the Holy Spirit documented in the Book of Acts that people actually "got" the message.

It seems that those who "get" it don't need an explanation, and that no explanation is possible for those who don't. Understanding the gospel is a function of faith.

---

29 See, *Marking God's Word—Understanding Jesus*, by Phillip A. Ross, Pilgrim Platform, 2005.

20. Don't Worry!

Therefore do not be anxious, saying, 'What shall we eat?' or
'What shall we drink?' or 'What shall we wear?' For the
Gentiles seek after all these things, and your heavenly Father
knows that you need them all. But seek first the kingdom of
God and his righteousness, and all these things will be added to
you. Therefore do not be anxious about tomorrow, for
tomorrow will be anxious for itself. Sufficient for the day is its
own trouble. —Matthew 6:31-34

J esus here takes another swing at concluding this important argument. Repetition in the Bible is a way of calling attention to
something important. And verse 31 repeats the admonition of
verse 25, except that the *therefore* in verse 31 is not the same Greek
word as the *therefore* in verse 25. Nonetheless, they are equivalent, and
they introduce the same conclusion to the same argument.

"Therefore do not be anxious" (v. 31).

Again, there are two parts to Jesus' admonition about anxiety, the
negative part—don't do this, and a positive part—do this (v. 33).

"Be not anxious for your life" (American Standard Version). "Do
not worry about your life" (English Majority Text Version). "Be
not carefull for your life" (Geneva Bible).

The idea is not to get distracted by the mundane concerns of life—food
and clothing. It is not that these things are unimportant. They are very
important. And I suppose that is why people tend to worry about them.
So, why does Jesus tell us not to worry about them? In order to under-

stand why this is so important, we must see this negative part in the light of its corresponding positive part found in verse 33:

> "But seek first the kingdom of God and his righteousness, and all these things will be added to you."

Doing what we are not to do—worry—gets in the way of doing what we are supposed to do—seek God and His righteousness.

Do This

Pursuing the kingdom of God is to be the top priority of every Christian, and we are not to get distracted from it. The first thing to notice is that it is very easy to get distracted from our pursuit of God's kingdom. In fact, the very things that we require for life itself—food and clothing—are the very things that most distract us from the concerns of God.

These concerns are always with us. We never outgrow our need for food and clothing, and when we neglect them, they immediately assert their importance and their demands upon us. We constantly get hungry and our clothes wear out. People who are caught in poverty spend their whole lives in active pursuit of these very things, and their poverty insures that they never get beyond these priorities because if they neglect them, they will suffer and perhaps die. The poor are consumed with their efforts to secure adequate food and clothing, and those efforts tend to keep them from pursuing the kingdom of God.

Poverty is a rut that individuals are not easily extracted from. And that is the issue here, at least part of it. Jesus was addressing the concerns of the poor, of those who are barely able to feed themselves. They work and toil on these mundane concerns and never get ahead. The rudimentary concerns of food and clothing capture their attention and time, such that it eclipses any time and attention that might be spent pursuing the kingdom of God. They are afraid to look up from the demands of the daily grind for fear of loosing whatever gains they think they have made.

This, however, is not merely a concern of the poor. Many other people find themselves locked in issues about food and clothing. It is a natural consequence of our humanity. Here it is not so much that people cannot afford to do anything else. Middle class people do it out of force of habit. But the wealthy seem to have been captured by pride and self-concern, which then serve as blinders that keep only these things in sight. Such people often (usually) fancy themselves to have "taste" and "refinement," and they spend much of their time preening and developing their tastes for fine wine, various delicacies, and fancy clothes. They tend to think that they are important, that they deserve to be pampered with such dandification. This is a different problem, but it has the same root and the same result. It is a product of deception and leaves no time or concern for God.

God knows about these temptations. They are universal. That's what Jesus meant when He said that

"the Gentiles seek after all these things" (v. 32).

These are the things that occupy the time and attention of the godless, of those who ignore, hate, and despise God. Those who don't care about Him don't think about Him. Concerns about food, drink, and clothing are not only universally common to all people, but they equally distract everyone away from God's remedy for the human condition.

INVERSION

Jesus explicitly told us to *not* focus on certain things. And when we do focus on them, they lead us away from Him. We tend to think that solving the problems of adequate and appropriate food and clothing contributes to our success in life. But it doesn't. It impedes it, according to Jesus. God knows that we need these things, and He will not fail to provide them. But He also knows that these bodily needs are secondary to our primary spiritual needs. Worldly people invert the order of these needs and think that people must have their bodily needs met before they can pay attention to their spiritual needs.

But that is wrong, according to Jesus. Our first and most primary need is the kingdom of God and His righteousness. And furthermore, by seeking these things, we will actually provide for our bodily needs as a byproduct of the development of God's kingdom and righteousness. How so? God's kingdom is driven by Christ's righteousness, which manifests in Christ's people as genuine love, honor, commitment, honesty, and integrity. These things—qualities, actually—provide the foundation for the development our God-given gifts and abilities so that we can be of service to Jesus Christ with what we call work (calling, occupation, career).

Let me say that again: Christ's righteousness produces love, honor, commitment, honesty and integrity, which are the basis for the development of our God-given gifts and talents, which are the means of human production. All of these things are the necessary ingredients for sustainable Christian capitalism.[30]

Inasmuch as we are distracted and dominated by our immediate bodily needs, we fail to trust that God will supply those needs. And not trusting God, we cut ourselves off from His grace and blessings. It becomes a self-fulfilling prophecy. Our self-concern constitutes a decision to not trust God. Christ's remedy for the problem of being distracted by our bodily concerns is the same for everyone, the poor, the rich, and the middle classes. Everyone needs to concern themselves with being who God has created them to be. Everyone has a calling in Christ. Our primary concern is to be the people that God created us to be, individually and collectively. And what precisely are we to be?

RIGHTEOUSNESS

"Seek first the kingdom of God and his righteousness" (v. 33).

We are to seek God's righteousness by endeavoring to be righteous ourselves. Seeking the kingdom of God is the destination or end, and seeking God's righteousness is the means to that end. So, here Jesus provides both means and end for solving this problem of excessive worry about our basic needs, this problem of being distracted from our primary purpose. He provides the means for joyful, productive, sustainable, and abundant human life on this earth. Our central purpose, our central aim and goal of life is to seek the kingdom of God and His righteousness. And one of the primary obstacles to this is worry and concern about our bodily needs. The problem is that people do whatever it takes to supply those needs, and too often it takes them away from God's righteousness and the virtues and values of God's kingdom. Self-concern distracts people from engaging this higher calling.

So, how can people do this? How can people drop their concerns about having adequate food and clothing, especially the poor! If you are barely able to feed and clothe yourself, how can you just stop doing the things that you are doing that provide for your next meal. How can the poor escape the rut in which they are trapped? How can people who are barely making ends meet stop worrying about how to make ends meet? Hasn't Jesus saddled His people with an impossible task here? It seems that way to many people.

---

30 Christian capitalism is capitalism that is guided by and dominated by genuine Christian virtues and values—love of God and service to Jesus Christ. It is not to be confused with secular capitalism.

However, the Lord does not require the impossible, unless He Himself will provide what is necessary. We can also say that the Lord always requires the impossible in order to force us to rely upon Him to provide it.

So, is trusting God some kind of magic trick? No, not at all. Well, there is a trick to it, but it's not magic. In order for God's plan to work, people—lots of people, not merely isolated individuals—must actually be the people that God created them to be, and to do so without sin (or with increasingly less sin). That is, people must actually seek first the kingdom of God. People must actually want what God actually provides.

And what is the kingdom of God? It is God's people living in His likeness, His righteousness. And what is God's righteousness? What does it mean to live in God's righteousness? How do people do that? Only through obedience to Christ by and through the grace of God.

So, is this a problem because we cannot *make* it happen to ourselves or to anyone else? We can only rely upon the grace of God to make it happen. If you are still engaged in what I am saying, if you understand what I'm talking about, it is probable that God's grace is already in your life. So, how do we know if God has graced us? Here's what Jesus said,

> "seek first the kingdom of God and his righteousness, and all
> these things will be added to you" (v. 33).

This is the answer. If we can actually seek the kingdom and right-eousness of God, we can do so only because of His grace which has already been given to us. God enables people to seek Him. There are three elements that we need to consider here:

1) wanting to do it,
2) engaging the process and
3) accomplishing it.

WANTING

The first element is the most important, and Jesus acknowledged its primary importance by calling it the first thing—seek first the kingdom of God and His righteousness. We are to *seek* (*zēteō*) it. This is an interesting Greek word. It is a Jewish idiom that means to worship. The object of worship—God—is implied because of the monotheism of the Jews. All worship was to be directed to Jehovah. The word also means to desire or endeavor, to inquire or require, and, of course, to seek or pursue.

To do any of this requires first that we actually want to do it. If a person doesn't *want* to engage this effort, it will not work. To fail to actually want to seek the Lord and His righteousness means at best that any engagement of it will be halfhearted and apart from the grace of God. So, if you actually want to do this, you are more than half way there because you cannot want it apart from God having already given you the desire. If you have the desire, you can trust God to complete what He began in you. If you actually have the desire, God has given it to you by His grace, and you will accomplish it by His grace through your faith, your effort.

I'm not suggesting that this is a team effort between you and God, or that success depends upon your effort. No, God does not require your effort or your faith to accomplish His purposes. God does it all, but He does it through our faith. He uses *our* faith as the means of *His* accomplishment. He gives us the faith. Then He gives us the desire. Then He gives us the opportunity and success. And it all happens with our willing cooperation. God could have chosen a different way to accomplish this, but He didn't.

Analogously, a person may have an opportunity to go to Europe, but lack the means. Or he may have both the opportunity and the means, but lack the desire. In order to insure His success, God provides all of the requisite elements.

Seeking God's *righteousness* (*dikaiosunē*) always involves God's grace. We have no righteousness of our own and there is nothing in our character from which righteousness can be built, forged, constructed, or grown. Getting righteousness from human beings is like getting blood from a proverbial turnip. It just can't happen. That's why we need Jesus. That's why it cannot be done apart from Christ. So, this seeking begins with Jesus Christ, who

"came to seek and to save the lost" (Luke 19:10).

We are only able to seek Him because

"He first loved us" (1 John 4:19).

He leads, we follow. He came to earth for the salvation of His people. That happened a long time ago. It is water under the bridge. It already happened. His grace has already been given. It's already a done deal.

If you understand this, you are probably already on board. But if you chafe at it, and doubt it, and find yourself contravening it, you are probably not on board (saved). But it is not my call that determines whether or not you move forward in grace. That's between you and Jesus. If you actually want what God actually provides, you probably already have it. If you doubt it, you probably don't. This is the need for personal faith that Jesus repeatedly spoke of. And that is why we must each take it up with Jesus.

ENGAGING

Let's suppose that you are on board God's grace train, that God has actually given you His grace. You actually desire to live by God's wisdom, and are ready to move forward to the next step, which is engaging it. What does it mean to engage God's righteousness? It means living according to God's Word. It is both simple and complex. There is a lot to it, a lot of implications and applications. And yet, it is never more than simple agreement with God.

God said,

> "all have sinned and fall short of the glory of God" (Romans 3:23).

All have sinned, therefore, you and I are sinners. God also said,

> "by grace you have been saved through faith. And this is not your own doing; it is the gift of God" (Ephesians 2:8).

Therefore, people are saved by grace through faith. Because you are reading or hearing these words, they are directed to you personally, this thought has been planted in your mind.

God said,

> "the fruit of the Spirit is love, joy, peace, patience, kindness, goodness, faithfulness, gentleness, self-control" (Galatians 5:22).

Therefore, these are the things that we are to engage. God said,

> "that the unrighteous will not inherit the kingdom of God ... neither the sexually immoral, nor idolaters, nor adulterers, nor men who practice homosexuality, nor thieves, nor the greedy, nor drunkards, nor revilers, nor swindlers will inherit the kingdom of God" (1 Corinthians 6:9-10).

Nor will enslavers, liars or perjurers (1 Timothy 1:10). Therefore, these are the things to avoid. None of this is difficult to understand. The Contemporary English Version puts it this way,

"But more than anything else, put God's work first and do what
he wants. Then the other things will be yours as well" (v. 33).

In verse 34, for the fifth time in ten verses, Jesus repeated the directive to not be anxious (v. 25, 27, 28, 31, 34). This may be the most
repeated directive He ever gave. Repetition signifies importance. But
why did Jesus give this idea of not worrying so much attention? Why is
it so important? Because it may be the most common method of faithlessness, the most common way of being distracted away from the
things that God says are important.

The contrast here is not between a little worry and a lot of worry.
He did not mean that we should worry in moderation. He said that
worrying is itself an act of faithlessness. The actual contrast is between
worrying and working. The solution to the problem of having sufficient
food and clothing is to work, not to worry. Work is the cure for worry.
Inasmuch as people work, they will have adequate food and clothing—
and not have the time or the need for worry. Work is therapeutic.

Of course, several other problems can enter the equation and goof
things up. People can be poor money managers, and run out of money.
Or people can get waylaid by drugs and alcohol, and spend food money
on these things. Or people can just have poor values and waste their
money on all sorts of distractions. But in general, people who work have
their basic needs taken care of. They have the means to supply their
basic needs. And that's the point.

Accomplishing

But when we add to this point that people are to be the kind of
people that God created them to be, they will excel in honesty,
integrity, and competence in some work related area (calling, occupation, career). This is a function of righteousness and God's gifts—spiritual gifts or gifts of the spirit per 1 Corinthians 12. When these things
are seriously engaged, people begin earning more than minimum
wages. When people work at jobs they love and are uniquely suited for,
and work with honesty, integrity, and purpose, they excel. And
excelling, they succeed. They make more money. And this is also part of
the Lord's point. When people are engaged in this way, food and
clothing—basic life needs—are simply not an issue. God supplies them,
not magically but through the economy (*oikos*).

This negative admonition not to worry is a positive call to work
excellence and advancement, which is the engine of Christian capi-

talism. The additional money that people earn from their competence and excellence serves as capital for investment and expansion. Economic growth is the result.

> "Seek ye first the kingdom of God, and his righteousness; and all these things shall be added unto you. Take therefore no thought for the morrow: for the morrow shall take thought for the things of itself. Sufficient unto the day is the evil thereof" (vs. 33-34).

The root of the Greek word *tomorrow* (*aurion*) is based on a root that means breeze or morning air. There are two Greek words that are translated as *tomorrow*. One of them (*epaurion*) is better understood as the next day, in the sense of one day following another. The other word, used in verse 34 (*aurion*), is more like *mañana*, in the sense of an indefinite time in the future. When people use the word *mañana* it suggests a kind of procrastination. And this is the sense that Jesus means here. He was saying, *Don't think in terms of mañana. Don't engage in procrastination.* Don't put things off until tomorrow because tomorrow never comes. It's always in the future. And Jesus insists that life happens in the present—do these things: seek God and His righteousness. Don't procrastinate. Don't put Him—God—off. Don't think that you can get to God's priorities tomorrow—*mañana*. If you put it off today, you will likely put it off tomorrow, as well.

The chapter ends with these words:

> "Sufficient for the day is its own trouble" (v. 34).

By this Jesus meant that each day has sufficient difficulties, troubles, and evil without adding to it by procrastinating about getting around to being the person that God wants you to be. When people put God's priorities off until tomorrow—*mañana!*—they are actually adding to the difficulties that will come upon them in the future. If you don't do today what must be done today, then it must be done tomorrow, along with all of the other stuff that needs to be done tomorrow. Procrastination today makes tomorrow all the more difficult. The habit of procrastination adds difficulty to difficulty. It makes life much more difficult than it actually is because it undermines work and integrity.

So, said Jesus, don't do this—worry. Rather, do this—seek the Lord and His righteousness. And don't wait until tomorrow. Do it now! Begin today!

21. Taking Heed

Judge not, that you be not judged. For with the judgment you pronounce you will be judged, and with the measure you use it will be measured to you. Why do you see the speck that is in your brother's eye, but do not notice the log that is in your own eye? Or how can you say to your brother, 'Let me take the speck out of your eye,' when there is the log in your own eye? You hypocrite, first take the log out of your own eye, and then you will see clearly to take the speck out of your brother's eye. Do not give dogs what is holy, and do not throw your pearls before pigs, lest they trample them underfoot and turn to attack you. Ask, and it will be given to you; seek, and you will find; knock, and it will be opened to you. For everyone who asks receives, and the one who seeks finds, and to the one who knocks it will be opened. Or which one of you, if his son asks him for bread, will give him a stone? Or if he asks for a fish, will give him a serpent? If you then, who are evil, know how to give good gifts to your children, how much more will your Father who is in heaven give good things to those who ask him!
                                                  —Matthew 7:1-11

Was Jesus politically correct in His condemnation against judging others? No. The politically correct interpretation of this verse is a modern interpolation of its meaning. While this verse does caution us about imposing our own values on others, it does not negate the idea of social values that do in fact apply to everyone. This verse is not about the negation of standards, but demands that we stop dissing one another. It insists that we stop assuming the worst of people, of casting aspersions upon one another. It forbids the

habit of putting people in a negative light, of falsely implying too great
a variance regarding social norms, of falsely implying that people are
beyond the pale. It forbids us to be overly suspicious of others because
suspicion undermines love.

This verse introduces a teaching section that concludes with what
we know as the Golden Rule,

> "whatever you wish that others would do to you, do also to
> them" (v. 12).

We would do well to understand the Golden Rule as not simply verse
12, but verses 1-12. To limit the Golden Rule to verse 12 is to invite the
same kind of misinterpretation that political correctness applies to verse
1—the abandonment of all social standards. The Golden Rule is not
about the abandonment of social standards, nor the replacement of
objective, social standards by individual, subjective standards.

The idea of not judging others means that we should not be
narrow-minded. Narrow-mindedness issues from a lack of graciousness
and toleration of viewpoints that are different from one's own. Nor does
the Golden Rule mean that whatever sins I want to engage should be
foisted upon others in the name of love. It does not mean to do the
sinful things to others that I want them to do to me.

The idea behind verse 1 is to refrain from using one's own subjective judgment and values as the standard by which all people should be
judged. I don't want to be judged on the basis of your preferences, nor
do you want to be judged on the basis of mine. That, however, does not
mean that there are no social standards by which all people are to be
judged. Indeed, the Bible insists that there are such standards. To withhold my standards does not mean withholding all standards. And it is the
abandonment of all universal social standards that constitutes the error of
political correctness. Nowhere does Jesus suggest the abandonment of
God's law. And everywhere Jesus reinforces the universal standards of
biblical law.

Judging Others

The problem with judging others on the basis of our own opinions,
preferences, and values is that is disrupts the fabric of social conformity
and trust that are essential for community harmony, not to mention
commerce and economic development. Currency and contracts require
individual honesty and integrity, and conformity to various objectively
true and mutually agreed upon social laws and customs that support

consistency and continuity. When the value of currency fluctuates too wildly or the trustworthiness of contracts is subject to personal whims, personal preferences, or personal values, societies loose the character and consistency that are required for sustainable economic development.

Indeed, verse 1 is a statement against the use of personal, subjective values as the criteria for making judgments about other people, or suggesting that other people cannot be trusted. That kind of judgment is not for individuals to make, but is to be a function of laws and courts, where people can get fair and just treatment.

We are not to taint the character of other people on the basis of our own views and values. Nonetheless, because all kinds of judgments must necessarily be made every day about all kinds of things, including people, verse 1 is, by implication, a statement of the necessity of using objective, or socially agreed upon universal values for all such judgments.

Judging others in the sense in which Jesus here forbids is a matter of not imposing our own morality upon others. But neither is it a matter of suspending all morality. Rather, the idea is that we are all to submit ourselves to biblical morality as the socially accepted morality for community standards because biblical morality is God's determination, not our own.

Life without moral standards is simply intolerable. Indeed, modern life would collapse, and is collapsing as various efforts are engaged to eliminate biblical moral standards from modern society. The point is that Jesus' command to judge not does not mean the suspension of all moral standards. Rather, it means bringing God's standards to bear, not on other people, but on one's self first and foremost. This caution about judging others is primarily a demand for self-judgment. Let's see how this idea develops in these verses. Verse 2 brings this idea front and center.

> "For with the judgment you pronounce you will be judged, and
> with the measure you use it will be measured to you" (v. 2).

Whatever standard for moral judgment we use on others will also be used on us. This idea reinforces the necessity for common standards that are mutually agreed upon because we must be willing to submit to whatever standards we impose upon others. If we want honesty and integrity from others, we must exercise honesty and integrity ourselves.

When the disciples asked Jesus about His parables, and how they should understand them, He said,

> "Pay attention to what you hear: with the measure you use, it will
> be measured to you, and still more will be added to you" (Mark
> 4:24).

Here Jesus alluded, not simply to moral standards and judgments, but
suggested the idea of just weights and measures that are required for
commerce and contracts. We are reminded of Proverbs 20:10:

> "Unequal weights and unequal measures are both alike an abomi-
> nation to the Lord."

And the demands of the Levitical Law:

> "When a stranger sojourns with you in your land, you shall not
> do him wrong. You shall treat the stranger who sojourns with
> you as the native among you, and you shall love him as yourself,
> for you were strangers in the land of Egypt: I am the Lord your
> God. You shall do no wrong in judgment, in measures of length
> or weight or quantity. You shall have just balances, just weights,
> a just ephah, and a just hin: I am the Lord your God, who
> brought you out of the land of Egypt. And you shall observe all
> my statutes and all my rules, and do them: I am the Lord" (Leviti-
> cus 19:33-37).

Note the insistence on one common law for all people, and its relationship to commerce and contracts.

In verse 3 Jesus points us to the central problem regarding this issue
of falsely judging others:

> "Why do you see the speck that is in your brother's eye, but do
> not notice the log that is in your own eye?"

Paul said the same thing to the Romans. After pointing out the wickedness of their own hearts in Romans 1, Paul concluded:

> "Therefore you have no excuse, O man, every one of you who
> judges. For in passing judgment on another you condemn your-
> self, because you, the judge, practice the very same things" (Ro-
> mans 2:1).

The spec is a mote (*karphos*) in the Authorized Version, and means a
dry twig or straw, which is contrasted to a log or beam (*dokos*) or
timber. These are not to be understood as different things, as if the
problem with your eye is different than the problem with mine. Rather,
these are to be understood as the same kind of problem, only one is
larger than the other.

HYPOCRISY

We all tend to notice the small problems with other people, and ignore the same things in ourselves, even when it is much worse. Here we find a kind of blindness. We easily find flaws in the ways that other people see things, but fail to find much greater flaws in our own way of seeing things. We are far too sensitive and concerned about the sins of others, and far to insensitive and unconcerned about our own sins.

The issue under discussion is human sinfulness, and how it pertains to judging others. People are far too eager to judge the sins of others and to ignore their own. And there are two common solutions to this problem, both of which are equally wrong. One is to ignore all sin and/or believe that the idea of sin is itself false. The other solution is the one that Jesus mentioned here, that of denying one's own sin while carping about the sins of others. The solution to this problem seems to be self-awareness. Jesus asked,

> "how can you say to your brother, 'Let me take the speck out of
> your eye,' when there is the log in your own eye? You hypocrite,
> first take the log out of your own eye, and then you will see
> clearly to take the speck out of your brother's eye" (vs. 4-5).

But can self-awareness cure hypocrisy? It cannot, even though the cure involves self-awareness. Hypocrisy is a kind of false or incomplete belief. The hypocrite thinks he is something he is not. He says one thing, but fails to act on it because he does not believe what he says he believes. As an expression of belief that is not supported by real conviction, hypocrites confess to believe something, but don't behave like they believe it. Sometimes people are aware of this conflict and do it anyway in order to secure for themselves some perceived advantage. And sometimes people are simply blind to their actual beliefs and actions. People often fail to see the conflict between what they say and what they do. Hypocrisy is a kind of psychological denial.

The difficulty with Jesus' recommended treatment for the log in one's own eye is that it cannot actually be done. We cannot work in our own organ of sight because we need our eye to see the log, but the log is in *our* eye. Yet, it is not in our field of perception. Indeed, the very idea of having a log in one's eye is so absurd that it forces us to under-stand it as an analogy. A log is larger than an eye. For the most part, an individual cannot even carry a log. A beam or log or timber can be larger than a person. The very idea of getting a log into or out of an eye is simply absurd. But the analogy isn't.

The analogy suggests that people are plagued with a problem that is larger than themselves, and not within their own subjective field of vision. It suggests a problem that is beyond their ability to fix. Jesus was pointing to a problem of perception that is related to sin and judgment. It is a problem that is so big and so close that it cannot even be seen. We can easily see it in others, but not in ourselves.

And yet He said that we should first take the log out of *our own* eye. We are instructed to do what we cannot do. And only when we have solved this problem for ourselves will we be able to help anyone else. First, we must solve our own problems of perception, sin, and judgment. And only then can we be of help to others with their perception, sin, and judgment problems.

Again, the central problem, which is not simply about motes and logs but is about judging and the Golden Rule, is false belief—hypocrisy. That is the context for these verses. Calvin thought that verse 6 is not related to the verses around it. Of verse 6 Calvin said that

> "Matthew gives us here detached sentences, which ought not to
> be viewed as a continued discourse. The present instruction is not
> at all connected with what came immediately before, but is en-
> tirely separate from it."[31]

I disagree. Let me explain. Jesus had just given an impossible instruction to remove the log from our own eye. This impossible instruction throws us on the grace and mercy of God, who alone can cure people of eye-log blindness. How can we do for ourselves what Jesus demands? We cannot! Curing this blindness falls to the prerogative of God—or not.

Calvin's explanation here is that we are commanded to preach the gospel to every creature (Mark 16:15), whether they like it or not (2 Corinthians 2:16).

> "The remedy of salvation must be refused to none, till they have
> rejected it so basely when offered to them, as to make it evident
> that they are reprobate and self-condemned."[32]

According to Calvin's argument here, once people have provided evidence that they are reprobate and self-condemned, then we can withhold the gospel. But prior to that, the gospel must be preached to all people indiscriminately. And Calvin is right about this, but this is not

---

31 *Calvin's Commentaries*, Matthew 7:6, public domain.
32 Ibid.

what Jesus was saying here. Again, this section cannot be understood literally or woodenly, but is subject to analogy.

The image that Jesus gave us about dogs and pigs is that of giving something of value to someone who cannot appreciate it.[33] His eye is all logged up. Being a dog or a pig, he cannot see or understand the gospel rightly, and we cannot help. The point that Jesus was making here is that we ought not to try to help those who are completely blind to the gospel—dogs and pigs. Receiving the gospel is not something that one human being can do for another. The gospel cannot be given to those who are blind to it. And if people insist on making the effort, they may get hurt. They may get trampled under foot or torn to pieces in the process. Why? Because the gospel is the stench of death to those who reject it, and their rejection can at times be violent.

EVANGELICAL HYPOCRITES

This is a caution about the dangers of evangelism. But who is Jesus talking to? He is talking to hypocrites, to people who believe falsely, people who fail to live up to what they confess. From the beginning of this chapter, He has been addressing unbelievers, people who had not yet understood what He had been talking about. In verse 2 He warned them that their false judgment against others would bite them back. In verse 4 He said that the log in their own eye would render them unable to help anyone else. And here in verse 6 He told them not to give what is holy to dogs or pigs.

But how would these people even know what is holy? The problem that He has been pointing out is that these hypocrites—and he was talking to His own disciples here—had no idea about what was actually holy. Hypocrites believe falsely or incompletely. They don't understand, though they pretend to, and that is the problem here.

When hypocrites instruct unbelievers in the things of God, they are likely to get hurt, trampled, or torn asunder. Hypocrites use the right religious words, so there is a sense that they are communicating something holy. But they don't actually know what they are talking about. They are self-deceived at best and liars at worst. The point is that self-deceived liars make poor evangelists of God's truth. The best they can do is to pretend to believe God's truth. But even unbelievers can spot a

---

33 This image is likely an allusion to Israel, but the application of it pertains to all who are blind to the gospel, whose minds are veiled. See *John's Miracles—Seeing Beyond Our Expectations*, Phillip A. Ross, Pilgrim Platform, Marietta, Ohio, 2019.

phony, and often they can do so better than other phonies who are caught up in phoniness themselves.

Phonies can fool other phonies, but they can't fool real believers or real unbelievers. So, when a phony believer tries to witness to an actual believer, the believer will call him on his phoniness, turn the tables and present him with the real gospel. But when a phony believer tries to witness to an actual unbeliever the unbeliever will be offended by the gospel and will figuratively tear the presenter apart. This is the danger that Jesus was talking about here, and it is very much connected with the verses that surround it.

GOSPEL

The issue in this section is how the gospel works. Paul said that

> "the gospel … is the power of God for salvation to everyone who believes" (Romans 1:16).

To those

> "who are being saved it (the gospel) is the power of God."

But is

> "folly to those who are perishing" (1 Corinthians 1:18).

So, how is the power of the gospel communicated? How is it received? If Paul was right—and he was—how is it that the gospel is so often preached or shared, but has so little effect?

Jesus was saying here in these first verses of chapter seven that His own disciples, at that point, were not only in danger of being ineffective in their evangelism efforts, but that they were in danger of being hurt or killed because they themselves were indiscriminately throwing—casting —the gospel at people who had no idea what they were talking about.

At this point the disciples were simply not ready to evangelize others. They had yet to assimilate themselves what Jesus had taught them. It is a curiosity that new believers are often eager to share what little they know with everyone they know, indiscriminately, and that the churches so easily encourage it.

Sure, new believers have gone from darkness to light, from death to life. Their hearts have been quickened, and they are overflowing with new insights, new visions, new revelations about all kinds of things. But for the most part, they don't really have any idea what they are talking about. They have more enthusiasm than wisdom, and that is a dangerous situation, said Jesus.

So, what was needed? What did the disciples need to keep them from this danger? Well, they were not in a position to instruct others. What they needed was instruction themselves. But have you ever tried to instruct someone who either didn't want to be instructed or who didn't think that he needed it? Instruction doesn't go well unless people actually want it, or at least are open to it. This is what it means to cast pearls before swine.

So, Jesus told them what they needed to do.

> "Ask, and it will be given to you; seek, and you will find; knock, and it will be opened to you" (v. 7).

You gotta wanna! They needed to inquire of the Lord themselves. Christianity is not a bunch of people telling others about God. Christianity is a bunch of people seriously inquiring about God themselves. Christianity is asking, seeking, and knocking. To be a Christian is to be consumed by the passion to learn about God, and to know Jesus Christ. And where we learn about God and Jesus is in the Bible.

EVANGELISM

Evangelism is not telling people what you know about God. It is confessing what you don't know, but that you know where to look. Evangelism is not instructing others about God, it is an invitation to look together for what only God can teach. It often seems that contemporary Christianity is primarily focused on this kind of broadcast evangelism, of telling others what *we* think, and of hiding our own ignorance.

But the truth is that most churches are struggling, and struggling churches often determine on their own that they need more members. They employ focus groups and ask themselves what they need. Or they take their focus groups to the heathen and ask the heathen what they think the churches need. They then compile the responses and turn their attention to evangelism, to giving the heathen what *they* want, rather than giving them what *God* wants for them.

The difficulty with this procedure is that struggling churches don't actually suffer from a lack of members. That is not their real problem. Their real problem is a lack of sanctification, a lack of growth and maturity. So, when such churches begin to evangelize, they export what they have—focus on self, immaturity, and hypocrisy. And like attracts like.

In verse 6 Jesus cautioned such Christians and their churches about the dangers of such evangelism. And in verse 7 He provided the cure. He said that before we export the gospel, before we share our testimony and our faith, we must ask, seek, and knock *ourselves*. Many Christians mistakenly think that their own conversion provided such a drastic change of life and worldview for them that their initial conversion represents a kind of high water mark for their new life in Christ. But, while we don't want to disparage the significance of initial conversion, it must be noted that the confession of Christ is not the end or goal of Christianity, but only the beginning.

It must also be noted that all Christians begin their walk with Jesus in hypocrisy. Yes, becoming a Christian reveals hypocrisy. Why? Because new Christians do not yet fully know or understand the Lord or His Word or His ways. New Christians claim to be Christian, but their lives, habits, and worldviews have yet to mature into full conformity with the teachings of Jesus Christ. We must understand that hypocrisy is a stage of Christian growth and maturity that all Christians pass through as they continue along the long path of sanctification. Spiritual growth involves the confession of hypocrisy as part of its cure.

DIFFICULTIES

Paul told the Ephesians to not lose heart because of the difficulties that accompany faithfulness. He called them to trust their roots in Christ to provide them with the

> "strength to comprehend with all the saints what is the breadth
> and length and height and depth, and to know the love of Christ
> that surpasses knowledge, that you (they) may be filled with all
> the fullness of God" (Ephesians 3:18-19).

Paul was saying that the fullness of Christ and God's plans for the world were greater than they knew or could imagine, but that God would see them to completion. Jesus assured the disciples:

> "For everyone who asks receives, and the one who seeks finds,
> and to the one who knocks it will be opened" (v. 8).

In other words, they were at that time not fulfilling their responsibilities as Christians because they didn't yet even understand where the fullness of God was leading them. But they could trust the Lord to complete in them what He had begun, and that the finished product would be good and great and beautiful beyond their wildest imaginations.

But the point is that prior to the fulfillment of God's plan, Christians have to deal with issues of hypocrisy because we are not yet being and doing all that we will eventually be and do in the fullness of Christ. In this sense Christians are hypocrites. Were the disciples pretending to be Christians? Yes and no. They were real Christians, but lacked maturity. They aspired and confessed themselves to be more than they actually were. We also claim faithfulness. We are like Peter, who claimed allegiance to the Lord, but denied Him repeatedly despite his profession and genuine love of the Lord. Peter wept bitterly when he discovered his own hypocrisy (Luke 22:62), but it was part of his spiritual growth.[34] We are all children playing grownup games as we endeavor to be the people that God has called us to be. And our play is an important part of growing up in Christ.

Jesus knew the truth of their immaturity and difficulties—and ours. So, He called attention to it.

> "Or which one of you, if his son asks him for bread, will give him a stone? Or if he asks for a fish, will give him a serpent? If you then, who are evil, know how to give good gifts to your children, how much more will your Father who is in heaven give good things to those who ask him!" (vs. 9-11).

We who are evil (*ponēros*), who are calamitous, morally diseased, and culpable, we who are derelict, vicious, and wicked, we who are yet children in the Lord want what is best for our own children. And God, who knows so much more than we do, will not lead His children astray any more than we would lead our own children astray. *But,* said Jesus, *you must ask.* We must seek. We must inquire. We must study God's Word diligently in order to become what God has called us to be.

There are three traditional means by which God accomplishes His purposes—Word, sacrament, and miracle. While miracles do continue to happen, they are not God's ordinary means. While we may hope for a miracle, that hope should not dull our involvement with regard to God's ordinary means—Word and sacrament.

God, who is our heavenly Father, will give good gifts abundantly to those who ask. So, we ask. We investigate God's Word. We plumb its

---

34 *Peter's Vision of Christ's Purpose in First Peter*, Phillip A. Ross, Pilgrim Platform, Marietta, Ohio 2011; and *Peter's Vision of The End in Second Peter*, Phillip A. Ross, Pilgrim Platform, Marietta, Ohio, 2012.

depths and probe its heights. We share our insights and listen to the insights of others. And yet, we do not approach this task as an obligation to be accomplished as a method to gain salvation or to establish a relationship with Jesus Christ.

Rather, we engage it as a response to God's gift of salvation in the same way that a child engages his relationship with his father. The child is not trying to become his father's son, he is simply relating to his father as the son that he already is. Neither do we approach our study of God's Word as academicians, seeking to prove or disprove it. We must not come to Scripture with an open mind, but with our minds fixed steadfastly on Christ Jesus our Lord. We simply approach God's Word with faith. Great faith or little faith doesn't matter, the size of our faith is irrelevant. The only criteria that matters is that our faith, our response to God is genuine, that our trust is real, that our fealty is actual. But how can we know that our response, our faith, is real?

To seriously ask the question is to fail the test. Imagine a woman who is being pursued by a suitor who wants her hand in marriage. Her suitor then confides to her that he is wondering whether his love for her is the real thing. Does his quandary about his love for her assure her? Or trouble her?

Similarly, do our questions about our own faith, about our own love of God assure God? Or trouble Him? It's not that faithful people don't have questions—they do! It's that the questions and issues of faithful people do not dwell on their own doubts, their own faithfulness.

22. In Sheep's Clothing

*So whatever you wish that others would do to you, do also to
them, for this is the Law and the Prophets. Enter by the narrow
gate. For the gate is wide and the way is easy that leads to
destruction, and those who enter by it are many. For the gate is
narrow and the way is hard that leads to life, and those who
find it are few. Beware of false prophets, who come to you in
sheep's clothing but inwardly are ravenous wolves.*

—*Matthew 7:12-15*

Because Calvin does not find these verses in chapter seven to be
connected, but to be a collection of independent ideas garnered
from many of the Lord's sermons, he finds the word *therefore*,
which introduces verse 12, to be superfluous. But because these verses
are actually related, at least in terms of their presentation by Matthew,
regardless of whether they came from different sermons, the conclusion
of verse 12 adds additional meaning and force to the argument that
precedes it.

The fact that Matthew introduced this verse with the word *therefore* suggests that he understood it to conclude an argument. Yet, Calvin
insists that verse 12 be read independently from the verses that surround
it. John Gill suggested that Calvin misjudged this section, that verse 12 is
in fact a summation of the verses that precede it and even a summation
of the whole of Christian doctrine itself. I agree with Gill.

Verse 12 provides an important conclusion for the verses that
precede it. Jesus was saying that, because whatever judgment that we
use for others will be used on us by others, we should use the basis of
judgment for others that we want others to use on us. Whatever rules
you want applied to you, you must apply to others. Verse 12 is not

239

about personal preferences. So, it doesn't mean that I should give other people black coffee because I like black coffee. It's not about those kinds of likes and dislikes, but is better understood as a universal standard of morality or social behavior. We need to make moral evaluations and determinations about other people on the same basis that we want them to make moral evaluations and determinations about us.

Most contemporary people understand verse 12 (and Jesus generally) to teach that people should *not* judge one another. That argument is: that because people don't want to be judged or morally evaluated at all by others, they should not judge or morally evaluate others. But that is not at all what the Lord means! Jesus was not pressing for the suspension of morality in the name of pluralism. Jesus was not a broadminded multiculturalist. And, in opposition to Calvin, when we see these verses as the development of a well-honed argument, that door is closed.

We see this in the final phrase of verse 12,

"for this is the Law and the Prophets."

The "Law and the Prophets" is a traditional phrase that means the Old Testament. Jesus meant that verse 12 was suggesting nothing more than Old Testament morality. However, it must be noted that Jesus understood the Old Testament Christologically, as must we. Thus, He was not simply pointing to Old Testament morality *per se*, but to Old Testament morality in the light of Christ, without the veil that so blinds the Jews (and others).[35]

Rather than pointing to an undefined, amorphous, multicultural morality, as contemporary people have been misled to understand this verse, it actually provides the foundation for traditional Christian morality, where Christ is the apex of all authority and power. Christianity is not multicultural, nor is it unicultural. Rather, Christianity is trinicultural because it is Trinitarian. What does this mean? It means that Christian culture shares—dimly, darkly, and imperfectly—the characteristics of the Trinity. Christian culture is culture in Christ, who alone provides for unity in diversity and diversity in unity. Apart from Christ, culture falls into either the anarchy of multiculturalism or the tyranny of monoculturalism.

---

35 *The Wisdom of Jesus Christ in the Book of Proverbs*, Phillip A. Ross, Pilgrim Platform, Marietta, Ohio, 2006.

HEAL THYSELF

So far in chapter seven Jesus has talked about the necessity of the universality of moral judgment in the sense that the way to deal with the problem of immorality in other people is to deal with our own immorality. The solution to the problem of the immorality of society is to cure ourselves in Christ. If everyone would do this, the problem would be solved. What Jesus was saying is that we cannot fix other people. All we can actually do is fix ourselves. And because the fix we need is actually a function of God's grace, there's not much we can do in this regard either—except ask, seek, and knock, which He mentioned in verse 7. Let us not overlook the importance of such personal inquiry.

So, how are we to inquire of the Lord? By the narrow gate, and not by the wide or broad gate (v. 13). The contrast here is instructive. The Authorized Version calls the one strait and the other both wide and broad. The right way or gate is like a straitjacket in the sense that it is constraining. It limits our options. The narrow gate suggests humility and obedience. The narrow way of the Lord keeps people in the strait and narrow, which means conventional and law-abiding.

The broad way, by contrast, is unconventional, deviant, and law-abridging.[36] This broad gate leads to death and destruction. And what is more, Jesus said that many people go that way—not intentionally, of course. They are blinded by their pride and ignorance of Jesus Christ. And in contrast, the right way is

> "narrow and the way is hard that leads to life, and those who find
> it are *few*" (*oligos*, v. 14).

One way is easy and broad, as in broadminded, and lots of people go that way. This can only be the multicultural, unshockable way (Jeremiah 6:15). And it is more than simply wrong or misguided. It is deadly because it ignores the only remedy for sin, the uniqueness and exclusiveness of Jesus Christ! The other way—the right way—is hard and narrow, as in narrow-minded, and only a few people go that way. The right way is founded and grounded on the uniqueness and exclusiveness of Jesus Christ. The two alternatives couldn't be more different or more opposed to one another.

The difference between these two ways must also inform our evangelism. Christian evangelism must be guided and modeled on how

---

36 For more on this, see "Queer Theory" in *Peter's Vision of Christ's Mission in First Peter*, Phillip A. Ross, Pilgrim Platform, 2012.

people come into the Christian fold. And Christ tells us here that the only way to enter is by the narrow gate. He abjectly denies the value of the broad or wide gate, and tells us to avoid it. So, Christian evangelism must respect this fact.

INDIVIDUALLY

The narrow gate suggests that people can only enter one at a time. People are not brought into the kingdom of God by groups. All group-ings, all classifications or social distinctions are equally useless before Christ. In addition, the difference between the wide gate and the narrow gate does not suggest the number of people who will come into the kingdom. Rather, it suggests a difference in mindset between believers and unbelievers. All who enter into life in Christ come by the narrow gate, and all who enter by the wide gate enter, not into life in Christ, but into hypocrisy and death apart from Christ. The illustration of the two gates is not about how many people get into heaven. It is about how anyone gets to heaven. It is about the Christian mindset or worldview. Are Christians to be narrow-minded or broadminded? Are we to follow Christ alone or follow the crowd in unison? In some ways we are to be narrow-minded and in some ways we are not to be broad-minded.

Christians are to stick steadfastly to God's Word and God's way, and to do so narrow-mindedly, in the sense of keeping God and His Word as our primary focus. We are to

> "seek first the kingdom of God and his righteousness" (Matthew 6:33),

rigidly keeping to the teachings of Christ. We are to seek God's right-eousness by exercising righteousness ourselves—Christ's righteousness, not our own. And we do that by receiving and submitting to the right-eousness of Christ by grace through faith, by studying God's Word and adhering to it.

That is to be our narrow-minded focus. But with regard to applying God's law (or Christ's righteousness) to other people, we are to be broadminded, patient, and gracious. We are to honor and endeavor to live our own lives by God's strict and narrow moral standards, atten-tive to every detail. We are to give ourselves no quarter, no room to fudge on our love of and obedience to God's Word. We are to be self-disciplined, taking the initiative to live in strict obedience to Christ to the best of our ability.

God's moral standards are to be the moral standards of all humanity because God is the Lord of all humanity. So, we are to judge others on the basis of God's Word, God's moral standards. But we are to do so patiently and graciously, as we want others to be patient and gracious with us as they judge us on the same basis. We are to be gracious toward others because we know from our own experience that we ourselves fall short of the mark. Yet, we must not abandon God's standards. So, we are to be tough on ourselves and easy on others, all the while honoring God's standards We are to use the same standard on ourselves as we use on others, but we are to hold ourselves to a higher degree of compliance than we hold others to. Why? Because we have more control of ourselves than we have of others. And because we want to present our higher compliance as the model for others to emulate. This is the method of Christian leadership and the method of Christian evangelism. We are to lead by example, and to inspire by example.

Calvin says that no one

> "will ever make great proficiency in it (the Doctrine of Christ) who has not learned to confine his senses and feelings, so as to keep them within those boundaries, which our heavenly Teacher prescribes for curbing our wantonness."[37]

The enemy to be overcome is not the immorality of other people, but our own habit of relying on our own senses and feelings, our own desires and preferences, to provide the standard of morality by which we judge. Other people are not the enemy! The enemy is the false standards of moral behavior that we so easily and naturally claim for ourselves.

The cure for the runaway social immorality that is undermining society is not found in getting other people to embrace Christ, but in actually embracing Christ ourselves. The cure for sin that Christ provides can only be applied from the inside out. It can only be applied by Christ Himself. We cannot apply it to other people, and our efforts to do so only exacerbate the problem. That is the lesson we are to learn from the mote and the log illustration. We must master Christian morality ourselves before we export it, because if we try to export it before we have mastered it we will only export our own morality, not Christ's.

Thus, the fix that the world so desperately needs is not the imposition of Christian morality upon others, but is personal submission to Christian morality in our own private lives. We cannot evangelize prop-

---

37 *Calvin's Commentaries*, Matthew 7: 13, public domain.

erly until we are properly evangelized ourselves. We cannot teach what we do not know, or share what we do not have.

Jesus has directed us away from the wide gate, away from following other people, away from relying upon ourselves, or others. We are not to rely upon any form of human morality, nor concern ourselves with what other people are doing or thinking. We are not to emulate other people, except that we are to emulate Paul and those who emulate him, which simply means to emulate Christ. We are not to be caught up in wide-gate concerns. But rather our attention is to be on the narrow gate, upon Christ Himself. We are to seek first the kingdom of God, knowing that the vast majority of people in this world are not seeking the kingdom of God. And because of that, we cannot rely upon them as examples or paradigms of morality or behavior. In fact, we must disregard them.

And we must disregard the morality of mass communication, as well, because mass communication in our day is a function of wide-gate mentality. It is interesting to note that in our contemporary world we are inundated with mass communication—TV, newspaper, radio, the Internet, etc. These vehicles of mass communication are almost all driven by popular, godless values, and are overwhelmingly opposed to Christian values and virtues.

At best they claim to be objective, broadminded, and neutral regarding moral values. But they are not any of these things! They are, in fact, best described as being worldly in character, in all of the various ways that Scripture discusses and discourages worldliness. They are not necessarily evil in and of themselves. Rather, they are simply dominated by worldliness.

I am not suggesting that people head for the proverbial hills or that we disassociate ourselves from all forms of mass communication. Rather, I am simply suggesting that we notice its character, and take appropriate action to protect ourselves from its corrosive effects. And how are people to do that? By applying the remedy that Jesus has given in this Sermon on the Mount, and particularly in verse 7,

> "Ask, and it will be given to you; seek, and you will find; knock, and it will be opened to you."

SAME OLD

We must inquire of the Lord, seek the Lord, turn to the Lord, accept the Lord. Inquiring of the Lord is a major biblical theme, and the failure to do so has been repeatedly pointed out in Scripture itself as the central problem that plagued ancient Israel. For instance, Zephaniah, speaking on behalf of the Lord, said,

> "I will stretch out my hand against Judah and against all the inhabitants of Jerusalem; and I will cut off from this place the remnant of Baal and the name of the idolatrous priests along with the priests, those who bow down on the roofs to the host of the heavens, those who bow down and swear to the Lord and yet swear by Milcom, those who have turned back from following the Lord, who do not seek the Lord or inquire of him" (Zephaniah 1:4-6).

These ancient Israelites had confessed their love and fealty to God, and yet they also honored the false god, Milcom (or Molech). And the attention they gave to Milcom testified to their abandonment of the exclusiveness of the God of Israel (Exodus 20:3). Their sin was syncretism, of mixing the Bible with other religions in violation of the First Commandment.

How is our contemporary world any different? It is not! But is our sin the result of engaging in mass communication? No and yes. No, the problem is not mass communication *per se*. However, we must acknowledge that contemporary mass communication serves as a primary conduit for the propagation or amplification of sin, worldliness, syncretism, and godlessness.

The Christian influence in contemporary mass communication channels is currently negligible. But neither am I lobbying for what passes for Christian broadcasting. For the most part, what currently passes for Christian broadcasting on TV, in the news, over the air waves, or on the Internet is for the most part Milcomian.[38]

For the most part much of contemporary Christianity does not represent or convey the central values and practices found in Scripture or in the Sermon on the Mount, but is compromised in the same ways that the ancient Judaism was compromised. The ancient Israelites proclaimed that Yahweh was their God, but also swore to Molech, which means that they were entangled in various national covenants and agreements, contrary to the dictates of Yahweh. Similarly, too many

---

38 Milcolm or Molech is the name of a heathen divinity whose worship figures largely in the later history of the kingdom of Judah as the national god of the Ammonites. The name can refer derivatively to any person or thing which demands or requires costly sacrifices, and is often associated in the Old Testament with nationalism or excesses related to civil government.

contemporary people claim to be Christians, but are dominated by the values of their politics, Democrat or Republican. Many people today are more Republican than Christian, or more Democrat than Christian. People too often put politics over Christ, rather than putting Christ first.

This is a huge issue and is fraught with difficulties. And Jesus knew this. It has always been a big problem, as is evidenced by both Jesus' reference to the prophets and the law, and the content of the prophets and the law. In fact, this is the central issue or central complaint of the prophets of old against various kingdoms of old. So, it should not be a surprise that it continues to be a problem today.

Knowing the history of the problem, Jesus next called attention to the central difficulty regarding the conflict between the prophets and the law.

> "Beware of false prophets, who come to you in sheep's clothing but inwardly are ravenous wolves" (v. 15).

The concern here is portraying what is not true as being true. That is what false prophets do. And the problem is a lack of integrity on the part of the false prophets. They are false precisely because they lack integrity. They are themselves not who they claim to be. Their actual private values and motivations are different than their publicly proclaimed values and motivations.

PRIVATE/PUBLIC

We can see this issue in our own day as the recent trend (over the past fifty or so years) to dissociate the public lives of our leaders from their private lives, as if what they do in private has nothing to do with what they do in public, as if their home life has nothing to do with their work life. But Scripture says differently. Jesus identified this practice with false prophets or lying leaders. The suggestion that our private lives have no impact on or relationship to our public lives is a central concern of Jesus' Sermon on the Mount, and has been a central biblical concern for thousands of years.

The lack of personal, individual integrity that results from the separation of private and public morality may be the central problem with contemporary American and Western society. It is at the heart of the current moral crisis, the current financial crisis, the current health care crisis, the current environmental crisis, etc. And yet, our politicians, public figures, and increasingly our religious leaders claim that their private lives have no impact upon their public lives or their leadership responsibilities. They proclaim loudly and boldly that their jobs are not impacted by their personal morality, that their personal moral failures have no impact on their ability to lead in government, business, education, or the church.

Nonsense! Said Jesus. But more than mere nonsense, such an idea is patently evil and wicked, and its practice is even more so. What makes a false prophet false is the lack of integrity between his subjective and objective values, the lack of integrity between beliefs and behaviors, between his private life and his public life.

Individuals do not have a subjective character and an objective character. People are whole beings, and our wholeness—including our unity in Christ—is broken by the false belief that our private and public lives can be separated. All such suggestions of moral compartmentalization are false, and what is more they comprise false religion and false prophecy because biblical Christianity teaches otherwise. The heart of Christian morality is the integrity of people as whole entities, as whole individuals and as Christians, united in Christ. Christianity teaches the unity and harmony in Christ of our private and public lives. Christianity teaches that this unity and harmony are absolutely necessary, and are found only in Christ.

The idea that wolves come in sheep's clothing means that vicious, ungrateful, and unmerciful people are pretending to be Christians. We know this because of the difference between sheep and goats mentioned elsewhere (Matthew 25:32-33). The distinction between sheep and goats points to a difference between Christians and non-Christians. So, the fact that Jesus said that these wolves masquerade in sheep's clothing rather than in goat's clothing suggests that they are pretending to be believers. Believers well understand the necessity for integrity between our private and public lives, but unbelievers don't. Thus, one of the telltale signs of the immorality of an unbeliever is his disassociation between private and public behavior.

We must beware of all such dissociation because it is false. Wherever such claims are made they are false claims and identify the claimants to be purveyors of falsehood and deceit, and ultimately of death and destruction. *Beware,* said the Lord,

> "sin is crouching at the door. Its desire is for you, but you must rule over it" (Genesis 4:7).

23. Knowing Fruits

You will recognize them by their fruits. Are grapes gathered from thornbushes, or figs from thistles? So, every healthy tree bears good fruit, but the diseased tree bears bad fruit. A healthy tree cannot bear bad fruit, nor can a diseased tree bear good fruit. Every tree that does not bear good fruit is cut down and thrown into the fire. Thus you will recognize them by their fruits.
—Matthew 7:16-20

What does it mean to judge a thing or person by its fruits? There are two concerns here: 1) what does the Lord mean by *recognize* or *know*? And 2) what does He mean by *fruits*? According to the Greek (*epiginōskō*), the kind of knowledge required here is both personal and experiential. It is not merely head knowledge, but is more akin to tasting a thing.

The fruit of a plant is the food it produces to nourish its seed. The fruit is the food that is harvested for our nourishment. And there are two kinds of fruit under consideration: good fruit and bad fruit, or nutritious fruit and poisonous fruit.

And yet, the issue under consideration was not simply good fruit versus poisonous fruit. People were not that dumb. These agrarian farmers could recognize poisonous fruit. They knew what to eat and what not to eat. That was not the problem. Rather, the issue was deception, wolves in sheep's clothing. The issue was one thing masquerading as another. The issue was pretense and deceit. The poison fruit of false prophets was disguised as good fruit.

Jesus was not talking about personal tastes here, whether we like or dislike a particular fruit, peaches rather than pears, or apples rather than oranges. Nor was Jesus talking about whether some fruit was ripe or

248

not. Fruit tends to sweeten as it ripens, and eventually its ripeness or sweetness turns to rot. But Jesus was not talking about a particular stage of fruit development, either. He meant to differentiate between fruit that nourishes and fruit that poisons.

FALSE PROPHETS FAKE FRUITS

We know this because this allusion to fruit was suggested as a method of judging false prophets. The false prophets were masquerading in sheep's clothing, so their real character was hidden. It was difficult to tell which prophets were true and which were false simply by looking at them. The false pretended to be true. Can people be tricked like this? Remember that Jacob had been able to fool his own father, who was half blind in his old age, by donning goat skins on his neck and hands to simulate Esau's hairiness (Genesis 27:16). Indeed, people are easily fooled about all sorts of things.

Because false prophets have plagued God's saints from the beginning of time, we must realize that telling the difference between true and false prophets is not as simple as we might first expect. Many people have been fooled over many generations about the same things. It happens over and over again. God's people are forever getting caught up in the lies of false prophets and the deceptions of self-deceit. If Christians are to make any significant progress beyond the temptations and failures of those who have preceded them, we must handle this matter of discerning between true and false prophets better than our ancestors have. Clearly, Scripture demonstrates that generation after generation God's people have been fooled by falsehood and deceit masquerading as truth and wisdom.

So, Jesus has given us this fruit test. We are to recognize prophets and teachers by their fruit. The principle of this measure is found in verses 17-18,

> "every healthy tree bears good fruit, but the diseased tree bears
> bad fruit. A healthy tree cannot bear bad fruit, nor can a diseased
> tree bear good fruit."

The contrast here is between a healthy tree that produces good fruit and a diseased tree that produces bad fruit. The Authorized Version translates this contrast as a *good* (*agathos*) tree that brings *good* (*kalos*) fruit and a *corrupt* (*sapros*) tree that brings *evil* (*ponēros*) fruit. We could also translate it as *a beneficial tree that brings beautiful fruit and a worthless tree that brings hurtful or malicious fruit*. The operating principle here is that like produces like. Goodness produces goodness, and poison produces death.

And because these categories are hard and fast they can be trusted to reveal false prophets from true. The categories do not overlap. Unfortunately, people jump to the conclusion that good fruit means lots of fruit and bad fruit means not much fruit. So, people mistakenly think that the false prophet has a small ministry with few followers and the good prophet has a successful ministry with a lot of followers.

But that is not at all what Jesus said or means. Jesus was talking about quality not quantity. And if history is the judge, many false prophets are often quite successful with huge followings. And yet we cannot make too much of this because it is also true that at various times true prophets are also successful, and false prophets are not. The point is that size means nothing here. The contrast was not a function of size, but of character.

When Jesus said,

> "For the gate is wide and the way is easy that leads to destruction,
> and those who enter by it are many. For the gate is narrow and
> the way is hard that leads to life, and those who find it are few"
> (vs. 13-14),

His point was not about numbers or size. He was talking about two different—opposite—mindsets or worldviews. He was talking about the dangers of being broadminded and the virtues of being single-minded. So, to try to impose size implications from this verse onto the idea of good and bad fruit is equally fruitless.

The point here is like the point in Matthew 6:22-23:

> "The lamp of the body is the eye: if therefore thine eye be single,
> thy whole body shall be full of light. But if thine eye be evil, thy
> whole body shall be full of darkness. If therefore the light that is
> in thee be darkness, how great is the darkness!" (American Standard Version).

The singularity of the eye here is an allusion to the uniqueness of God and the exclusive demand of the First Commandment—loyalty to God alone. And the contrast is the disloyalty related to paganism's pantheons. Of course Jews and Christians are too smart to simply fall for pagan gods *per se*, when they are in plain sight. So, they are hidden—occluded. Similarly, the light and the darkness are kinds of spiritual fruit.

The practice of truth fills the body with light, as the practice of false-hood fills the body with darkness.

The extremes of light and dark are easy to discern. Unfortunately, the traditional error that Jews and Christians make is more subtle. The error that is so often repeated by monotheists is syncretism, blending together what must be kept apart in the name of oneness or unity. And this amalgam of light and shadow, truth and error, arises from the failure to honor the First Commandment. It pollutes the purity that God demands. Isaiah said it so well that Jesus quoted him.

> "Well did Isaiah prophesy of you hypocrites, as it is written, 'This people honors me with their lips, but their heart is far from me; in vain do they worship me, teaching as doctrines the command-ments of men. You leave the commandment of God and hold to the tradition of men'" (Mark 7:6-8).

FRUIT IS FAITH

So, what is the fruit that Jesus was talking about? In a word, the fruit of the gospel is faithfulness. So, the bad fruit would be faithlessness, and faithlessness in disguise as faithfulness is hypocrisy or agreement without conviction, faith without obedience. The bad fruit is not a little faith, because a little faith is like the mustard seed that grows into a giant plant (Matthew 13:31). The bad fruit is faithlessness, which grows into corruption, chaos, and death.

We will recognize false prophets by their faithlessness, but only if we correctly understand that faithfulness always produces obedience to God's Word—not perfect obedience, of course. Human sin is not so easily overcome. Rather, the fruit of faithfulness is the willingness to accept God's Word as truth, and the honest effort to comply with it. So, the fruit is not mere obedience, but is growth in Christ, sanctification and maturity of both belief and behavior. We can also call it love, as John did.

> "Whoever says 'I know him' but does not keep his command-ments is a liar, and the truth is not in him, but whoever keeps his word, in him truly the love of God is perfected. By this we may know that we are in him: whoever says he abides in him ought to walk in the same way in which he walked" (1 John 2:4-6).

> "No one born of God makes a practice of sinning, for God's seed abides in him, and he cannot keep on sinning because he has been born of God. By this it is evident who are the children of

God, and who are the children of the devil: whoever does not
practice righteousness is not of God, nor is the one who does not
love his brother" (1 John 3:9-10).

The Greek word *karpos* simply means *fruit* and is used in the same
ways that we use the word today. Fruit is what we harvest from fruit
trees. Similarly, the fruit of a manufacturing process is the product
produced. The fruit of one's hands is the result of one's labor. A fruitful
exchange suggests a good that is gained. So, to know a person by his
fruits means that whatever he produces, or whatever the result of one's
experience with him, will be of the same character as his heart or spirit.
Thus, the idea of knowing people on the basis of their fruits brings us
back full circle to the first verse of this Sermon on the Mount:

"Blessed are the poor in spirit, for theirs is the kingdom of
heaven" (Matthew 5:3).

Because one's fruit reveals the condition of one's heart we also come
back to Matthew 5:8:

"Blessed are the pure in heart, for they shall see God."

In His Sermon on the Mount Jesus has described the kind of people who
are faithful—the poor in spirit, those who mourn, the meek, seekers of
righteousness, the merciful, the pure in heart, the peacemakers, and
those who are persecuted for righteousness' sake. These are the kinds of
people whom God blesses, and it is God's blessing that is the particular
fruit by which we can know God's people. God blesses His people, He
blesses faithfulness. And God's blessing is, then, the fruit of faithfulness.

Faithless Fruit

Conversely, where we don't see God's blessing—God's truth, the
light of Christ, the love of God and neighbor—we find the fruit of faithlessness. At this point we need to be careful not to confuse God's
blessing with our own ideas of success and progress. Such was the error
of the Corinthians, who mistook their own thinking, their own
wisdom, their own desires to naturally be in harmony with God's.

They assumed that what they called success in the academy and in
the marketplace (academics and economics) were the blessings of God.
The church at Corinth had produced much fruit in the sense that it was
large, successful, and influential. But at the heart of that enterprise was
falsehood, deceit, and deception. Perhaps it was self-deception on the

part of the leaders, whom Paul labeled as false prophets. Consequently, the fruit of the Corinthians was not the kind of fruit that Jesus described in this Sermon on the Mount. What the Corinthians called success, Paul called failure. What they called truth, Paul called falsehood. What they called wisdom, Paul called foolishness.

But God is not opposed to wealth, success, or influence. However, neither do such things in and of themselves constitute God's blessing. The problem in Corinth was not the wealth, success, or influence, but the falsehood, deceit, and deception. The leaders were engaged in unrepentant and heinous sin, and pretended or genuinely believed that there was no conflict between what they taught and what they did. The lack of integrity between belief and behavior—intentional or not—constitutes deceit, deception, and error. It does not matter if people sincerely believe in what they are teaching and doing. Sincerity is not a measure of truth. People can be and often are sincere, but wrong.

Jesus' Sermon on the Mount provides a clarification of God's law and was modeled on Deuteronomy 28, which itself discussed the fruits of faithfulness and faithlessness by setting them in stark contrast. When Jesus calls us to judge people on the basis of their fruits, He is referring to Deuteronomy 28, not exclusively, but essentially.

Deuteronomy 28 describes God's blessings and how those blessings will come to those who are faithful to Him, faithful to Yahweh, the God of the Old Testament. Everything that faithful people do will be blessed by the Lord. The first thing to note about this section of Deuteronomy 28 is that God was speaking to Israel as a people, as a nation, and not simply to particular individuals within that nation. It is important to see this because those who fail to see this turn these blessings into a faulty understanding of wealth and prosperity. The blessings are both corporate and individual, neither of which can be excluded, and both of which necessarily come together because of the trinitarian character of humanity.

A casual reading of Deuteronomy 28 does suggest that God blesses His people with wealth and prosperity—and He does! However, that does not mean that wealth and prosperity are always a sign of God's blessing. Nor does it mean that every faithful person will always be blessed with superior wealth and prosperity. The blessing to be sought is not the wealth or the prosperity, but God's favor, because apart from God's favor wealth and prosperity become the means of God's curses. The real blessing is not the wealth or the prosperity, but the favor of

God, God's love—and that is always a blessing, regardless of one's financial or material situation.

Sharing The Fruit

This is a hard lesson for people to learn and to hold on to. And it may be an even more difficult lesson to pass on to our children. People who grow up in the lap of wealth and prosperity nearly always adapt themselves to it, assume it to be the norm. Human beings are very adaptable, that's one of our strengths—and one of our weaknesses. The poor tend to adapt to poverty, and the rich tend to adapt to wealth. And by adapt I mean that they come to expect it. By and large the poor expect to be poor and the rich expect to be rich.

People normally expect things to always have been in the past as they now are, and to continue in the future to be what they have always been. People tend to think of themselves as normal and their experience as normative. And in both cases those expectations and tendencies are problematic to the gospel of God's grace. God's grace is an intrusion into history, an encroachment into personal experience. It is extraordinary, not usual.

This problem of the norming of our individual experience, of thinking that things have always been the way they presently are, and will always be so, is at the very heart of Jesus' Sermon on the Mount message. The heart of Christ's message is His character and resurrection, the demonstration that He came to change the world—because He could, so He did. Christ came to change the human norm, to change human beliefs and behaviors that are shaped by our hopes and dreams—yes, of course.

But our hopes and dreams tend to be tethered to our expectations and presuppositions about what is real, about what is possible, about who we are. And it is at this point that the gospel of Jesus Christ inserts itself and its change. The gospel is about new life in Christ. It destroys our natural expectations and presuppositions about the nature of reality, and then gives us new expectations and presuppositions in Christ that are completely unknown and unknowable by the old standards. The gospel changes our social norms.

Jesus Christ explodes our earth-born and earth-bound human expectations. That is what His miracles are all about. Miracles change our expectations about what is possible. That is what His resurrection did. It broke the most fundamental belief about the nature of human experience—that people are born, live, and die—end of story. And broke it, He did! Christ's resurrection began a process of change, a way of thinking about who we are in Christ, about who we are as a people, about the inheritance of heaven. And this new thinking in Christ will eventually dominate the world. Great progress has already been made.

This is what Jesus meant when He said,

> "I did not come to judge the world but to save the world" (John 12:47).

He didn't mean that the world would not be judged. It will be judged by the disobedience and disregard of unbelievers, who are even now storing up God's curses. The more unbelievers there are, the greater the curses will be. But this is true regardless of Christ. This was God's Old Testament threat, and our human situation.

New Fruit

Christ, however, provides an antidote, a cure, a fix—salvation. Jesus Christ is a game changer. He changes our beliefs, our expectations, and presuppositions about what is possible for ourselves and for humanity. Christ changes our understanding of who we are. In Christ we become greater—more whole, more complete—because we find ourselves in unity with Christ and with His people.

Our identity as individuals becomes trinitized in Christ. In Christ we become who we were created to be in the image of God. In Christ our likeness to God, our original created nature becomes clearer. We don't become Christ. We don't become God, not even little gods. We don't become perfect, but in the light of Christ we do become better than we used to be, where *better* means more humble, more loving, more of service to the Lord. We are always human, but in Christ our humanity becomes more like it was created to be.

This is the fruit of the gospel of Jesus Christ. And where this fruit isn't, where it doesn't exist, neither has the gospel taken hold. We know this fruit by knowing the gospel, and we know the gospel better as this fruit ripens in us. Our recognition of this fruit in others requires its development and maturity in ourselves. That's how we know it. We recognize it in others because we know it in ourselves.

24. THE MUD DELUSION

Not everyone who says to me, "Lord, Lord," will enter the kingdom of heaven, but the one who does the will of my Father who is in heaven. On that day many will say to me, "Lord, Lord, did we not prophesy in your name, and cast out demons in your name, and do many mighty works in your name?" And then will I declare to them, "I never knew you; depart from me, you workers of lawlessness."

—Matthew 7:21-23

We come now to some of the most disturbing verses in the Bible. If these verses don't make you shake in your boots, you have failed to understand them. And yet the idea found in these verses is one of the most central ideas of the Bible. It's not that it is a difficult idea to understand. Rather, it is a difficult idea to accept because it offends and contradicts our most dearly held assumptions about ourselves, about God, and the nature of salvation. In fact, one of the basic consequences of reading the Bible is its challenge to, destruction of, and reshaping of our most dearly held yet faulty assumptions about ourselves, about God, and about reality.

Very early in our reading of the Bible we find the story of Satan's deception and its infectious consequences in humanity—sin and the Fall. The story tells us that Eve and Adam were deceived and all of their posterity have been infected with the error of dissembling, of pretense, and self-deceit about the very thing Jesus mentioned in these verses. We have not only been deceived about who we are, about who God is, and about how reality actually works, but the deception has been so successful that apart from personal regeneration we don't even know that we have been deceived because the deception convinces us to trust ourselves, to trust our own perceptions, and our own analysis. And more than simply not knowing that we have been deceived, or how we are even now still being deceived, people categorically reject the mere consideration that Satan's deception infection has already permeated their own perception. And failing to see this, people deny and ignore the only possible correction—Jesus Christ.

And, Jesus tells us in these verses, this problem has even infected our perception of Him—of God. Jesus was saying here that people apply this very error to their perception and understanding of Him and the salvation that He provides. Why do I say this? Because Jesus said it. Just a few verses earlier He said that

> "the gate is wide and the way is easy that leads to destruction, and those who enter by it are many. (And) the gate is narrow and the way is hard that leads to life, and those who find it are few" (Matthew 7:13-14).

Many take the wide way. What was Jesus talking about? What is the gate He was talking about? The gate is the entrance to the kingdom or the entryway to salvation. And the fact that the gate is wide suggests a common, almost universal understanding and approach. The wide gate is the way that most people—even most Christians—think about salvation. The wide way is the popular way of thinking about it.

The other way, the way that Jesus called attention to, is the narrow way or the narrow gate. The Greek word translated as narrow (*thlibō*) literally means to crowd together, and figuratively suggests a rut or footpath that is wide enough for only one person at a time. The point is that people are saved (or enter the kingdom) individually, not by groups.[39] Paul called attention to this:

> "There is neither Jew nor Greek, there is neither slave nor free, there is no male and female, for you are all one in Christ Jesus (Galatians 3:28), neither circumcision nor uncircumcision counts for anything, but only faith working through love" (Galatians 5:6).

People are not saved because of who they are, because apart from Christ people are mistaken about who they are.

Unbelievers don't see this at all, and believers often—even usually— misunderstand it because they have not abandoned their attachments to

---

39 Salvation puts people into a group—the church. But going to church does not cause people to get saved.

sin. Even Christians who are actually saved still sin. Too many Christians continue to misunderstand themselves, their God, and how salvation works because we are still embroiled in sin. We are all embroiled in sin because our world is embroiled in sin.

Created in God's Trinitarian image, our identity as human beings is not merely personal and individual, but is caught up in the social culture in which we live. We are both individuals and social beings—both at once and at the same time. We cannot live apart from society, and the society in which we live has a significant personal impact on us. People are always defined in part by the social context in which they live.

MUDOLOGY

To be freed from sin by the grace of God through faith in Christ is a fundamental reality that all Christians acknowledge. In Christ we are free indeed! In Christ we are washed clean, and yet we continue to live in the social mud pit of the world. I'm not saying that Christians are not completely saved by the grace of God. We are! It's a done deal. But look around! We are still in the mud pit, and it is tough to do anything while still in the mud pit without getting muddy. I'm equating the mud with sin. It's dirty, messy, and life threatening because the mud is actually toxic sludge.

What has this to do with the verses under consideration? What has this to do with Satan's deception? Simply this: people don't see the mud. People don't believe that sin is real, or they don't believe that it is as extensive as God says it is. People deny God and don't honor Him as God or give thanks to Him, but they have become futile in their thinking, and their foolish hearts have been darkened (Romans 1:21). And this even applies to some Christians when they believe that sin no longer has any effect on them. People think that in Christ they have been washed clean—and they have been! Christ's forgiveness is efficacious, complete and real. In Christ human purity will indeed be restored one day. In Christ we are free at last and free indeed.

Yet, we continue to live in the mud pit—in the world. And we are called to do everything we can to keep from getting muddy again, to avoid sin. That's what sanctification or growth in grace is all about. But we live in a mud pit and most of our neighbors continue to think that the mud is not toxic, that it is just a normal part of being human, that mud is no big deal. And so, like pigs, they wallow in the mud because it feels good, and everyone does it. So, they think, it must be normal. People want to wallow in the mud with their friends, because they love them and want to share the good feelings and common bonds of mud wallowing with them.

So, Christ has come and hosed down His people who dwell in the mud pit. And suddenly they have come to see that mud is not part of their skin. People had never seen skin before Christ hosed them down because all human skin has been covered with mud all of their lives. From our earliest recollections, we know only mud covered skin, our own and that of our fellow mud dwellers. Even the water that people bathe in is muddy because its source is the mud pit. People have adapted to the mud. They actually like it. They think that mud shields them from the bright light of the Son. And it does!

Nonetheless, Christ's water of baptism is clean and pure, and people are genuinely cleansed and purified by it. But we continue to live in the mud pit. And in our day the pit has gotten so big that we cannot escape it. Everywhere we go, we are still in it. And besides, there is nothing that we could do to get ourselves out of the pit even if we wanted to. The walls are too high and slippery. And all of our tools are made of mud.

But Christ has washed us with His pure water. He has marked us with the blood of the covenant and promised to return one day with a new city (Revelation 21:1-2), a New Jerusalem that will come down from heaven, which means that it will not be from the muddy pit in which we live. On that day we will truly be washed completely clean and set in the city without mud. We cannot build such a city for ourselves because all of our tools are made of mud and are covered with mud. Everything we touch becomes muddier with the mud of our own hands. We mine and refine the mud to make all kinds of wonderful things that titillate our senses and inspire our imaginations. But no matter what we do with it or to it, it is all still mud.

Satan's original deception was that God's plan to get us out of the mud was a lie, that God was trying to trick us because He doesn't want us to get out of the mud, because we will track mud into His house and He cannot abide any mud in His house. And the only way for God to keep mud out of His house, argued Satan, is to keep us out because we are covered in mud.

So, said Satan, *God doesn't want us to be like Him—without mud— because He's jealous and narrow-minded. But,* said Satan, *I've got some mud free water here.* And he reached into a mud pond and scooped out a handful of almost clear water. *If you just wash in it yourself, you can be just like God—mudless and able to see things without mud in your eyes,* or so he said.

THE PHANTASY

Did you see Satan's deception? Eve didn't. She believe the Serpent was telling the truth. She believed that she could wash herself in Satan's muddy water and become like him. He was the most mudless being she had ever seen. And so she did. And, lo and behold, she became more mudless than she had ever been before. So she told her husband what the Serpent had said. And he saw her as he had never seen her before. Her nearly mudless skin was radiant and uncaked.

Wow! he said, *let's wash in Satan's dirty water together.*

And, lo, they did. And the muddy water washed mud from their eyes, and they were sort of like God, except for the mud residue. But they didn't notice it, nor did they care. They couldn't see it because they were distracted by their own relative mudlessness, and the supple cake-lessness of their skin.

Enough of the analogy, already! You get the point, don't you? The Serpent was a false prophet, a false teacher, even a false savior because he told them what was not true. Like any good poison, what he said was 99.9% pure truth, and only .1% false. Rat poison has to be good enough for rats to mistake it for food. Even a rat is smart enough to reject what smells like poison. And the rat is not killed instantly either. It takes a while for the poison to work its way through his digestion and into his blood.

So, what is the essential falsehood that Satan peddles as truth, but God says is poison? It is the idea that we can get clean by washing ourselves or washing one another in Satan's water, by doing what God has prohibited, by following Satan's advice, by ignoring God. It is the idea that we can save ourselves or save other people. It is the idea that we can do for ourselves all that we need—and even do it in the name of Jesus Christ!

SAVED BY...

Today this has become the idea that people are saved by baptism, or by confession, or by understanding, or by theology, or by the sacraments, or by repentance, or by church membership, that people can be saved by the behaviors of faithfulness, that doing faithful things is a method of salvation. Let's examine this idea.

Are people saved by baptism? Or perhaps a better way to ask the question is: are people saved apart from baptism? Is baptism necessary?

We know from the story of the thief on the cross that salvation can happen apart from baptism. However, the story of the thief on the cross is not intended to be normative. Without getting distracted by issues of believer's baptism or infant baptism, we can simply say that for both parties baptism is an act of thankfulness and obedience to God's salvation. And because baptism is not a necessary element of salvation, what is important is *that* it happens not *when* it happens. People often overemphasize baptism by expecting baptism to produce the fruit of salvation. But it doesn't. Salvation is always by grace alone through faith alone in Christ alone according to Scripture alone to the glory of God alone. Christ alone saves, not baptism.[40]

So, are people saved by confession or belief, understanding or theology? No one is saved apart from belief, or apart from confessing that Jesus Christ is Lord. But does our own belief cause us to be saved? Or does God's salvation cause people to believe? Does the cart push the horse? Or does the horse pull the cart?

If people are saved by their own belief, if people are saved by believing correctly, then all we need to do is to teach about Christ correctly and people will come to faith. In this case the correct content of the salvation message would push people into salvation. By hearing God's truth people would be compelled to respond with faith.

I am very tempted to believe that this is true because Paul said that

"everyone who calls on the name of the Lord will be saved" (Romans 10:13).

If that's all there is to it, then all people need to do is call on the name of the Lord and they will be saved, not *might* be saved, but *will* be saved. I am also tempted to believe this because people cannot possibly hear the gospel right unless it is rightly preached. Preaching wrongly about the gospel doesn't help people hear it rightly.

Surely those who asked,

"Lord, Lord, did we not prophesy in your name, and cast out demons in your name, and do many mighty works in your name?" (v. 22)

believed this. They had not only called on the name of the Lord, but they had already taken it to the next level. They were preaching and

40 See Footnote 18, p 163.

casting out demons and doing mighty works—and doing it all in Jesus'
name! Such people would be deemed not just faithful, but fruitful by any
standard. Right? Such people would not just be pew sitters. They would
be pastors, evangelists, and missionaries who labored in the name of
Jesus Christ. At least they would think of themselves as such, and who in
the Christian community would think differently?

Well, Jesus thought differently. But why? Paul asked and answered
the question.

> "How then will they call on him in whom they have not be-
> lieved? And how are they to believe in him of whom they have
> never heard? And how are they to hear without someone preach-
> ing? And how are they to preach unless they are sent?" (Romans
> 10:14-15).

Follow Paul's logic: you can't call unless you believe. And you can't
believe unless you hear. And you can't hear unless someone tells you,
unless some information that you do not possess comes to you. Turning
this into a positive progression we see that telling people about Christ
leads to hearing, and hearing leads to believing, and believing leads to
people calling on the name of the Lord. Paul's progression is: telling,
hearing, believing, and then calling on the name of the Lord. This
progression suggests that people must believe before they can call on the
Lord, that belief precedes reception of grace. While this progression
begins with telling, which leads to hearing, it ends with calling, which is
preceded by believing. The *calling* in this case is what people usually
think of as asking for God's grace and mercy, which is the mechanism
by which God's grace is provided. We ask, God gives. But we cannot
truly ask unless we truly believe. Asking apart from belief is the definition of hypocrisy.

But what is it that people must believe? They must believe that God
has already provided His salvation by the propitiation of Christ on the
cross before they can call on Him and ask for it. We must believe that it
is real before we can really ask for it. People do not ask for what they
believe to be imaginary and unreal.

People can't believe until they hear with ears to hear. We must hear
the Lord before we can call upon Him. We cannot answer a question
that we have not heard. Thus, our own salvation actually precedes our
calling on God, such that our response is simply agreeing with God.
And Paul concluded,

"So faith comes from hearing, and hearing through the word of Christ" (Romans 10:13-17).

But Paul does not mean that faith comes from the physical ability to hear. It is not a matter of hearing ourselves think about Christ. But rather, it is the object of our hearing that carries the power, and that object is the Word of God transmitted by the Holy Spirit. Paul said to the Corinthians,

"For the word of the cross is folly to those who are perishing, but to us who are being saved it is the power of God" (1 Corinthians 1:18).

The Word of God is the power of God to save.

Consequently, it is not our decision to receive Christ that saves us, though everyone who is saved does make such a decision. Christ does not follow our decision. The Lord leads! He doesn't follow. Rather, it is our decision that follows the leading of the Lord. We hear Him. We hear His call to us, and then respond.

"We love because he first loved us" (1 John 4:19).

Upon hearing the Word of the Lord, our old assumptions and presuppositions about God, about ourselves and about the world, are shattered by Christ, the of Rock of salvation. And in utter helplessness, with nothing in our hand, we see that God has reached out and, for some inexplicable reason that has nothing to do with us personally, the Lord has changed our hearts and minds. We suddenly see that He is not only real, but we see His reality only because He has changed us by giving us eyes to see and ears to hear.

In response, we cry out,

"Abba, Father!" (Romans 8:15)

because our adoption has already been initiated. But to call our response to God's adoption the decisive element of our salvation is a travesty of language. It is not *our* decision to receive Him, but *His* decision to receive us that is the critical factor. And that decision was made by the Lord, who had sent Jesus Christ to atone for our sins. That's the important decision, and it was made by God, not us. Without God reaching out and changing us, we would have nothing to respond to.

So, if you understand this message, that God sent Christ to propitiate for your sins, if you "get" that, if you hear it at all, it is because you have been given "ears to hear" (Luke 8:8). It is because of God's grace alone. It is not because you are special. It is because Christ is special.

I'm not saying that God doesn't respond to our prayers and pleas. He does. But He doesn't respond to all prayers and pleas (Jeremiah 7:16, Matthew 6:7). Sometimes God chooses not to respond. And that is the distressing point about these verses in the Sermon on the Mount.

God doesn't meet our expectations. God doesn't change (Malachi 3:8, Hebrews 13:8). People change—thank God that people change! But God doesn't. He is always the same. And He always saves people the same way, by grace through faith. Grace is the power and faith is the means. But it is not the act or the decision to have faith that saves. It is the object of faith that saves, which is none other than Christ alone.

...By Christ

This verse teaches that people are not saved because they want to be saved, even though everyone who is saved actually does want to be saved. Rather, this verse teaches that God saves who He wants to save, and everyone He wants to save actually gets saved. Listen again to Jesus' words,

> "On that day many will say to me, 'Lord, Lord, did we not prophesy in your name, and cast out demons in your name, and do many mighty works in your name?' And then will I declare to them, 'I never knew you; depart from me, you workers of law-lessness'" (Matthew 7:22-23).

Why are these people *not* saved? They wanted to be saved, and *they* thought that they were. What was missing in their plea or in their relationship to Jesus?

They were essentially saying that the Lord owed them salvation because they had been working for Him. Note the lack of any expression of love, appreciation, or thankfulness in their languager. They had been naming and claiming the Lord, but *He* did not reciprocate. They had done various things in the name of the Lord, even had what appeared to many people to be the power and Spirit of the Lord, but neither they themselves nor those who mistakenly thought that they had such power and Spirit knew the truth of the situation.

And because they didn't know the truth about their own salvation, they were false teachers. It is not that they failed to truly believe what they thought was true. Nor were they doing bad things. Rather, they were themselves convinced that their lie—their own understanding—was true. They were self-deceived because they did not know the truth.

But they could not share what they did not have, nor could they teach what they did not know. They did not actually believe what Christ said was true. People are saved by Christ, not by their belief in Christ. Christ is never wrong, but our belief can be wrong.

Are people saved by the sacraments? The Roman Catholic Church says *yes*, but we know better. Are people saved by repentance? Fundamentalists certainly think so, but we know better. Are people saved by church membership? A lot of people think so, but we know better. I'm not saying that these things are not important. They are all very important. But they are not salvific. So, how are people saved? By grace alone through faith alone in Christ alone according to Scripture alone and to the glory of God alone. It is God's doing start to finish, top to bottom.

Am I saying that Christians are robots who have no roll in salvation? Not at all! If anything, I'm saying that non-Christians are the robots who have no roll in salvation because they are slaves to sin and blind to the truth of the world in which they live. By rejecting Christ, unbelievers reject the only real decision that actually make things different. I'm saying that Christians respond to Jesus Christ. They choose to accept Christ, to agree with God. I'm saying that in Christ alone people are free from bondage and slavery to sin. Christians are the people with ears to hear. Christians are the people who are not in denial about their own sin or about what God's Word actually says, including the difficult verses.

But, said Jesus in these verses under consideration, *some people who think that they are Christians, some people who make every effort to think like Christians and act like Christians are in fact not Christians!* This is not my opinion, it is the Lord's. I'm not interpreting the verse to suit myself. I'm simply understanding what was said.

How can this be? How can Jesus say such a thing? Think of the Lord's concern regarding the deception of the Pharisees. He chastised them:

> "Woe to you, scribes and Pharisees, hypocrites! For you tithe
> mint and dill and cumin, and have neglected the weightier mat-
> ters of the law: justice and mercy and faithfulness. These you
> ought to have done, without neglecting the others. You blind
> guides, straining out a gnat and swallowing a camel! Woe to you,
> scribes and Pharisees, hypocrites! For you clean the outside of the
> cup and the plate, but inside they are full of greed and self-indul-

gence. You blind Pharisee! First clean the inside of the cup and
the plate, that the outside also may be clean" (Matthew 23:23-26).

The Pharisees were very religious by every standard except Christ's.
They thought they were right, but Jesus knew better.

Satan convinced Eve that she could be like God, not by living in
obedience, but by an act of self-righteous disobedience. But did Eve
know that the fruit of the tree of the knowledge of good and evil was
forbidden? She did. She said that God had forbidden the fruit, that God
had told them not to eat it.

Or touch it, she added, *lest we die.*

You won't die, the Serpent retorted.

And it sounded plausible to her, as it still does to many.

> "The tree was good for food … it was a delight to the eyes, and
> … was to be desired to make one wise" (Genesis 3:6).

So,

> "she took of its fruit and ate, and she also gave some to her hus-
> band who was with her, and he ate" (Genesis 3:6).

Where is the sin in any of this? This sin was disobedience to God's
Word, plain and simple.

But who sinned? How did Eve sin? Eve sinned by not checking
with Adam first. Eve was a derivative being. She had been

> "taken out of Man" (Genesis 2:23).

She was made from Adam's rib. As well as being factually true, this
means that Adam had preeminence. He was older, if you will. The little
sister should not have been leading her big brother, but should look to
the leadership of her big brother. Her sin was usurpation. Deciding to
eat the fruit was not a decision that she should have made alone. They
were a team—one flesh. And the team had a captain. A team without a
captain doesn't work, and neither does a team with two captains. But
was it fair that Adam was the captain? Who appointed him? Who
indeed!

Adam also sinned. His sin was abrogation because he, by neglect or
denial, failed to obey God's prohibition. God said *don't*, and he did
anyway. The fact that his action was a loving response to his loving wife
who had baked him up a sweet and delectable pie of forbidden fruit was
no excuse for dereliction of duty. The fact of the matter is that Adam

decided to decide on his own, just as Eve had done. And that is the problem that Jesus was dealing with in Matthew 7:21-23. Those people, too, had decided to decide on their own. Jesus was talking to people who decided that they were Christians because they decided to be Christians, who began to work as Christians, and teach as if they knew what Christians know. But they didn't. In all likelihood, they believed what they said they believed, that they were Christians, that they were faithfully carrying out God's will. They thought they were right. But Jesus told them that they were fooling themselves because He didn't know them. Their names weren't on His list.

Damned Fools

A sermon on these verses can't end positively for those who refuse to believe God's Word. I can ask people to close their eyes and bow their heads, and raise their hands if they love Jesus. I can ask people to come forward and commit their lives to Jesus. That's essentially what these people had done in one way or another, but Jesus rejected them. Read the words. It's plain and simple, though a mite discomforting for the doubtful.

And what was the sin of these self-chosen believers? Lawlessness (*anomia*). The Authorized Version translated it as *iniquity*. The Greek word means illegality or not lawful, or more generally, wickedness and unrighteousness. But what is so bad about preaching and healing and working wonders in the name of Jesus? Nothing if you know what you are doing, and everything if you don't. Teaching truth is great. Teaching falsehood isn't. And it doesn't matter if you believe in what you are doing. It doesn't matter if you have the best intentions in the world. The Pharisees had good intentions and believed that they were right in their beliefs and actions.

What matters is Jesus Christ. What matters in the first and final analysis is not our love of God, but God's love of us. Don't get me wrong. I don't mean that our love of God is unimportant. It is very important! But it is secondary. Our love follows, it doesn't lead. It's a response. God leads and we follow. God is sovereign and gets what He wants. We aren't, and we don't get what we want for ourselves. We get what God wants for us. The problem with these people was that they were following their own lead, not God's.

We are mere children holding on to Daddy's hand. And though we hold on with all our might—as we should, we are not kept from slipping away by our grip on Him. Rather, it is Daddy's grip on us that keeps us safe. It was Daddy's idea to adopt us, not our idea to get adopted by Him. But, of course, all whom Daddy decides to adopt do come to love, appreciate, and agree with Him.

Our response is in fact very important, but it is secondary. Our response is like Eve's authority in her marriage to Adam. It is very important, very valuable. But it is secondary. Our response is like Adam's response to God's covenant. Adam's response was very important, very valuable. But it was a response, not an initiation. God initiates, we respond—or don't. Christ is primary, we are secondary.

25. HARD RAIN

Everyone then who hears these words of mine and does them will be like a wise man who built his house on the rock. And the rain fell, and the floods came, and the winds blew and beat on that house, but it did not fall, because it had been founded on the rock. And everyone who hears these words of mine and does not do them will be like a foolish man who built his house on the sand. And the rain fell, and the floods came, and the winds blew and beat against that house, and it fell, and great was the fall of it.　　　　　　*—Matthew 7:24-27*

This final illustration provided in the Lord's Sermon on the Mount is about two houses, two homes. One was built on rock, which represents a stable foundation, and one was built on sand, which represents an unstable foundation. Little was said about the homes, which means that for the purposes of the comparison they were identical.

We can assume that the labor involved in building them was roughly the same, that they were of similar size, had similar features and were constructed of similar materials. The only difference mentioned was their foundation. They may have been right beside one another, or some distance apart. Their location was unimportant, other than its relationship to their different foundations. A casual observer would not notice any significant difference.

The two houses were set up as analogies relating to different responses to hearing Jesus' Sermon on the Mount, two different ways of hearing the Sermon. The first response was obedience to the instructions Jesus had given. That response of obedience was characterized as building on a solid foundation. Paul likened Jesus Himself to be the

Rock of this parable. Speaking of the ancient Israelites who had been baptized in the desert as having been under the influence and instruction of Christ.

> "For they drank from the spiritual Rock that followed them, and
> the Rock was Christ" (1 Corinthians 10:4).

Remember the story. Moses had taken Israel out into the desert. Food and water were limited, unlike their experience in Egypt where they had been provided with food and water as provisions of their slavery. In the desert, they remembered the "good" times in Egypt, the leeks and onions, and began to grumble against Moses and his leadership. They were hungry and thirsty and looked to Moses for their provision. The Lord told Moses to strike a particular rock, and water gushed out from it (Exodus 17:6). The particular rock that Moses smote was on Mount Sinai, the mountain from which he had received the Ten Commandments. Moses' striking the rock and the consequent water for the people of God symbolized the life-giving and sustaining character of God's law.

CHRIST THE ROCK

Paul then identified the particular Rock that Moses struck as Christ. And by doing so Paul identified Christ as the One who had given Moses the original Ten Commandments, as God Himself. Paul's identification of the Sinai Rock as Christ was an allusion to Christ's divinity and to the Trinitarian character of God. As the Son of God, Christ is eternally existent, and so Jesus Himself instructed the disciples on the road to Emmaus about His presence in Scripture and of His eternal existence.

> "And beginning with Moses and all the Prophets, he interpreted
> to them in all the Scriptures the things concerning himself" (Luke
> 24:27).

At that point in history, only the Old Testament existed.

By tracing Himself to the earliest expression of God's law Jesus tied His own teaching to the ancient teaching of the Old Testament, and to the issues of obedience and disobedience that had plagued Israel from the time that Moses came down the Mountain with God's law in hand only to find the Israelites dancing to the Golden Calf (Exodus 32). From the outset, Israel's heart had been sinfully bent to prefer the ecstasies of idolatry to faithful obedience to the only God who actually exists. And this was the concern of these last verses of Jesus' Sermon on the Mount—obedience to the Word of God.

Jesus described these two houses, one built on the rock and one on the sand. The house built on the rock was an analogy to the household established on Christ, the Rock of salvation. The physical house, the structure, is the abode of a family, a household. And the household is the main object of the analogy. Jesus' concern was not architecture, but social structure. So, the house that was built on the rock (v. 24) alludes to the household that is established on Christ, who is the Rock according to Paul (1 Corinthians 10:4). And the fact that Paul testified that Jesus Christ was the Rock from which Moses smote water also suggests that all that Paul wrote about Christian social structure was itself established on this Rock of Christ. Indeed, Paul Himself was building a house on that very Rock.

Family Household

Paul's household cannot be under emphasized. Though Scripture tells us nothing about Paul's biological family, whether he was a widower or never married. We know a bit about Paul's father, who had himself been a Pharisee and a tentmaker from Tarsus, but nothing else. And we don't need to know anything about Paul's biological family because that was not what was under consideration here.

Remember that Jesus had redefined the family on the basis of gospel obedience. Someone told him (Jesus)

> "'Your mother and your brothers are standing outside, asking to speak to you.' But he replied to the man who told him, 'Who is my mother, and who are my brothers?' And stretching out his hand toward his disciples, he said, 'Here are my mother and my brothers! For whoever does the will of my Father in heaven is my brother and sister and mother'" (Matthew 12:47-50).

The church is the family of Christ. And in the church we may have blood relatives or maybe not. It doesn't matter because the family of the church is not a function of blood, but of bread, not of race, but of grace.

Why do I say grace rather than obedience, since Jesus was talking about obedience to the gospel, and Moses brought the Ten Commandments for obedience, and Jesus said that His new family members were identified by their obedience? Isn't the issue obedience rather than grace? Well, the issue is obedience. However, it is not obedience rather than grace, but the grace of obedience. Scripture does not set grace and obedience in opposition. The point is that obedience is a fruit of God's grace.

Unfortunately, many Christians are confused about this. Many contemporary Christians believe that Paul taught that the gospel is a matter of God's grace and that Christ's propitiation on the cross put an end to the law—and it did, but not in the way that many people think. Paul, arguing for the transfer of God's blessings from the Jews to the Gentiles said,

> "What shall we say, then? That Gentiles who did not pursue righteousness have attained it, that is, a righteousness that is by faith; but that Israel who pursued a law that would lead to righteousness did not succeed in reaching that law. Why? Because they did not pursue it by faith, but as if it were based on works. They have stumbled over the stumbling stone, as it is written, 'Behold, I am laying in Zion a stone of stumbling, and a rock of offense; and whoever believes in him will not be put to shame'" (Romans 9:30-33).

The Gentiles were coming to righteousness (right behavior) by faith, where the Jews, who had been pursuing righteousness through God's law for generations had failed to achieve it through obedience to the law. The Gentiles received by faith what the Jews could not achieve by law. And what was it that the Gentiles received, but the Jews could not achieve? Righteousness (*dikaiosunē*) or justification. We can also call it salvation because it is the ground (or foundation—Rock) of salvation. Paul's point was that it came through faith in Christ, not through obedience to the law. Righteousness comes by grace through faith, not from the imposition of the law.

So, did the Old Testament law fail to do what God had in mind for it? Not at all. Remember that according to Paul the Jews failed to understand the law because

> "to this day whenever Moses is read a veil lies over their hearts" (2 Corinthians 3:15).

That veil hid the purpose of the law from them. And its purpose was Jesus Christ. God knew full well that the Jews would not be able to achieve righteousness through obedience to the law. But had the Jews known that, they would not have tried, and their trying was essential to God's plan. So, God's purpose for them was to try to live according to the law in and of themselves, by themselves, apart from regeneration and the power and presence of the Holy Spirit. How do we know this? Because the dispensation of the Holy Spirit came after Christ, not before.

The ancient Jews had been involved in a mission of sacrifice in order to set up the ultimate sacrifice of Christ and propel the gospel to the Gentiles, to the whole world. History has never been a haphazard unfolding of events, but the unfolding of a particular plan and purpose. The Jews had built their society, the Temple, and the capital of their nation, on the basis of God's law, which would to fail to bring them into compliance.

This is the knowledge that was veiled from the Jews. It is not that God's law is flawed—it is not! Rather, the flaw is found in the sin of humanity, and the laws, worship, and practices of ancient Israel were intended to make the problem of sin clear to humanity, to demonstrate that only Christ's propitiation on the cross can cure the sin problem.

But the ancient Jews could not know this without such knowledge interfering with their own efforts to give it their best shot. God veiled their hearts, occluded this information from them. But it wasn't so much that God hid it, as the fact that it simply was not available to history until Christ had actually come. Only in the light of Christ, only following Christ's propitiation and the wider dispensation of the Holy Spirit was this information, this idea, even thinkable.

This is what Paul saw (2 Corinthians 12). The purpose of the law, of the Old Testament establishment—the law, the Temple and the customs —was to reveal the degree to which sin had affected humanity and the fact that sin had but one solution—Jesus Christ. Nothing else would suffice, not the law, not the prophets, not the Temple, not the nation, not the schools and scholars, not the marshals or the military, not the wealth or wisdom of Solomon—nothing but Christ alone, through faith alone according to Scripture alone to the glory of God alone.

THE END

The verse that many Christians cite as demonstrating the opposition between grace and law is Romans 10:4—

> "For Christ is the end of the law for righteousness to everyone
> who believes."

But this verse does not teach the opposition between grace and law. It teaches the harmony between them. How can I say that? Because the Greek word translated *end* is *telos*, and the word does mean end, but not end as in the cessation of a thing, but end as in the final purpose for a thing. Christ is the *purpose* (end purpose) of the law for righteousness to everyone who believes. The purpose of Christ is the grace of God that was released by Christ's propitiation on the cross.

Because of Christ God has withheld judgment on sin that would have otherwise resulted in the death of humanity. But because of the righteousness of Jesus Christ all those in Christ are protected from the final judgment that would otherwise destroy them. Why would God do this? Because He trusts Christ to bring His people into perfect sanctification and obedience to His immutable law through regeneration and by the power and presence of the Holy Spirit. That process began in earnest with the birth of the Christian church and will be fulfilled in glory. Thus, grace facilitates the final purpose of the law.

The first purpose of the law was the conviction of sin. But the final purpose of the law is the establishment of righteousness by Jesus Christ through the forgiveness of sin and the sanctification of His people. We are not forgiven in order that we can do or be whatever we want. Rather, we are forgiven in order that we may be what God intends for us to be. Everyone and everything else will be destroyed, not saved.

So, the only real question is about what God intends for His people to be. And this is the question that Jesus was answering in His Sermon on the Mount. Jesus did not oppose the Old Testament or its laws. Rather, He fulfilled them Himself by living in obedience to them. And He continues to fulfill them in us as His people live in obedience to Christ—to the "law of Christ" (Galatians 6:2). God's purpose has always been the love, care, and longevity of His people on the earth, or as we say today: sustainable human culture.

God's model for that culture hasn't changed. But in Christ it has been fulfilled or clarified. God's various covenants throughout history do not evidence any change in God's purpose or intent. They only evidence the slow growth of human maturity and the changing needs of people as that maturity has developed. The final covenant in Christ represents the goal of human maturity as people engage and confront the perfection of obedience in Christ.

That perfection was accomplished by Christ in the flesh of Jesus. And while Christ's propitiation on the cross was much more than a model of human obedience to the Word of God, it also stands as a model of human obedience to the Word of God. Following Christ means being like Him in our thoughts, actions and deeds. Christians are to imitate Jesus Christ, not His death on the cross, nor His carpentry, but His willing obedience to the will and Word of God.

The Means

So, the question that Jesus answered in His Sermon on the Mount is: what does righteousness look like? In Christ God's people are poor in spirit—humble. They are patient and kind. They do not envy or boast. They are not arrogant or rude, do not insist on their own way, are not irritable or resentful, do not rejoice at wrongdoing, but rejoice with the truth. They bear all things, believe all things, hope all things, and endure all things (1 Corinthians 13:4-7).

Those who mourn are comforted by the love of Christ through one another. And the comfort that they receive is not for themselves, but is for others. Christians are to pass on to others the comfort that they receive in Christ.

Christ's people are meek, not mousy and timid, but strong and courageous. A racehorse is called meek when it responds to the subtle commands of its rider. Such a horse is not merely obedient, but is willingly and gladly obedient.

Christ's people also hunger and thirst for ... what? Truth? Great preaching? Good music? No, righteousness! They pursue righteousness like other people pursue food and drink. Just as food and drink are necessary for survival, so is Christ's righteousness. We pursue Christ's righteousness because there is no other. Christ alone stands righteous before God.

God's people are merciful. Because God is merciful to them, they pass that Spirit of mercy forward to others. We receive mercy in order to know it, so that we can be like God—merciful, not perfectly so, but increasingly so.

God's people are also pure in heart. This means that God's people have pure motives. But what does it mean to have pure motives? For a thing to be pure it must not have any impurities in it. If it is gold, it's all gold. If silver, all silver. The difficulty with people is that people have mixed motives, and the truth is that people will always have mixed motives this side of glory.

So, this does not mean that God's people will have any kind of moral purity anytime soon. Nonetheless, it does mean that we will grow in purity day by day. Over time Christians become better people. But this does not mean that we are better than others. It simply means that we should be better than we used to be, probably not a lot but a little.

We must understand that these qualities that Jesus has laid out in this Sermon are all important. It's not that we can pick and choose between them, but that we must embrace them all. As we grow in purity, we must also grow in humility, love, joy, peace, patience, kindness, goodness, faithfulness, gentleness, and self-control (Galatians 5:23).

God's people are also peacemakers, not war mongers. And yet, we are to be salty. We are to have a definite taste, so we are not to be bland or tasteless. God's people are also bright! The light of the world must be bright. Christ wants us to shine forth His grace and goodness in all that we think, say, and do. Christ is the foundation of the peace we are to make.

One of the primary ways that we can be successful in our efforts to imitate Christ in these things is to control our anger. Jesus said that the expression of anger is morally equivalent to murder. It is bad enough to feel anger, worse to express it, and worse yet to make accusations on the basis of it. Anger is a negative emotion. But the positive emotions aren't any better.

The Lord also demands that we not lust, that we control our sexual urges and behaviors. He told us that adultery and other forms of covenant faithlessness begin with the wrong desires. This does not mean that Christians cannot have a healthy sex life. It means that all sexual expression must be covenantal—within marriage. Period. End of discussion.

The problem with sex outside of God's covenant is that it violates God's covenant. People may not like this restriction, and they may not understand it. But it doesn't matter what people like or understand because God provided the stipulations of His covenant. And those stipulations are not negotiable. They just are. To even question this is to lust for a power that is not ours. Such a question is itself the evidence of covenantal disobedience because its expression reveals the sin of lust for power. We are not to stand in judgment of God.

One of the consequences of breaking God's covenant, like breaking the marriage covenant, is spiritual divorce. Christians should not divorce or be divorced. But the world is not a perfect place, and God is merciful. The point is that divorce should not be a tolerable option. There should be social stigma attached to divorce because it always falls short of the ideal. Then again, there should be social stigma attached to all sorts of sin. But don't get me started. However, we must also understand that our sin is not greater than God's forgiveness. Divorce, like other sin, can be forgiven.

God's people are not only people of God's Word, we must also be people of our own word, in the sense of saying what we mean and doing what we say. Christians must be faithful to their own promises, just as God is faithful to His promises. Oath taking is neither forbidden nor required. We should simply be honest in what we say. Failure here leads to dishonesty and widespread social corruption and deterioration.

To say that God's people turn the other cheek simply means that we don't take revenge. All revenge belongs to the Lord. Our job is grace, mercy, and forgiveness. And to make sure that we understand how far we are to go with our grace, mercy, and forgiveness, Jesus insists that we love our enemies, that we love those who do us harm, those who persecute us.

Have you ever actually tried this? It's not only hard to love your enemies, it's impossible apart from Christ. It is impossible to work up mushy feelings for someone you hate. And Jesus knew this. That's why He demanded it. As well as being a call to end the cycle of insult and revenge, this commandment challenges our definition of love. And that is part of its purpose. Love—real love, Christian love—is not mushy feelings or syrupy attractions. Love is a kind of behavior. It is the behavior of commitment, not romance. Romance is about sex, not love. Love—real love, Christian love—is always about God, who is the Author and Administrator of love. This, of course, does not mean that people cannot be romantic within the confines of marriage. In fact, they should be! Nonetheless, romance is not a substitute for the discipline of love.

Loving our enemies does not mean feeling all emotional about them. It means treating them in accord with God's instructions. It means giving them, not what they want for themselves, nor what we want for them, but giving them what God wants for them.

CHARITY

Related to this concern is charity. Jesus demanded that His people be charitable. We are to give generously, and not to keep accounts about our giving. The spirit of account keeping and the Spirit of charity are completely different. Our own left hand is not to know what our right hand is doing regarding our charitable giving. What does that mean? It means not keeping accounts. It means that charity must be both personal and confidential. We are to know personally the recipients of our charity, but we are not to make our gifts to them known publicly. Charitable giving should be kept private in order to protect the

giver from undue pride and the recipient from unnecessary embarrass-
ment.

FASTING

Christ's people are to fast, to occasionally abstain from food and
pleasure. The Lord approved of every element of traditional fasting,
except that Christians are to fast in such a way that no one knows about
their fast. It is to be part of our own personal, private discipline. We are
not to engage it in order to appear to be religious. In fact, none of our
personal spiritual disciplines are to be engaged in order to appear to
others to be religious. For the most part, no one else should know about
our spiritual disciplines. They are to be like prayer, matters for our
closets, done in secret.

Christianity is not to be engaged as a method of self-improvement
—even though self-improvement will result. Self-improvement is not
the proper motivation for Christian discipline anymore that self-
improvement is the proper motivation for love or marriage. Rather, the
practice of Christian discipline, like the practice of love and marriage,
must be for the sake of the other, for the sake of the loved one(s). The
proper motivation is self-sacrifice, not self-improvement. Self-sacrifice is
other directed, whereas self-improvement is mere selfishness.

Neither are Christians to be anxious about anything. Anxiety
reveals a lack of faith and trust in God to provide for what we need. God
always provides for His people—not always with what we want, but
always with what we need.

This is not a teaching against being a mature and productive
member of society. The Lord very much insists that His people be
responsible for themselves, their families, and their churches—and the
poor among them. In fact, it is the corporate character of the church that
provides the context for genuine human maturity and productivity,
which then reduce anxiety for the basic needs of life.[41]

But we are not to join a church or become Christians for these self-
serving reasons. These things are byproducts of Christianity, and we are
not to come to the Lord for the byproducts of a relationship with Him.
Rather, we are to

> "seek first the kingdom of God and his righteousness, and all
> these things will be added to you" (Matthew 6:33).

---

41 See page 221, regarding Christian capitalism.

Seek God and His righteousness first and foremost. Keep your attention here. Keep your eyes on the cross, on the Lord, not on the things that will be added. These added things are not to be our primary concern, and making them a primary concern puts the proverbial cart before the horse.

Christians are not to judge others on the basis of their own thoughts, ideas, values, etc. We will be judged with whatever measure we use when we judge others. And we are to judge others—God commands it! However, we are to make those judgments on the basis of Scripture, not on the basis of our own personal likes and dislikes. Scripture is the standard for all judgment, the only reliable standard.

And the way this works is to use the standard of Scripture *on ourselves first.* After we have mastered the biblical demands regarding faithfulness in our own lives, then we can apply that same measure to others. But always, we must approach the task of judgment with grace and mercy, following God's lead. And we should always be tougher on ourselves than we are others. We should also seek the judgment of others about ourselves, as a matter of personal accountability.

Christ also admonishes us to ask, seek, and knock. We are not to think that we can stand by and let God send us what we need. We are not to become religious dependents, depending on the church or the state or whatever to provide for our basic needs. We are to be proactive, to anticipate, to have initiative for the things and values of Christ, and for His people. That initiative is a matter of asking, seeking, and knocking or inquiring. Christians are to be leaders and leaders must get out ahead of the pack. Christians do that through service. Having a spirit of service means anticipating the needs of others, and meeting them. This attitude is also known as love.

DOERS & DON'TERS

This is the Rock upon which the households of Christians are to be built—these attitudes, these qualities, these behaviors. Jesus cited two groups of people for this comparison: those who hear Him and obey, who comply with His teachings, and those who hear Him and don't. Excuses, reasons, or justifications for noncompliance are irrelevant. What people believe is only important inasmuch as it leads to compliance. So, whatever people believe that does not produce compliance is false. The measure for true or false teaching is not words but behavior—fruit.

Note also the way that this fruit is known: it is tested and revealed. And what is the test? Floods and winds—storms. The geography of ancient Palestine was full of ravines and susceptible to flash floods. The point is that genuine piety and faithfulness cannot always be distinguished from false piety and faithlessness until trials, temptations, and difficulties come. Difficulties, like storms and flash floods, expose and test the foundations of our faith, or our lives. At that point everything depends on the foundations. If they are strong and sufficient—built on the Rock, they will support the storm-tossed household. And if they are built on anything other than the Rock, the house will be washed away.

The lesson here is that the only thing that we can do to protect our households from ruin and destruction, which will inevitably come, is to build on the Rock long before the storm hits. Once the storm is upon us, it's too late to do anything about the foundation. So, the way to make it through the hard times is to build on the right foundation during the good times.

And this lesson is not simply about individuals and nuclear families, but also has application to communities and societies. The storms of life don't just hit particular individuals or families, but God

> "makes his sun rise on the evil and on the good, and sends rain on
> the just and on the unjust" (Matthew 5:45).

We are social beings, and our lives and fortunes are intertwined with our communities and societies. Jesus was talking to everyone because His gospel is intended to go out to the whole world, to all humanity.

But note also that Jesus distinguished between two groups of people. God is not concerned about the human groupings that we determine for ourselves—male or female, rich or poor, slave or free, black or white, etc. These groupings mean nothing to God. But there is one grouping, one division among people that is important: those who build on the Rock, and those who don't—believers and unbelievers, covenant keepers and covenant breakers.

Because the great storm is not upon us right now, there is still time. But it's always on the horizon. It's coming. We are closer to God's final judgment than any other generation to date. The time to work on our foundations is now.

> "We must work the works of him who sent me while it is day;
> night is coming, when no one can work" (John 9:4).

26. WHO INDEED?

*And when Jesus finished these sayings, the crowds were
astonished at his teaching, for he was teaching them as one who
had authority, and not as their scribes.*   *—Matthew 7:28-29*

*'What have you done?' (asked Pilate). Jesus answered, 'My
kingdom is not of this world. If my kingdom were of this
world, my servants would have been fighting, that I might not
be delivered over to the Jews. But my kingdom is not from the
world.' Then Pilate said to him, 'So you are a king?' Jesus answered, 'You say that I am a king. For this purpose I was born
and for this purpose I have come into the world—to bear witness to the truth. Everyone who is of the truth listens to my
voice.'*   *—John 18:35c-37*

The people were astonished at Jesus' teaching in this Sermon on
the Mount. They were surprised, filled with wonder. They were
amazed and bewildered. They were shocked and a little
confused. Why were they astonished? Because He taught these things
with authority and power. He seemed to criticize the traditional Old
Testament teachings of the Pharisees, and at the same time He did not
contradict them. He appeared to know exactly what He meant, and
exactly what was true and what wasn't. His teaching had authority. It
was authentic. And in this regard it was unlike the teaching of the
scribes and Pharisees.

The scribes (*grammateus*) were educated people. They were gram-
marians. They could read and write, and spent time studying the Scriptures. They were the people who had "book learnin'." They had what
we call degrees, positions of social power, and community influence.

When the scribes preached and taught, their approach to the task of teaching was to master and regurgitate the great biblical commentators of the past and of their own day. They taught in the tradition of the scholars. Their approach to teaching was scholastic, philosophical, and intellectual.

Matthew's point was that that this was not the way that Jesus taught. Something was very different about the way that Jesus taught, and about the content of His teaching. Whatever it was that Jesus did and said, His approach, His method, His doctrine was not like that of the scribes. He wasn't teaching about the kingdom of God as if He was a tour guide who was distant from the times, events, and landscape of which He spoke. He seemed to have direct authority and knowledge of the things He had talked about. Where a tour guide would stand on the outside of the times, events, and landscape being described as an observer, Jesus spoke as if He was part of the times, events, and landscape, as if He had stepped out of a page of history as it was unfolding, as if He had somehow made history itself come alive. His connection, His teaching, His doctrine seemed to be direct rather than mediated, as if He was the author, and not as if He was representing the author.

It may have been like one of those historic moments that are burned into our consciousness and memories. One of those "Where were you when the planes crashed into the World Trade Center on nine eleven?" moments. There are certain important events that seem to force us out of our heads, out of our dreams and imaginations, out of our schedules and plans and activities, and make us starkly aware of our immediate circumstances. Something about Jesus seemed to make people particularly aware of their immediate circumstances and the content of their lives against the context or backdrop of a much larger story.

Jesus spoke as if He had power and authority because He actually had power and authority. He spoke of the kingdom of God as if He knew it personally because He did. It was not an abstraction to Him. It was not a matter of His having studied about the kingdom—though He did. Rather, He spoke of it as if He knew it personally and intimately. It wasn't an abstract memory to Him. It was an immediate reality.

CHRIST'S PURPOSE

Later, when Jesus was being interrogated by Pilate, He told Pilate the central purpose of His mission on earth. Pilate asked Him,

"What have you done?" (John 18:35).

Why do your own countrymen disown you? What have you done to deserve the wrath of the Jews? What is all this ruckus you have stirred up about? Pilate was attempting to get to the bottom of the issue. And because the issue had landed on Pilate's desk, so to speak, it had become a political issue because Pilate was the chief political figure in the region. Because the matter had come before Pilate, it had become both political and official. At this point Christ's mission became an official part of Gentile or world history. A charge had been made, a court had been convened, and Pilate was forced to make a formal decision in the matter.

Jesus was aware of Pilate's position and predicament, so He answered Pilate's question honestly and in political terms. The Jews had suggested that Jesus was a political threat to the Roman occupation of Jerusalem because Jesus either claimed to be a king or because He was playing the role of the anticipated Messiah, who was to be a king to the Jews. The Jewish understanding of the anticipated Messiah was that the Messiah would be a political figure—not just a king, but the long expected king. And a land could not have two kings. The Jews believed that the Messiah, whether a pretender or the real thing, actually threatened Rome's power. This wasn't the first rabble rouser that Rome had to deal with. There had been many before, and there would be many more.

The Jews who had been persecuting Jesus understood this. So, they brought Jesus to Pilate knowing that Pilate could not countenance a rival political authority in Jerusalem. They knew that Pilate was a ruthless political leader, who would dispose of any rival authority to Roman domination in order to maintain the peace. Roman peace was always a peace imposed by the domination of Roman power. *Pax Romana* was maintained by insuring that nothing challenged Roman authority.

But when Pilate looked at Jesus, and investigated His activities, he didn't find a political rival. Pilate saw a beaten man who had no connections to powerful people. Sure a few poor souls had hailed Him as some kind of Messiah, but most people seemed to reject Him and His authority and His teachings. The Jewish leaders most certainly rejected Him. So, what was the real problem? Pilate wanted to get to the bottom of it.

What have you done? He asked.

Jesus assured Pilate that His kingdom was not of this world. And to prove that it wasn't, Jesus noted that, if His kingdom had been of this world, His people would have been fighting on His behalf. But no one was. No one came to His defense. No one.

Curiously, Jesus' response was not a denial of His kingship. In fact, Jesus acknowledged that He was indeed a king, and that Pilate himself had acknowledged it.

> "Pilate said to him, 'So you are a king?' Jesus answered, 'You say that I am a king'" (John 18:37).

Pilate wasn't asking if Jesus was a king. Pilate's statement was not a question, he simply offered the statement, as if it was an observation. *So, you are a king.* If anything, Pilate was mocking Jesus, who stood before him, beaten, broken, and undefended. If Jesus was a king, it most certainly was not any kind of king that Pilate knew about. Pilate simply responded to Jesus' statement,

> "my kingdom is not from the world" (John 18:36).

The word *world* is not in the Greek. The Authorized Version translated it

> "my kingdom not from hence."

Jesus was telling Pilate that His authority was not in conflict with Pilate's authority. It wasn't that Jesus doesn't have political authority, after all, all authority in heaven and earth would be given to Him. But His jurisdiction would be the

> "new heaven and a new earth, for the first heaven and the first earth" (Revelation 21:1)

would pass away. Jesus' authority was not the authority over a country, or a land, or a place, not Jerusalem or Judea, not Rome, or Geneva.

Rather, Jesus' authority was a function of time, not place. Jesus was the king of a new world, of a new age, of a new people. To Pilate Jesus was king of the future. Jesus was not concerned about Pilate or Roman power or occupation. Those things would all soon pass away. Jesus was not Pilate's rival. Pilate's authority was worldly, temporal, and temporary. Jesus was not after Pilate's position as political ruler, nor Rome's. If anything, He was after Pilate's soul. He wasn't after Rome or Greece—or empire. He was after the hearts and minds of people everywhere, the whole world.

Jesus acknowledged that He had been born for this purpose. For what purpose? To be the king of truth itself. Notice that Jesus connected His kingship with His witness to the truth. The truth, to which Jesus witnessed and of which He is king, is another word for reality. Jesus is king of reality, the state of actuality. When we speak of the truth we mean that which actually is the case. The hard, cold, objective fact of existence or life.

THE TRINITY

Scripture equates truth and God. What is true is real, and there is nothing more real than God. And the witness of Jesus and the witness of Christianity is that the reality of God is Trinitarian, which means that truth is Trinitarian. The thing which most uniquely defines Christ as both human and divine, the thing which most sets Christianity apart from other religions is the reality of the Trinity.

Christ was born for *this* because Christ is the second Person of the Trinity. Earth and heaven before him bow, Christ was born for this. The Trinity is not real apart from the reality of Jesus Christ, who is both God and man, both human and divine. It is precisely because of Christ's role in the reality of the Trinity that He was able to speak with authority, an authenticity that the scribes did not know.

Much can be known about Scripture intellectually, scribally, if you will. Much can be known about Jesus Christ intellectually, as a matter of study. But there is a great deal of difference between knowing about Jesus intellectually—abstractly—and knowing Him personally—directly. And even more difference between knowing Him and being Him. Jesus' authority was not a function of His knowing God, but of His being God by the reality of the Trinity.

Christians sometimes talk about the difference between knowing about Jesus and knowing Him personally. That difference cannot be bridged intellectually. Those who know the Lord personally can learn much about Him intellectually. But those who only know Him intellectually cannot study their way into a personal relationship with Him. That relationship can only be initiated on His side.

In all likelihood, what astonished people about Jesus' teachings was His familiarity with His subject. He seemed to know and understand personally all of the mysteries He spoke about. He had a familiarity and an intimacy with God that shocked people—even those who had been close to the Lord in an Old Testament sense. It seemed unreal *to* them because it was unreal *for* them. It seemed as an affront to accepted religious propriety. And it was, because His manifestation in the flesh was a new thing in human history. They thought that Jesus must be making it up, because no one could have such intimate knowledge of God and His mysteries. Or so they thought.

But Jesus was not making it up. He was simply speaking the truth. And it is not an error or an offense if it is true—and it is! Christians today experience something vaguely similar because people are still offended when we speak of Christ as divine. But for those who actually know Him personally, it is not an offense to speak of their personal experience of the Triune Lord. But it is an offense for people who don't know God personally to speak as if they do. It is offensive to pretend to know the king when you don't actually know Him. The king is offended when He finds out that you have been dropping His name without His permission This is the offense of Matthew 7:21-23:

> "Not everyone who says to me, 'Lord, Lord,' will enter the king-
> dom of heaven, but the one who does the will of my Father who
> is in heaven. On that day many will say to me, 'Lord, Lord, did
> we not prophesy in your name, and cast out demons in your
> name, and do many mighty works in your name?' And then will
> I declare to them, 'I never knew you; depart from me, you work-
> ers of lawlessness.'"

These people spoke as if they knew Jesus personally, but He did not know them as they said they did. Their fake witness to His real truth offended Him because it undermined the virtue of Truth. They testified to God's Truth with a lie, and their lie clouded God's Truth. The witness of a known liar in court is worthless.

In fact, if the truth be known, only Jesus Christ Himself can witness to the truth of His role in the Trinity because only He is sinless. Only He can be trusted to tell the Truth, the whole Truth and nothing but the Truth. The rest of us are sinners. We don't know the whole Truth and much of what we say is not true, for a variety of reasons.

The Truth is not complete or whole apart from Christ, and to suggest that it is is a lie of the highest order. Those who deny Christ deny His authoritative and unique witness as the second Person of the Trinity, and falsely claim for themselves ultimate authority, and doing so they speak a lie. They claim for themselves an objectivity that they do not have in order to deny the objectivity of the Son of God as He witnesses to the Truth of His Father, a Truth that is itself Trinitarian in character. To miss the Trinitarianism of Truth is to miss Truth alto-gether.

Christ was born for *this*, for the testimony and the manifestation of the Trinitarianism of God's Truth in human history. He has opened the heavenly door, And man is blessed evermore. Christ was born for *this*!

And what is more: everyone who is of the truth listens to His voice. It is not just that they listen to it, but that they can hear it. Those who listen have ears to hear. Those who can't hear the Lord don't have the ears for it.

THE GOOD & THE BAD

This is the good news that is also the bad news. The good news is that everyone who is of the truth listens to Jesus Christ because they hear the Lord. And the bad news is that only those who are of the truth listen to the Lord. Those who are not of the Truth cannot hear the Truth because they do not—and will not—listen. They willfully refuse. And their refusal, their unwillingness is the source of their damnation.

Sure, God has damned all who will not listen to Him. But those who refuse to listen do so of their own accord. They willingly choose not to listen. They prefer to deny Jesus Christ as Lord and Savior. They do not have ears to hear because they refuse to listen. They *will not* receive and therefore cannot have God's free gift. They will not abide God's grace because they will not surrender their supposed—but false—objectivity.

They correctly understand that God requires the death or surrender of their supposed objectivity, an objectivity which they understand to be their own personal heart and soul, an objectivity that they have worked hard to achieve, an objectivity that is the result of much study and effort, an objectivity that they believe to be endemic to their personal and social identity—but which is an objectivity that is actually an abstract figment of their own imaginations, that has been garnered for themselves by themselves and is all about themselves. It is an objectivity that places them at the top of the apex of all authority because they know—and they know correctly—that Truth is always objective. They correctly understand the importance of Truth, but mistakenly claim the ability and the right to determine that Truth for themselves, apart from Christ, apart from the Trinity, apart from the Trinitarian character of reality.

So, Christ, who is Himself the Truth by virtue of the Trinity, refuses to recognize them because they are unwilling to recognize Him. He denies them because they deny Him. By denying Christ, they deny the Trinitarian character of reality itself, which is the cornerstone of all Truth. Apart from knowing Christ, and knowing Him personally and Trinitarianally, Truth cannot be known.

Not just religious truth, not just biblical truth, not just spiritual truth —as if Truth can be divided or separated or abstracted from the wholeness of the fabric of reality—but all truth, including scientific truth. The central characteristic of reality—the Trinity and Christ's role in it—cannot be denied without having that denial effect all aspects of the Truth. The denial of Jesus Christ and all that the Bible teaches about Him is like denying gravity or the existence of the sun. Such a denial reveals a blindness and a stubborn pridefulness that is beyond belief and beyond instruction. So, Christ rejects those who reject Him.

And Christ was born for *this*, too. Good Christian men can rejoice! Oh, that the world were filled with good Christian men! What a joy that would be! Someday it will be, and that is the message and the hope of the gospel. Jesus Christ was born to save! He calls us one and calls us all to gain His everlasting hall. Christ was born to save!

Jesus Christ is related to salvation like wet is related to water. Jesus Christ is related to truth like solar flares are related to the sun. They are always found together and never found apart. So, the good news of salvation in Christ is also the bad news of damnation apart from Christ. The good news of Christ's Truth is horribly bad news for those who deny it.

The birth of Jesus Christ is the central watershed of history. The birth of Jesus Christ has changed the world forever. That change is already established in this world, and is nearly finished. The birth of Christ makes the Trinity undeniable because Christ has revealed the Trinitarian character of the reality in which we live.

The world cannot go back to what it was before Christ, but it can only continue becoming what it will one day be because of Him. The announcement of the birth of Christ is the announcement that the world has already entered into salvation because God has chosen to save it, and nothing can thwart God's will. It's a done deal. The die has been cast.

> "Remember this and stand firm, recall it to mind, you transgressors, remember the former things of old; for I am God, and there is no other; I am God, and there is none like me, declaring the end from the beginning and from ancient times things not yet done, saying, 'My counsel shall stand, and I will accomplish all my purpose, calling a bird of prey from the east, the man of my counsel from a far country. I have spoken, and I will bring it to pass; I have purposed, and I will do it'" (Isaiah 46:8-10).

This was shocking news—astonishing—for those who had been waiting for the Messiah to come. Those who had gotten comfortable with waiting, refused to stop waiting. They had accommodated them-selves to the wait. They were used to waiting, and many of them did not want to stop waiting. Just who did Jesus think that He was to tell them that the waiting was over? Who indeed?

> "And he said, 'The God of our fathers appointed you to know his will, to see the Righteous One and to hear a voice from his mouth; for you will be a witness for him to everyone of what you have seen and heard. And now why do you wait? Rise and be baptized and wash away your sins, calling on his name'" (Acts 22:14-16).

Scripture Index

Alphabetical Index

www.ingramcontent.com/pod-product-compliance
Lightning Source LLC
LaVergne TN
LVHW051454080426
835509LV00017B/1757